Sacred
Geometry
and
Spiritual
Symbolism

Sacred Geometry and Spiritual Symbolism:

The Blueprint for Creation

Donald B. Carroll

4th Dimension Press ■ Virginia Beach ■ Virginia

To my children
Jeremy, Chase,
and
Corwin

Contents

Acknowledgments

There are so many to thank in the bringing of this book to fruition. I would like to thank all of the staff and volunteers of the Association of Research and Enlightenment and the Edgar Cayce Foundations, these organizations and individuals have kept alive and expanded on the amazing material that can be found in the Edgar Cayce readings. I have been the recipient of their unwavering support, assistance, and inspiration that has been a vital part of this work. There are many to thank and I list just a few in the following: Kevin Todeschi, John Van Auken, Henry Reed, Peter Woodbury, Jennie Taylor Martin, Alison Ray—thank you for your faith, Cassie McQuagge, Carol Hicks, Susan Lendvay, Kevin Grant, Vanessa Darling, Renee Branch, James Mullaney, and the Wayshower organization. I give many thanks to my copy editor, Stephanie Pope, who was vital in channeling my streams of consciousness into fertile, organized growth and coherence. To Carol Hicks whose graphic illustrations were so important for visualizing the content. If I have missed anyone, please forgive me; it seemed in any direction I turned there were wonderful people. To all the authors of books, articles, and images cited in this work I thank you; such works are the lamps that helped guide me on this journey, shining light onto the shadowed ideas in my mind, acting like photosynthesis for them to grow. I hope I have added a little light for others.

Thanks to all my family, particularly my sons, Jeremy, Chase, and Corwin who are some of the people I most admire in the world, and my brother Chris for always being there.

Signposts of the Journey

All roads lead to an interconnected Oneness. Signposts, to me, are those phrases or thoughts in writings that catch our attention and help us choose the path that is right for us. It may not be the one that any author of said writings is traveling, yet these thoughts provide direction to the same destination through a different landscape. The journey is ours.

In the study of ourselves in relation to the Whole lies the awakening of the inner man to a full consciousness of our respective part which we must play in the scheme of creation. Here again man is baffled by what seems to be a great division of force. This is due to the limitations of the conscious facilities by space-time. Yet there is open to every individual a door through which he may pass to obtain a new vision. This door leads to the inner self. 'We must, in spite of our three-dimensional, finite, physical viewpoints, understand the inner, infinite, higher-dimensional experiences that the inner subconscious mind may be induced to bring through imagination into our consciousness, but which visioning, hunches, premonitive or intuitive thoughts, experiences, or spontaneous ideas we will fail to understand, unless we know something of the logic of the higher-dimensional viewpoint.'[1]

Thanks to God, in his infinite wisdom, who has provided the knowledge for those who seek.

Ecclesiasticus 39: 1-8 (New Revised Standard Version)

¹He seeks out the wisdom of all the ancients, and is concerned with prophecies;

²He preserves the sayings of the famous and penetrates the subtleties of parables;

³He seeks out the hidden meanings of proverbs and is at home with the obscurities of parables.

⁴He serves among the great and appears before rulers; he travels in foreign lands and learns what is good and evil in the human lot.

⁵He sets his heart to rise early to seek the Lord who made him, and to petition the Most High; he opens his mouth in prayer and asks pardon for his sins.

⁶If the great Lord is willing, he will be filled with the spirit of understanding; he will pour forth words of wisdom of his own and give thanks to the Lord in prayer.

⁷The Lord will direct his counsel and knowledge, as he meditates on his mysteries.

⁸He will show the wisdom of what he has learned, and will glory in the law of the Lord's covenant.²

I shall not call you servants anymore, because a servant does not know his master's business; I call you friends, because I have made known to you everything I have learned from my Father.   John 15:15³

As above, so below.   Hermes Mercurius Trismegistus

Science without religion is lame, religion without science is blind.   Albert Einstein

Everyone who is seriously involved in the pursuit of science becomes convinced that a spirit is manifest in the laws of the Universe.   Albert Einstein

All knowledge is to be used in the manner that will give help and assistance to others, and the desire is that the laws of the Creator be manifested in the physical world.   254-17

Though the evidence, both physical and thoughtful, may be found throughout the world, as guideposts, it is through the temple within where the finite may merge with the infinite when we see the footprints of God.

Preface

At some point in our lives we ask ourselves what is our purpose, what is our meaning, why do we exist? Why have we been endowed with self-consciousness and self-recognition and the ability to even ask these questions? We can surmise that these questions stem from our feelings of separation and the lack of wholeness we experience, which cause us to *hope* that there is a greater existence than just our finite time on earth, and not just those feelings. On occasion we also experience heights of joy and unity which cause us to *know* that there is a greater infinite existence. Unfortunately, we tend to regress from these knowing moments and live in doubts that lead us back to hoping there is something more, some greater unifying consciousness in the universe.

This knowing and hoping has been the impetus for the disciplines of science and religion to seek meaning and order for and in our existence. Religion generally espouses a belief of a greater, all-encompassing infinite consciousness that we have the ability to become one with through faith. On the other hand science seeks the mysteries of the creation of the universe and life through strictly observable and repeatable data that may or may not prove the existence of such a higher infinite consciousness. Religion knows through feeling experiences; science can have hopes through observed measurements.

Is there any evidence that the knowing of religion can be unified with the hoping observations of science? Can the doubting Thomas of science observe the substantiation of God? I say, "Yes!" Yes, through two geometric symbols consisting of the triangle and the arc and their aspects. It will be shown how, through the millennia, religions have intuited the importance of these shapes and incorporated their symbolism throughout their beliefs. This goes beyond shared collective consciousness archetypes limited to spiritual beliefs. It will also be shown how this geometry is being found by modern science in the essence of life and the cosmos. It is hard to believe that this shared geometry is merely coincidence and that the same two geometric forms found at the symbolic cores of religions all over the world and through the ages are now, because science has been able to advance far enough, being discovered in the fabric of the universe and life itself. I believe that once we explore these signposts, we will be able to **know,** with a synthesis of science and religion, that there is a higher consciousness and a Oneness for us all in the universe.

Note to Readers: Religion versus Spirituality: a Guide for Readers

In my discourse, the concepts of religion and spirituality are used often and to a certain extent can be considered interchangeable. Please, before the protest start over such a statement, allow me to clarify my meaning. Traditionally, being religious and being spiritual have been one and the same. In more recent times, more and more people are differentiating between the two terms. An example of this would be recent polls taken in the United States. In a February 11, 2003 Gallup poll, 50 percent of the people asked considered themselves to be religious, while 33 percent considered themselves not religious but spiritual. Perhaps more telling is a survey reported on by *USA Today* in an October 14, 2010 article reporting from a survey of that same year, where 72 percent of the age group of 18 to 29 said they are "really more spiritual than religious." It is clear that these two terms are no longer being considered equivalent and that people are making a differentiation between them.

From what I have gathered, I believe people who call themselves religious vs. spiritual are usually involved in an organized religion, attend a church/temple of that religion, and feel a strong affiliation toward that religion over other religions (often feeling that theirs is the only true religion). People who call themselves spiritual vs. religious, may or may not attend a church/temple or be involved in organized religion, but if they are, they often feel there may be truth in more than one religious sect. Their religious beliefs are not usually what are referred to as "fundamental" or "orthodox" even within their own religious following.

One simple example, if one looks at the core of just three major religions: Christianity, Judaism, and Islam, will be found the spiritual concept that God is love and Godly love is something to be practiced and shared by all. This is not something to be constrained in only one religion's parameter. As the Persian Islamic poet Rumi put it: "O lovers! The religion of the love of God is not found in Islam alone. In the realm of love, there is neither belief, nor unbelief."[1]

Spiritual masters brought forth spiritual ideas and truths that later became codified into religions by followers of these ideas. Though some may feel these ideas have been skewed by attempting to place them within finite parameters, the infinite divine reality from whence they originate remains in unity and oneness, and if one goes deep enough into any religion, the spirit and spirituality will still be found. In this shared Divine ground will also be found the roots of the symbols used by each religious philosophy and what will be seen is that these symbols are shared archetypes of a core unity.

Introduction

The breathtaking beauty and mystery of the universe, including our world, have inspired many people. Our cosmos has motivated poets, writers, and scientists, noting just a few, to try to grasp its enormity and magnificent mystery. I would hazard a guess that every single one of us has, at least once in our lives, looked up at the stars or out over the waters at a sunrise or into the eyes of a newborn child and felt both awe and inspiration. An awe that we may not be able to define, but a feeling that there is a greater design than just a mechanical universe winding down, with our only purpose being to procreate for our species to survive on this speck in the universe called Earth. Deep within us we feel a touch of infinity, of eternity; it whispers to our minds and hearts that we are so much more than what we see. We feel, to varying degrees, that there is more meaning to the universe and to ourselves than just survival. We sense greater patterns and laws that govern not only the material, but also the ethereal. Even if we consciously deny these feelings within ourselves, one cannot help but believe that it is just that—a denial. We seem born with an intuitive sense that there is more beyond than what we see—that our being goes beyond our years on earth, beyond space and time. Whether we feel a leaning toward spirituality or science, ultimately either avenue is seeking the answers to the same questions: our meaning, our purpose, our being. Every single person has felt this yearning in one form or another. In *Hamlet* Shakespeare expresses this idea with his line: "There are more things in heaven and earth, Horatio, than are dreamt in your philosophy."[1] In his poem "Excelsior" Longfellow calls to this feeling of seeking, going ever upward, expressing that even when our physical bodies fail, our spirit continues.[2]

Does this innate feeling we experience that there is more to us and the universe than a purposeless, accidental, random mixing of primordial soup have any basis? Is the search being done by science and religion truly an antithesis to each other? Is this feeling that our consciousness is more than just a chance occurrence of chemicals in our physical brains, just a defense against the prospect of mortality? These are the questions so many struggle with in addition to even why is there such a struggle. Some will say, because we cannot produce concrete, tangible evidence of God beyond faith, that at best God and consciousness beyond physicality remain a hypothesis. Ironically if you push scientists back to the most core tenets of their disciplines, they will admit that in the end theirs are based on hypotheses and assumptions also. While physicists, neurologists, and biologists plumb the mysteries of quantum science, fractals, the beginnings of the universe, how energy becomes matter and then energy again and what makes inert matter become alive, religions examine the mysteries of how spirit becomes flesh, becomes living stones of the temple of God, the jewels in the lotus, and how the flesh can become spirit again.

Is this actually the case for science and religion? Is there an uneasy draw between these two schools? Is there any evidence of a greater meaning, a shared universal consciousness that embraces the entirety of science and religion that unifies them in their goals?

There is evidence that surrounds us both in its simplicity and its complexity. The evidence is represented in two geometric forms that span the millennia in religion and science, forms that can be found at the very foundations of both schools of thought. These geometric shapes are the triangle and the parabola (arc), and these shapes will be shown to represent the shared primal archetypes behind the archetypes of science and religion. They are the patterns or the building blocks of the universal laws and a conscious living universe that science is discovering and religion has intuited. They are the archetypes that permeate all the aspects of both in one form or another.

The shapes of the arc and the triangle are some of the most basic forms in two-dimensional geometry. The arc is a simple curve that we see formed in a rainbow or a tunnel through which we pass. It is an arc that creates a section of the path of a celestial object on its journey through the heavens. The triangle is the simplest polygon—three closed sides defining an area. It is a shape that is intrinsic to all other polygons. We see triangles every day in the roof shape of many of our homes and the supporting structures of numerous bridges we pass over. The curve (arch) and triangle are fundamental building blocks in architecture used for their strength and simplicity. They also are found in the core of biology and the fabric of the universe. The archetypes of the arc and triangle with their power and straightforwardness also exhibit themselves in religious and mystical symbolism throughout the world in various ages.

What follows here is an exploration throughout civilization of the aspects and multidimensional forms of the arc and triangle, both in their science-based arenas and the realms of spirituality. As so often happens when finite minds attempt to interpret the infinite, rifts occur over misunderstandings and different perspectives. Think of religion and science as two explorers who have landed unbeknownst to each other at opposite poles of a planet, trying to get to the center. Each traveler has only a basic compass and a radio to communicate with. Each thinks the other is somewhere out of sight, yet in the same hemisphere. Radioing to each other to meet at the center, one tells the other he must go south, while his compatriot advises that it is north that will lead them to where they want to go. Neither one is grasping the other's viewpoint that each one, from his perspective, is correct. If they will both follow their own compasses, they will meet in the center.

This in-depth examination of the arc and triangle in science and religion will show that they create an encompassing and unifying link between these two disciplines. Schools that so often seem in conflict are, in actuality, two sides of the same coin. Both of these belief systems each fundamentally share the same vision of life and the cosmos. When this is realized, it can be a beginning for the healing of this schism of misunderstanding which may lead to a wholeness and unity for all.

This research came from humble beginnings but took on a life of its own and blossomed into what could be called an elegant equation involving arcs and triangles. These patterns in life often surround us so implicitly and explicitly that we no longer see them consciously. They create an equation which shows that science and spirituality reflect our underlying Oneness—what the ancients formulated "As above, so below."

These forms will be shown to be linchpins of cosmology and biology from which the essence of life and religious symbolism are spawned. Their examination will show that the frequency of occurrence throughout history and the cultures within their spirituality are significant.

The triangle and the arc emerge as cosmic archetypes that manifest at the core of science and human consciousness. They are two forms that clearly show the yin and the yang, the masculine and the feminine, perfectly containing their opposite counterparts in balance. From the triangle the arc can be drawn, and from arcs triangles can be created. Such is the reach and influence of these apparently simple forms that together they create a fusion for uniting science with spirituality. They are the archetypal forms that are the warp and woof of the universe, intrinsic symbols of both religion and science creating an elegant equation of unification. Elegant equations are what theorists call formulas such as Einstein's $E=mc^2$ and Newton's every action has an equal and opposite reaction. Other such examples of elegant equations include "God is Love" (1 John 4:16 NRSV) and "you reap whatever you sow." (Gal. 6:7 NRSV) Elegance is a term that applies to formulas that are uncomplicated and symmetrical, yet within such formulas are great scope and power.

It is for the readers themselves, of course, to determine the level of profoundness this discourse evokes. Perhaps they will see the source of a theory beyond a Holy Grail–type of scientific search for a unified theory of everything and find the basis of a unified theory of science and God. This would, beyond a doubt, be a unified theory of All.

For sciences and religions both have multiple branches that, in essence, are seeking the same thing—an understanding of the Creative Forces of the universe, of God, of our meaning. What will be shown here is that the basic natures of both sides' pursuits have exhibited the expression of such forces and meaning in the symbolism of the triangle and the arc. These symbols actually identify the unity of religion and science.

In my small way what is being presented here is a perspective of the Perennial Philosophy put forth by such luminaries as Leibniz and Huxley. The concept of this philosophy is that the divine reality (divine ground) is the source of spiritual insight and higher consciousness throughout the world's ages and cultures. In addition the varied religions have interpreted this infinite ground through finite minds creating only skewed parts or aspects of it.

From a science–based viewpoint of this alpha, divine reality, the physicists have their own search for a "theory of everything." Here science is also interpreting the infinite with finite lenses and grasping only limited parts. Using a scientific analogy, their quandary could be compared to a shattered hologram. A hologram has the unique property that the film from which it is projected can be divided into pieces, yet each piece will project the entire hologram, only with a narrower, skewed perspective.

Ultimately the evidence put forth here is that the geometry employed both by spiritual philosophies and science are used to explain life and the cosmos, the microcosm and macrocosm. Science may try to say this is not evidence of a higher collective consciousness or of Creative Forces, but then how was this shared symbolism which threads through both sciences and spirituality and was intuited thousands of years before science confirmed these same geometries explained with other than a shared higher consciousness of the whole?

The irony of both their searches is that they regularly focus on external surface phenomenon. There is a degree as well as a need and purpose for this, but it is not the conclusion. Whether it is Newtonian physics that works on the surface versus quantum physics that works in the essence or dogma versus spirituality, the final leg of the journey is within. In both schools history has shown their paradigm-shifting illuminations have invariably been through an inward intuitive experience.

> That is why anybody who has the gift of tongues must pray for the power of interpreting them. For if I use this gift in my prayers, my spirit may be praying but my mind is left barren. What is the answer to that? Surely I should pray not only with the spirit but with the mind as well? And sing praises not only with the spirit but with the mind as well? Any uninitiated person will never be able to say Amen to your thanksgiving, if you only bless God with the spirit, for he will have no idea what you are saying. However well you make your thanksgiving, the other gets no benefit from it. (I Corinthians 14:13-18)[3]

The Journey Begins

So from where would such concepts about geometric figures and the depth of their significance germinate? In the introduction spiritual and scientific laws were touched upon. So let us begin with some of the oldest laws recorded—those brought down from Mount Sinai.

This examination began as a thought experiment about what was the actual shape of the biblical Ten Commandments and why their shape would be of consequence. It takes us back to a time when religious leaders and scientists were one and the same. Moses, the leader and patriarch of the Israelites, prophet to Christians and Moslems alike, is an example. He is known as the giver of the Law. Often the vision of a great figure standing on a mountain veiled in smoke and illuminated by lightning flashes comes to mind. Can you envision him standing there, face aglow, holding the two tablets of the Law, the Ten Commandments, given to him by God? Moses was also raised as a prince in the royal household of the Egyptian pharaoh, and such an upbringing would bring with it the highest possible education in the sciences.

Though most are familiar with the commandments being written on stone referred to as tablets, the Hebrew word *luah* translates as both tablet and table. Table is the term used in the King James Version of the Bible. Luah also translates as "house of the soul."[1] The translation of luah as house of the soul and its symbolism as this house leads to the hypothesis of triangular tablets being addressed here.

Fig. 1.1—Moses with the Tablets

The Ten Commandments is also known as the Decalogue—meaning ten words or utterances. It may be considered a symbolic, spiritual core of Mosaic Law, much as the periodic table of the elements in science categorizes the discovered fundamental substances that make up the universe. These ten words written on stone symbolize, in essence, the way to act with both God and man, but are meanings engraved in more than just the words on these stone tablets? Are there meanings in the shapes of the tablets themselves? In Exodus 32:15 it states that the tablets had writing on both sides, that the writings could be seen through the tablets. Could this indicate that there are meanings for us in the words and the shape of the tablets as well as through the very stone itself? Remember, literacy of the general population is a recent event in humankind's history. Nowhere in the Bible are these shapes described. My intuition is that they are two triangular tablets or tables.

The search to validate or invalidate this premise and its significance turned into an exploration that expanded beyond the Tables of the Law. It led down a path that wound through myths, science, religions, and ancient mystery schools. The quest was one that ultimately joined all of these facets through shared symbolism and meaning and became an investigation not just of the triangle but also of the parabola, commonly known as an arc. It ended with the discovery of a strong unifying pattern between these symbols that creates a bridge both in the macrocosm and the microcosm of humankind's experience. The key to seeing this pattern is in the deeper meanings of the triangle and the arc. The meanings can be found in their different manifestations, aspects, and dimensions. Such triangular aspects can be seen in many forms including pyramids, stars, and diamonds. The parabola or arc, best known from geometry's conic sections, appears in circles, spirals, ellipses, and such shapes as the Christian ICTHYS symbol and its more ancient brethren, the vesica pisces. Within their combined symbolism is a vital universal message—a message in a glyph-like language barely remembered, but still imprinted upon the fabric of spacetime and our consciousness. We, similar to children learning the meanings of their surroundings, need to discover again the archetypal meanings of these symbols to gain their messages.

P.D. Ouspensky writes of the difficulty of grasping the essence and incorporating the meanings of such symbols within us and trying to communicate that meaning to others. He speaks of this when one is attempting to transmit to another "objective knowledge," that is knowledge "based upon ancient methods and principles of observation, knowledge of things in themselves, knowledge accompanying 'an objective state of consciousness,' knowledge of the All."[2] He states:

> . . . But objective knowledge, the idea of unity included, belongs to objective consciousness. The forms which express this knowledge when perceived by subjective consciousness are inevitably distorted and, instead of truth they create more and more delusions . . . Realizing the imperfection and weakness of ordinary language the people who have possessed objective knowledge have tried to express the idea of unity in myths, in symbols . . . The transmission of the meaning of symbol to a man who has not reached an understanding of them in himself is impossible . . . (If he does know) a symbol becomes for him a synthesis of his knowledge .[3]

In Dr. Mark Thurston's book *Experiments in SFG: The Edgar Cayce Path of Application*, he explains the concept of such innate knowing with a quote from Walter Starcke.

(It is) . . . to understand it from all levels: to see it, to compre-
hend it, to understand it both spiritually and physically, to
experience it, to identify with it, and, above all, to discern
what it is 'for' . . . [4]

Aldous Huxley in his book *The Perennial Philosophy* describes this con-
cisely as: "What we know depends also on what, as moral beings, we
chose to make ourselves."[5]

This puzzle of receiving such knowledge from what we need to already know or have spiritually experienced will be explored and ex-
pounded upon. Fear not these Zen koan–like statements, for like such
koans the purpose is to move the thought process out of the rational
state to the intuitive state where such knowledge lies dormant, waiting
to be awakened. Think of the koan: "What is the sound of one hand
clapping?" Now think of it as potential, the unmanifested waiting to be
made manifest, of God and God moving, manifesting, the clapping creating vibration. And vibration creates the universe, as will be seen in
Chapter 6. Think about the left hemisphere of the brain, generally considered the logical, linear side of the intellect and the right side of the
brain, generally considered the holistic, intuitive side of the mind. Now
as they are brought together equally, they create a unity, a Oneness to
be likened to heaven on earth. One might wonder if the meaning of
sitting on the right hand of God infers to thinking more in the right side
of the brain, the side considered more holistic and intuitive, and to
manifest exactly that.

What follows here is a quest through lands, people, and symbols.
The purpose is to arouse the sleeper in all of us. For once aroused such
pilgrims can, with informed purpose, follow their road home, toward a
home of wholeness and completeness, of Oneness. This birthright home,
buried in our memories, calls to us just as the cries of seagulls over the
ocean in the dark of night tell the sailor that land, though unseen, is not
far off. There is that yearning to be home, that pull within us to find a
course to our own mansion which is waiting for each of us in His house.

For the pilgrims looking to come home, the aim is to make clearer
these signposts, which lead us on a path to our own door in a house of
many mansions. Just such a pilgrim will recognize within such symbols
that the journey home is through the knowing which resides within us
all. This effort is a synthesis of research into many avenues, culminating
in conclusions that ideally will give a fresh map to all such seekers in

the world. Like many maps, the information has been collected from varied sources. Once the information is processed and integrated, a legend of symbols is created to act as guideposts for one looking for such direction.

One source of information researched is from the printed readings of Edgar Cayce—America's famous clairvoyant who came to renown in the first half of the twentieth century. These readings, numbering more than fourteen thousand, were transcribed while he lay in an altered state of consciousness brought on by a type of self-hypnotic suggestion. Among the great volume of information the readings provide is the story of our original Oneness with God, then the fall, our separation, and our ongoing journey back to a knowledgeable Unity with God. Other sources include evidence left behind in ancient Egypt, the Judeo-Christian and Hindu-Buddhist religions, early mystery schools, architecture, science, and sacred geometry.

This quest includes not only the hypothesis that the Ten Commandment tablets were triangular but also other hypotheses that this research led to as well. These suppositions include the importance of the triangle in the ancient world as supported by the triangular shape of sections of the spinal canal and the spinal column's resemblance to a serpent which led to an Egyptian royal cubit of the Great Pyramid being derived from the length of the spine. A similar type of spinal cubit can be seen in the Mayan *zapal* measurement for their pyramids. Moreover, evidence is shown that this "spinal" cubit could have been used at Stonehenge as well. The length of this spinal cubit was actually documented in the readings of the Edgar Cayce. What's more, evidence is presented that the shape of the ancient Egyptian crown stemmed from the form of human vertebrae and that the King's and Queen's Chambers of the Great Pyramid are symbolic of the pineal and pituitary glands of the human brain. Furthermore, headpieces, such as the cone-shaped dunce's cap, a wizard's hat, and even the Pope's mitre whose symbolic purpose was to imbue the wearer with wisdom, can trace their shapes to the triangle and arc. Also postulated is the fact that the baptism of Jesus can be traced back, in symbolism, to the ancient Egyptian obelisk. The findings about the obelisks may well explain why the Roman Catholic Church had such monuments, generally considered pagan, moved and relocated in front of some of the most eminent basilicas in Rome, such as Saint Peter's, and why Rome has more standing Egyptian obelisks than anywhere else in the world.

Ultimately it will be seen that religion and science are not at odds or exclusive of each other. They are in fact united by an unseen bridge, a bridge created from the symbols and the profound meanings of the triangle and the arc in both their disciplines. It will be shown that these symbols are not only in the world around us, the stars above us, and our spiritual beliefs, but are also in the fabric of the universe and our very DNA itself. These two symbols can represent light itself—both the spiritual light immanent in heaven and earth and the technical phenomenon of light and of matter that the latest scientific theories consider to have both wave and particle aspects and functions.

Triangular Tablets of Wisdom

In researching illustrations of the Tablets of the Law, we find that they are in–variably shown as rectangular in shape or rectangular with rounded tops. Many of us remember Charlton Heston, in the Cecile B. DeMille movie *The Ten Commandments,* coming down the Holy Mountain as Moses with these depicted tables. I did come across two interesting presentations where the tables of the law were rectangular, but with a triangular cut top.[1]

Those portrayals stirred in me the memories of wisdom writings and symbolism represented in triangular formats—the triangular formats of the Tetractys of the Pythagoreans, the Tetragrammaton of the Judaic Kabbalah mystics, and the Ennead of the ancient Egyptians. It makes one consider if these could have derived their shape and symbolism from one or the other, or perhaps they all share the same divine inspiration.

The Pythagorean Tetractys was represented by the shape of a triangle with ten symbols (commas) arranged as one would picture bowling pins. Pythagoras, born in the fifth century BCE, taught that everything was related to mathematics and that numbers were the ultimate reality. He taught that through mathematics everything could be measured in rhythmic patterns, geometry, or cycles. You may be familiar with his name from the Pythagorean Theorem, used for finding the lengths of the sides of a right triangle: $A^2 + B^2 = C^2$.

About Pythagoras and the Tetractys author Manley P. Hall writes:

> The teachings of Pythagoras indicate that he was thoroughly conversant with the precepts of Oriental and Occidental esotericism. He traveled among the Jews and was instructed

by the *Rabbins concerning the secret traditions of Moses, the lawgiver of Israel* . . . Pythagoras was initiated into the Egyptian, Babylonian, and Chaldean Mysteries.[2] [Author's emphasis]

Theon of Smyrna declares that the ten dots, or Tetractys of Pythagoras, was a symbol of the greatest importance, for to the discerning mind it revealed the mystery of universal nature.[3]

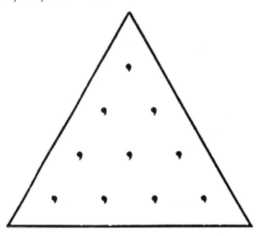

Fig. 2.1–Tetractys

The Judaic Kabbalists, who follow mystical rabbinic teachings based on an esoteric interpretation of Hebrew scripture, study the Tetragrammaton. The Tetragrammaton plainly means "four-letter word." The four-letter word it addresses is the Hebrew name for God, *Yod Heh Waw Heh*, again represented in a triangular format. P.D. Ouspensky goes into detail on the study of the Tetragrammaton:

> The study of the Name of God in its manifestations constitutes the basis of the Cabala . . . These four letters have been given a symbolic meaning . . . According to the Cabalists the four principles permeate and compose each and everything . . . The idea is quite clear. If the Name of God is really in everything (if God is present in everything), then everything should be analogous to everything else, the smallest part should be analogous to the whole, the speck of dust analo-

gous to the Universe and all analogous to God. "As above, so below." . . . In Alchemy the four principles of which the world consist are called the four elements. These are fire, water, air, and earth, which exactly correspond in their meaning to the four letters of the name Jehovah.[4]

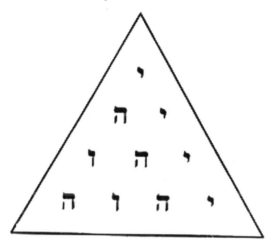

Fig. 2.2–Tetragrammaton

This treatise will show that Ouspensky's description is exactly the case—a case for Oneness. The Cayce reading 288-27 concurs with Ouspensky, the alchemists, and Plato as to the four principles that make up the world:

> Q-4. What are "the forces of the natural elements?"
> A-4. Fire, earth, air, and water. These are the natural elements
> in the physical plane, and—as the forces of these have influ-
> ences—as the spirit of the air . . . the spirit of each! See?

The Ennead, Greek for nine, is a group of nine related Egyptian gods and is mentioned in the Pyramid Texts which are a collection of ancient Egyptian religious writings dating from at least 2200 BCE and from which *The Egyptian Book of the Dead: The Book of Going Forth by Day* evolved. The Ennead is usually represented in the shape of a pyramidal (triangular) hierarchy of gods or principles that they represent.

Author and student of Egyptology Marie Parsons comments on the Ennead:

. . . the group of nine gods that embodied the creative source and chief forces of the universe (though this number was not always nine; at some times it was as few as five, and other times as many as twenty or more; and often, the traditional Ennead includes a tenth god, Horus the Elder).[5]

Author John Anthony West in his book *Serpent in the Sky* describes it as:

The Grand Ennead emanates from the Absolute, or "central fire" (in the terminology of Pythagoras). The nine Neters (Principles) circumscribed about the One (The Absolute) becomes both One and Ten. This is the symbolic analog of the original Unity; it is repetition, the return to the source.[6]

While within the Pyramid Texts themselves it states:

Utt. 442
    The king becomes a star.
    Truly, this Great One has fallen on his side, He who is in Nedyt was cast down. Your hand is grasped by Re, Your head is raised by the Two Enneads . . . Who live by the gods' command, You shall live! You shall rise with Orion in the eastern sky; You shall set with Orion in the western sky.[7]

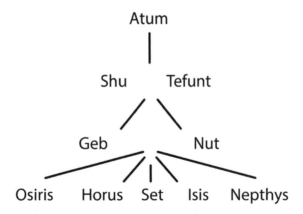

Fig. 2.3–Ennead

The fact that the title of the quote is "the king becomes a star" and in said quote it states that " . . . Your head is raised by the Two Enneads . . . Who live by gods' command, you shall live!", then it is not difficult to picture two triangular tablets of commandments ("god's commands"), which, when overlapping each other, create the King's Star, a six-pointed star similar to the Star of David, also known as the Seal of Solomon and the Creator's Star. Such a star could be considered akin to a spiritual periodic table of the makeup of the universe and humankind, not only in laws but also in the way it represents the four principle elements of fire, water, air, and earth.

The Bible itself confirms Moses' awareness of such Egyptian esoteric knowledge. In Acts 7:22 (KJV) it states that Moses was instructed in all the wisdom of the Egyptians. Along these lines, the laws of the Ten Commandments as found in the Bible also have comparisons to the Egyptians' negative confession found in their Book of the Dead—a book Moses would have had familiarity with. In the Ten Commandments when a law states "Thou shall not . . .," the negative confession laws of ancient Egypt state "I have not . . ." (See Appendix 1 for a comparison of the two documents.)

I also find it curious that it seems confirmation of Moses' understanding of Egyptian wisdom is noted in Acts 7:22 which when the numbers are listed as 22/7, they become pi? Pi is an important, advanced mathematical constant necessary to determine different aspects of a circle, and the circle often is a representation of God and eternity. Though the concept of pi seems to have been known to the Egyptians, it is still debated today as to whether it is represented in the Great Pyramid. Is this a hint in the Bible of the importance of geometry, particularly sacred geometry and the universal wisdom contained within it?

An Egyptian hieroglyph adds further support to the framework of this triangular tablet hypothesis. This hieroglyph, pictured on the following page, appears as a bowl with a diamond shape or the shape of two triangles placed base to base etched in its center. One of its translations is an alabaster bowl, but this bowl with its triangular shapes is also at the core for another translation which is a scroll or a priest carrying a scroll.[8] Moses, the Hebrews' lawgiver, could easily be identified as "a priest carrying a scroll," or in this case, two triangular tables.

**Fig. 2.4–"A Priest Carrying a Scroll" Hieroglyph–
Temple at Edfu, Egypt**

The bowl by itself in hieroglyphs means "lord," and I wonder if by adding the diamond in the bowl that such a stone or jewel is being signified within ourselves as houses of the soul? This meaning could be similar to the New Testament quote calling us living stones and reminiscent of the Buddhist mantra *Om mani Padme hum*, behold the jewel in the lotus. Such connections will be explored in more detail in later chapters. Interestingly there is biblical New Testament writing where Jesus has an alabaster bowl or box of unguent poured over his head. This "baptism" is in his preparation for fulfilling the laws and becoming the covenant. In the biblical Old Testament perhaps there is another clue at the beginning of Moses' life. As written in the New Jerusalem Bible, the King of Egypt instructed the midwives to watch the two stones (possibly birthing bricks) at birth (Ex 1:16 New Jerusalem Bible), and if a boy was born, they should kill him, but all girl infants could live. Is this a symbolic reference for the coming of the two tablets of the Ten Commandments and identifying the future lawgiver who is to receive them? At this point Moses the infant, the future high priest and lawgiver of the Hebrews, is placed in a papyrus basket (bowl) and placed in the river Nile. So right from his beginning we have two stones and a basket/bowl that are linked to Moses, an apparent connection that seems more than coincidental in symbolism both in the Egyptian hieroglyph for a priest carrying a scroll and the two stone tablets of the commandments carried by Moses.

Besides the Tetractys, Ennead, and Tetragrammaton, there are additional writings referencing divinely inspired triangular tablets. Author Manly P. Hall mentions similar triangular tablets found in the writings of Josephus in *Antiquities of the Jews*. It states that the patriarch Enoch:

> . . . placing in the deepest vault a triangular tablet of gold bearing upon it the absolute and ineffable Name of Deity. According to some accounts, Enoch made two golden deltas. The larger he placed upon the white cubical altar in the lowest vault and the smaller he gave into the keeping of his son Methuselah . . . [9]

The case for similarities and the crossing paths of these three different schools and the biblical Decalogue are evident. Hall ties Pythagoras to Egyptian and Judaic traditions, West links the Ennead with Pythagoras, and all the above-cited authors connect their meanings to the unity of the Creative Forces in the universe. This evidence in turn lends itself to support the theory that the tablets are triangular.

You may ask why the shapes of the tablets are important enough even for discussion since the tablets are merely the modern day equivalent to paper that a contract is written upon. In today's world only the words of the contract have significance. Remember, literacy in the general population in the ancient world was not common. The ability for the majority of a population to read is a modern day event and long before written language was commonplace people could grasp symbols. Symbols could cross boundaries of different languages and alphabets and be shared by the populace. The phrase "A picture is worth a thousand words" is an adage for a reason. The shapes have a spirit of meaning in themselves.

The essence of spiritual law and core principles was not only in the ten words but also in the shapes. These two proposed triangular tablets, these "houses of the soul," create the six-pointed star, the Seal of Solomon, the Creator's Star. This star combines the individual symbols representing the four ancient elements of the universe: fire, water, air, and earth. (See symbols on the following page). They make an early symbol of the unification of the spiritual and physical forces, of heaven and earth.

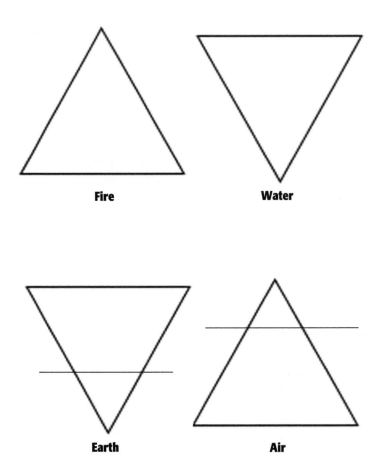

Fire   **Water**

Earth   **Air**

The Stars Above and Holy Mountains and Pyramids Below

According to Jewish, Christian, and Islamic tradition, the biblical Mount Sinai was the location where Moses received the Ten Commandments. The actual location of Mount Sinai has been in a long-standing dispute with scholars and archaeologists. Adding another layer of complexity to the discussion is the fact that this important mountain was referred to as both Mount Sinai and Mount Horeb. In the book of Exodus, the Torah, and the Quran, Moses received the Ten Commandments on Mount Sinai; however, according to the book of Deuteronomy in the Hebrew bible, the Ten Commandments were given to Moses by God on Mount Horeb, though both may have been different names for the same location. What will be explored here is the possibility that Mount Sinai and Mount Horeb are two distinct locations. In other words, there may actually be two holy mountains rather than a single Mount Sinai. What will be analyzed is the existing evidence that one is a mountain near Serabit el-Khadim, a town from antiquity in the Sinai Peninsula where the remains of an ancient temple for the Egyptian goddess Hathor can still be found today and that the other Mount Sinai is actually referring to the Great Pyramid in Giza.

The most widely accepted candidate for Mount Sinai according to biblical scholars is Gebal or Jebel Musa, a mountain in the Sinai Peninsula of Egypt. Its name literally translates to "Moses' Mountain" or "Mount Moses." While the Torah lists several places where the Israelites stopped on their journey out of Egypt, their exact route continues to be the source of debate. The most obvious routes for travelers through the region were the more major roads; however it is quite likely that the Israelites used a less obvious route to avoid the Egyptian army. While this information is still debated among scholars, the southern route which goes past Jebel Musa is the most traditionally accepted.

Dr. Robert Schoch, a Boston University professor with PhDs in both

Fig. 3.1—Exodus Route

geology and geophysics, shares a different theory in which he uses his expertise to date the Sphinx closer to 10,000 BCE, almost 6,000 years earlier than is generally accepted by archaeologists.[1] During an A.R.E. Conference in 2004, Dr. Schoch presented evidence to support his assertion that the ancient city of Serabit el-Khadim (also Serabit al-Khadim, Serabit el-Khadem) with its Temple of Hathor is a likely site for Mount Sinai.[2] His evidence was in support of earlier theories such as those described by Lina Eckenstein in her book *A History of Sinai* that this was the site of the holy mountain of Moses.[3] His lecture put forth reasons that the most likely route for the Exodus would have been a southerly route through the Sinai and that the band of travelers stayed at Serabit el-Khadim, which is far enough away for the Israelites not to be pursued or harassed by the Egyptians. It should be noted that Serabit el-Khadim is on the same traditionally accepted southern Exodus route.

The primary Egyptian goddess of the city was Hathor, known as the Mistress of Turquoise and the Lady of the Sycamore Tree, who is some-times represented as a sycamore fig, and is often recognized as a protec-tor in desert regions and the patron goddess of miners. Hathor is commonly depicted as a cow goddess with a sun disk set between the horns on her head. It is interesting to note that according to the Hebrew Bible, the idol made by Aaron while Moses was away at Mount Sinai, was a golden calf, possibly representing Hathor.

Other researchers have also named this city as a possible stopping place of the Israelites during their exodus. Sir Flinders Petrie, an early twentieth century archaeologist and Egyptologist, felt that not only

Fig. 3.2–Statue of Hathor in the Cairo Museum

would the Israelites already been familiar with the city but also be-lieved that it was one of their stops during their exodus.[4] This area was well known in antiquity for mining and trade of turquoise and copper. To mine the turquoise, the Egyptians would carve large tunnels and caverns into the mountains.

Author, historian, and researcher Laurence Gardner, a Fellow of the Society of Antiquaries of Scotland, went a step further and validated Petrie's research and presented evidence that Serabit el-Khadim is the site of Mount Horeb.[5]

Ralph Ellis is a biblical researcher, Egyptian historian, and the author who presented evidence for the assertion that the biblical Mount Sinai is actually the Great Pyramid.[6] His conclusion is based on a number of facts including the following: that Mount Sinai is traditionally described as the tallest of three mountains and is named for the sharpness of its peaks, that it would have been possible to guard the entire base of the Great Pyramid as the Israelites were commanded, but not a true mountain, and that Moses was commanded to go *into* Mount Sinai. From *Tempest and Exodus*: "And the Lord said unto Moses, Come up to me *into* the mount, and be there; and I will give thee tablets of stone, and a law, and commandments which I have written; that thou mayest teach them, and Moses rose up and his minister Joshua: and Moses went up the mount of God."[7]

Later he continued to build upon the idea with his statement: "It would appear that the Great Pyramid itself might have played a central role in some of the early Hyksos–Israelite rituals . . . It also contained the god of the Israelites."[8] His book also correlates the Star of David symbol with the Great Pyramid. He continues, "it is of no coincidence that the Magen David . . . which more popularly known as the Star of David, (a.k.a. Seal of Solomon) one of the most potent symbols of modern Judaism is formed from two interlocking pyramids (one being inverted)."[9]

Not only do they give appealing and persuasive arguments, but evidence does exist to support both sites simultaneously. Moses could have climbed the Great Pyramid, as one would a mountain, before entering into it and following the passages, making his pilgrimage with God. Serabit el-Khadim would have been similar since it was filled with caverns and mining tunnels for turquoise and copper which could be used the same way.

The mineral turquoise is found from a gem–quality to a chalk–like category. According to Dr. Schoch and other sources, Serabit el-Khadim was known for mining a very pure turquoise gemstone, unique and valued for its sky blue color. Moses was raised by the royal Egyptian family and surely with the esoteric knowledge of Egypt along with the Great Pyramid and all its symbolism, as referred to earlier by Acts 7:22. He would also then have knowledge of this Egyptian outpost for mining and the importance of the gemstone turquoise.

In Exodus 24: 9–10 of the Bible, Moses, Aaron, and seventy elders went up the holy mountain to meet God. The ground God was standing on was described as "a sapphire pavement pure as the heavens themselves."[10] Rather than referring to the blue gemstone sapphire, it is possible that it was turquoise instead. An ancient miscommunication or error in translation could have easily caused the substitution. It is likely that the quality of the turquoise-laden mountains found at Serabit el-Khadim may indeed have resembled or be depicted as a sapphire pavement. This would also fit in with the goddess Hathor, not only as the golden calf, but as the Mistress of Turquoise of the area.

It is also likely that the tablets containing the Ten Commandments brought down by Moses from a mountain filled with turquoise would have been carved from turquoise laden stone. (This theory of turquoise tablets including the significance of turquoise and its structure will be discussed in the next chapter.) According to the Bible, the tablets were kept in the Ark of the Covenant and transported by the Israelites with Moses. It has been suggested that the dimensions of the Ark fit perfectly inside the coffer in the King's Chamber of the Great Pyramid,[11] thus the tablets may have been housed in the granite sarcophagus.

Again the six-pointed star could have meanings at multiple levels and also represent both the Mount Sinai at Serabit el-Khadim and the Great Pyramid. The upright triangle can represent the spiritual mountain of the Great Pyramid, and the inverted triangle the natural physical earth mountain. The Tablets of the Law also represented both the laws involving God and those involving man. Observing these laws perfected man or made man whole in all aspects: "as above, so below" to use the phrase from *The Emerald Tablet*, a cryptic text reported to be the foundation alchemists attributed to Hermes Trismegistus.[12]

It is also interesting to note that a search of the authorized King James Version of the Bible for the word Horeb results in seventeen verse references and Sinai appears in twice that number at thirty-four. (See the chart below.) Could this be a coded identification to mark both sites?

Sinai[13]

KJV Verse Count	
Exodus	13
Leviticus	4
Numbers	12
Deuteronomy	1
Judges	1
Nehemiah	1
Psalms	2
Total	34

Horeb[14]

KJV Verse Count	
Exodus	3
Deuteronomy	9
1 Kings	2
2 Chronicles	1
Psalms	1
Malachi	1
Total	17

Further, the total adds to 51, curiously the angle of the sides of the Great Pyramid (51 degrees). Pictured below are two pyramidal-shaped peaks that can be seen as a person approaches Serabit el-Khadim. Perhaps the twin peaks each represent seventeen verses, totaling 34, while Horeb (Sinai) represents 17 (34). The number 17 also appears in the Cayce readings for the seventeen missing years of Jesus, accordingly both he and John the Baptist went to the Great Pyramid for their final initiation. Also, the Egyptian Pharaoh Akhenaten, the heretic pharaoh who attempted to bring a style of monotheism to Egypt, had a reign that lasted seventeen years.

Fig. 3.3–Serabit al-Khadim

The different names for the holy mountain of God may also help identify the two sites. Sinai translates as *thorny*, where these pictured twin peaks can be found while Horeb translates as *desert and/or sword*, not only identifying the shape of the Great Pyramid, like a tip of a sword or Benben stone and desert to link it to Serabit el-Khadim. A synonym for thorn(y) is spine and an important connection of the Great Pyramid being on the Giza Plateau which was dedicated to Osiris, whose symbol, the Djed, represented his spine, thus could be linking Serabit el-Khadim back to the Great Pyramid. The cubit to the human spine and central nervous system with these links will be discussed in a later chapter. Choosing a site because close-by mountains are pyramidally shaped is not unprecedented in Egypt. Egyptologists believe that is why the site of the Valley of the Kings was chosen to bury their royalty with a pyramid-shaped mountain looking over it. (See color Fig. 1.) This King's Valley pyramidal mountain was named Ta Dehent (the peak) by the Egyptians and was inhabited by Meret Seger (she who loves silence), an Egyptian serpent goddess who protected the area. The importance of the symbolism of the serpent and its inhabiting a pyramidal mountain will be elaborated upon in detail in Chapter 11.

Another possible reason for two sites can be inferred by their positioning and symbolic relations to the sun and moon. The Egyptians can be considered sun worshipers through their god Ra or Re represented as the sun. The Great Pyramid in its original state of white, polished tura limestone would gleam brilliantly, reflecting the sun, whereas the twin peaks of Serabit el-Khadim would represent the moon. It was shown that Hebrew translates Sinai as thorny, but the Middle Eastern translation of Sinai relates to Sin, the moon goddess of the Sumerians, Assyrians, and Babylonians. For these culture the twin peaks are found in the "wilderness of Sin" (see previous map), and they could be representative of the horns of a crescent moon. Thus the masculine and feminine aspects of God are represented. This can be seen in the headdress of Hathor herself with the sun (Ra) nestled between her crescent horns.

As a final note, the fact that the mountain region of Serabit el-Khadim was mined almost 9,000 years ago for copper and turquoise brings up an interesting possibility. It is known that the turquoise of the area was prized for its pure sky blue color representative of the heavens. The "fallen sky stone" is a common appellation for turquoise. Copper may also be extremely significant. Not only is copper one of the oldest mined metals and the precursor of the Bronze Age, but it is also associated with the evolvement of civilization and has some unique qualities. Copper, freshly sheared or smelted, has a distinct odor similar to that of fresh blood—an analogy used historically by murder mystery authors. You can experience this phenomenon by rubbing two copper pennies (prior to 1992 when they were mainly copper) together for about thirty seconds and you will experience this odor.

Even the color of copper, with its reddish hue, connects it to blood. The very ore in the mountain itself is described as being in veins! (See color Fig. 2.) It would not be too farfetched to believe that an ancient people, so close to nature, would not have recognized the similarities between blood and copper with copper representing the lifeblood of the mountain. The Egyptian hieroglyph for copper is the ankh symbol, which is the Egyptian symbol for life.[15] With turquoise representing the heavens, what better material than copper to represent the Earth's blood or life force—a place where heaven and earth meet.

Another aspect of copper is that it is an excellent conductor of electricity. Tie this to a statement from the Cayce readings: "Life in its manifestation is vibration. Electricity is vibration. 1861-16" On other occasions Cayce added: "Know then that the force in nature that is called electrical or electricity is the same force ye worship as Creative or God in action. 1299-1" as well as "Electricity or vibration is the same energy, same power ye call God, not that God is an electric light or an electric machine, but vibration that is creative is of the same energy of life itself. 2828-4" Could such mountains veined with copper be opportune sites for the manifestations of God's Creative Forces?

Perhaps these suggested connections by ancient humankind were the reasons for blood sacrifices on mountains to replace the copper "blood" that had been removed. As civilizations built their own pyramid mountains and mounds around the world, some cultures continued such sacrifices.

On the other side of the world, copper metallurgy was flourishing in South America, particularly in Peru around the beginning of the first millennium AD. Ceremonial and ornamental objects show the use of hammering and annealing. Copper was most commonly alloyed with gold and silver during the time when the Mayans, Incans, and Aztecs reigned in Central and South America.[16]

Author Adrian Gilbert has pointed out that researchers have found that one primary purpose of the Mayan pyramids was to symbolize mountains. Like the Great Pyramid, the pyramid of Kukulcan in Chichen Itza has two interior chambers. [17]

The Egyptian hieroglyph for mountain is *djew*, ⌴ depicted by which is symbolic of a universal mountain with *two* peaks holding up the heavens. A similar carving can be seen over the original entrance to the Great Pyramid. (See color Fig. 3.) Perhaps this is another clue linking the sites as if they were the two holy mountain peaks of the *djew* representing a oneness, a unity portrayed in the symbols of a universal mountain.

If we consider the area as a place for initiation, let us go back to the 51 degree angle of the Great Pyramid which has a sine of .777.[18] In a right triangle, this is the ratio of the side opposite of an acute angle (less than 90 degrees) and the hypotenuse. John Van Auken's research on the Gnostic community with Judaic influences using Kabbalistic numbering quantified the heart chakra as 777 and signified this as the cross.[19] This assertion is supported by the fact that the Great Pyramid is at the longitudinal and latitudinal cross or "heart" of the land masses of the world. Therefore, the Great Pyramid of Giza is arguably found at the center of the earth's landmass (30 degrees north, 31 degrees east)—both north–south and east–west.[20]

The Great Pyramid "cross" connection is possibly further strengthened celestially with the research done by author Andrew Collins. The answer as to whether the Cygnus–Giza overlay is any more valid than the Orion–Giza correlation lies in the fact that the match between the *cross stars* of Cygnus and the pyramids of Khufu, Khafre, and Menkaure is precise and meaningful. It is a perfect expression of the celestial influence on the ground of Dwn-'nwy, who as Sokar is also ancient Egypt's oldest funerary deity, whose abode was Rostau, Giza itself.[21] These aspects will be discussed in greater detail in Chapter 11.

In addition Mr. Collins states: "Strangely as Cygnus sets, its four main stars, called the *triangles* by astronomers, have the distinct appearance of a perfect four-sided pyramid, a casual observation which is unlikely to have been missed by Old Kingdom (Re: Egypt) astronomer priests."[22] It should be noted that he puts these Cygnus alignments during the age of the pyramid builders (approx. 2600 BCE). Even with these date differences, Cygnus and its stars seem to play a significant role with their symbolism as both a cross and triangles through the ages.

Personal observation suggests that these four main star triangles and the four-sided pyramid fit also into a diamond-shape or base-to-base triangles. The Cygnus constellation is also known as the Northern Cross or the Cross of Calvary, representative of the site of the crucifixion of Christ—a cross atop a mound. Terrestrially the Great Pyramid can also be seen as a cross point at the *heart* of the land masses of the earth. It lies at the center of a land mass where the east/west parallel crosses the

most land and the north/south meridian crosses the most land intersect. Later chapters will discuss the Great Pyramid and its initiations in
greater detail.

These star alignments also give a very interesting perspective when
viewed from the Cayce reading 5748-6 text:

> (Q) What was the date of the actual beginning and ending of
> the construction of the Great Pyramid?
> (A) Was one hundred years in construction. Begun and com-
> pleted in the period of Araaraart's time, with Hermes and Ra.
> (Q) What was the date BC of that period?
> (A) 10,490 to 10,390 before the Prince entered into Egypt.

There has been much discussion and controversy over the date of
construction of the Great Pyramid. Mainstream Egyptologists place its
construction at approximately 2500 BCE, but there are several researchers who suggest it is much older and date the pyramid closer to 10,000
BCE. The Edgar Cayce readings were very specific about the dates, placing the building of the Great Pyramid from 10,490 to 10,390 BCE.

Some of the methodologies employed in establishing its date of construction use the astronomical positions of the stars for the time periods championed by each school of researcher. These experts debate the
alignment of stars and constellations to such points as the north entrance of the Great Pyramid and the north and south "airshafts" from
the King's and Queen's Chambers. Because of precession—the movement of the earth's axis—there is a shift in the position of the stars.
Because the precessional cycle is approximately 26,000 years, we can
calculate historical dates based on star alignments. For example, our
current polestar (North Star) is Polaris. But this star changes as we move
backward or forward in time. In 3000 BCE our polestar was the star
Thuban, located in the constellation of Draco while in 12,000 BCE it was
Vega of the constellation of Lyra.

During the construction dates of the Great Pyramid gleaned from the
Cayce readings (10,490–10,390 BCE), there was no specific polestar. There
was instead a trinity of stars spinning around the celestial North Pole.
During this ancient time, this star trinity was circumpolar, meaning that
as viewed from this north latitude they never set below the horizon.[23]
The Egyptians called them the "Imperishables." This trinity of stars,
through thousands of years, has shifted in our view of the sky and now

dips below the horizon during the year. Today the trinity, known as the Summer Triangle, consists of three stars—Deneb, Vega, and Altair—each connected to a separate constellation known as Cygnus, Lyra, and Aquila, respectively. (See color Fig. 4.)

Through different ages and cultures, each of these three constellations has represented birds. It is easy to imagine the ancients looking into the sky above the Great Pyramid in 10,400 BCE and seeing a slowly turning triangle with three birds circling the center, one for each point of the triangle, centering this starry triangle in a celestial circle. (See color Fig. 5.)

The symbolic image of the bird above the Great Pyramid in this stellar triangle of the North is repeated in the Egyptian Benben stone, the pyramidal stone atop an obelisk or the apex of a pyramid. This important stone represented the Benu bird, believed to be the original phoenix, later adopted by the Greeks, depicting rebirth and resurrection.

The Cayce readings also state that the Great Pyramid was oriented in

Fig. 3.4—A Benben Stone

association to the locations of various stars: "Then began the laying out of the pyramid and the building of same . . . to be the place of *initiation* . . . It was formed according . . . to the position of the various stars . . . "(294-151)

For the date that the Cayce readings set for the building of the Great Pyramid, what better example of "as above, so below" could be provided in the stars than this stellar triangle that also represents three celestial birds circling above. These would not only represent the pyramid itself, but the Benu bird of rebirth and resurrection. Such representation would fit aptly for the initiation purposes of the Great Pyramid from the Cayce readings.

> (Q) Please describe Jesus' initiations in Egypt, telling if the Gospel reference to "three days and nights in the grave or tomb," possibly in the shape of a cross, indicate a special initiation.
> (A) This is a portion of the initiation—it is a part of the passage through that to which each soul is to attain in its development, as has the world through each period of their incarnation in the earth. As is supposed, the record of the earth through the passage through the tomb, or the pyramid, is that through which each entity, each soul, as an initiate must pass for the attaining to the releasing of same—as indicated by the empty tomb, which has *never* been filled . . .
> 2067-7

As stated in this reading an initiation is "part of the passage through that to which each soul is to attain in its development . . . " The word initiation, at its roots, means a going in, a beginning, participation. Often it is used in relation to rite of passage ceremonies or involvement with secret rites. In the context of this work initiation can be considered the movement on the path towards a higher consciousness, a unification of the spiritual with the physical. This would be considered the journey of the awakening of the Oneness that is shared in all. This would be the bringing of Heaven and Earth together, in an evolvement in mind, body, and spirit in mutual participation with God. The ultimate realization that the microcosm and microcosm not only reflect it in each other, but that they are one with each other.

Again the number 3 is noted in this rebirth-and-resurrection initiation matching the trinity of stars above, the symbolism of the three-bird constellations, and the Egyptian Benu bird. Interesting to note is even at 10,500 BCE this triangular trinity of stars still incorporates much of the aspects of Mr. Collins' Cygnus observations. This theorized date of construction receives more validating evidence in that at 10,500 BCE the Sphinx, which faces due east, would have been greeting the constellation Leo rising directly east in the night sky. Dr. Schoch notes that Bauval's research (see *The Orion Mystery*) on the alignment of the three stars in Orion's/Osiris' belt in 10,400 BCE shows: "that the pattern of Orion's belt seen on the west of the Milky Way matches, with uncanny precision, the patterns and alignments of the three Giza pyramids!"[24] So as Egyptologists and researchers look to the stars above to help validate their theories of the construction date and purpose of the Great Pyramid below, we are provided with insight to the Pyramid's true purpose and are given another validation from the Cayce readings.

When looking and mapping the celestial sphere of the heavens, the earth's round surface is projected on it. Declination is considered the equivalent of measuring degrees of latitude on the earth's surface. In a very curious "coincidental" event of measuring the difference of degrees of said latitude between these three polar stars, the results are 11, 22, and 33. In numerology these are considered "master numbers": 11 = symbolizing psychic illumination, 22 = the master builder, illumination with grounding, and 33 = Christ Consciousness or Master Teacher. This 1-2-3 power punch through the stars declinations certainly emphasizes the significance of the trinity triangle of the North stars. The number 7 will also be seen as a significant number in ancient times representing the achievement of spiritual awareness, and its use is found in many aspects such as the seven days of creation, the seven ancient planets, the seven chakras, the seven deadly sins, the seven virtues, the seven sacraments, among others. Dr. Schoch notes that the number 7 was sacred to the Egyptians, "as a cosmic number, one that joined earth and sky."[25] The significance of such numbers being incorporated within the Great Pyramid and Stonehenge will be discussed with greater detail in Chapter 11.

By many people these facts have to be called "coincidental" in that it is not believed ancient civilizations at the time, let alone 10,500 BCE, had the ability to make such measurements, and again the ancients are not given the credit they are due with the hubristic thinking that our current civilization must be the most advanced in all aspects.

Uncannily the Edgar Cayce readings actually address this apparent remarkable ability to measure longitudes and latitudes at such an ancient date:

> There were begun some memorials in the Nubian land which still may be seen, even in this period, in the mountains of the land. Whole mountains were honeycombed, and were dug into sufficient to where the perpetual fires are *still* in activity in these various periods, ***when the priest then began to show the manifestations of those periods of reckoning the longitude (as termed now), latitude, and the activities of the planets and stars, and the various groups of stars, constellations***, and the various influences that are held in place, or that *hold* in place those about this particular solar system. [Author's emphasis]   294-150

This is from a reading about the time in ancient Egypt and Nubia prior to the construction of the Cayce reading date of 10,500 BCE for the Great Pyramid. The earlier cited reading told of the use of stars and celestial alignments incorporated in its construction, while this readings speaks of the time such abilities were acquired, including the reckoning on longitude and latitude and eerily concur with such alignments for this ancient date!

Summer Triangle Difference in declination 10490 BCE[26]

Angular Separation

From object or point:	Deneb
To object or point:	Altair

Difference in declination:	**–11° 08' 17.9"**	**11 degrees**
Location name:	Egypt, Cairo	
Location coordinates:	Lon: 031° 15' 00" E, Lat: 30° 03' 00" N	
Local time:	02/03/10490 BC 05:10:23 AM	
Universal time:	02/03/10490 BC 03:10:23	
Julian date:	–2110016.36779	

Angular Separation

From object or point:	Deneb
To object or point:	Vega

Difference in declination: +21° 54' 55.4"   **22 degrees**
Location name: Egypt, Cairo
Location coordinates: Lon: 031° 15' 00" E, Lat: 30° 03' 00" N
Local time: 02/03/10490 BC 05:10:23 AM
Universal time: 02/03/10490 BC 03:10:23
Julian date: −2110016.36779

Angular Separation
From object or point: Altair
To object or point: Vega

Difference in declination: **+33° 03' 13.2"**   **33 degrees**
Location name: Egypt, Cairo
Location coordinates: Lon: 031° 15' 00" E, Lat: 30° 03' 00" N
Local time: 02/03/10490 BC 05:10:23 AM
Universal time: 02/03/10490 BC 03:10:23
Julian date: −2110016.36779

For due diligence the differences of these three stars were also checked at different dates using the same program to confirm that these degree declinations were specific and unique to 10,500 BCE. The results were as follows: at 3000 BCE, Altair to Deneb was 26 degrees, Vega to Deneb was 7 degrees and Vega to Altair was 34 degrees. Measuring the declinations of 2012 AD the results yielded were: Altair to Deneb, 36 degrees, Vega to Deneb, 6.5 degrees, and Vega to Altair 30 degrees.

It has been pointed out how the stellar asterism of the "Summer Triangle," during the period around 10,400 BCE, was a trinity of circumpolar stars. Further we saw that this triangle of "Imperishable" stars could represent the Great Pyramid itself and the immortal Benu bird. It was also shown how the differences of degrees between these three stars were 11, 22, and 33 degrees. It should be noted that even if the ability of ancient Egyptians to measure these degrees is debated, it would be well within their ability to measure the distance ratio or proportion between these three stars. Such a ratio would be, pointedly, 1-2-3.

Now looking to the southern sky using the Cybersky 5 planetarium program for this ancient time of 10,400 BCE in Egypt another triangle asterism of stars can be found. This trinity of stars we know today as the winter triangle. It consists of the stars Sirius, Procyon, and Betelguese.

The Betelguese star is in the shoulder of Orion and the two other stars are separate from Orion. What is stunning is that when the differences of degrees are measured between these three stars the results are 8 degrees, 16 degrees, and 25 degrees! What this means is that, like the Summer Triangle stars, the distance ratio between them, for all intents and purposes, is also 1–2–3. It is noted that to be perfectly exact it should be 24 degrees, rather than 25 degrees.

I would like to offer my deep gratitude to author and astronomer James Mullaney FRAS for confirming for me that such ratios and proportions between the stars in each of these celestial triangles could be measured and noted in a 1–2–3 fashion with even basic instruments.

So in the sky to the north of the Great Pyramid you have a triangle of stars that match, in this ratio, a triangle of stars in the southern sky. While this is occurring around 10,400 BCE, you have the constellation Leo, the celestial lion/sphinx, coming up in the sky, due east, to face his terrestrial brother on the Giza plateau, then padding across the sky between these two triangles of stars.

Now, remembering that pyramids were considered symbolic mountains, reflect that these two starry triangles could well have shared the same meaning, but as cosmic sky mountains. At this point it is time to review the meaning of the Egyptian hieroglyph djew.

The djew glyph is depicted as two rounded hills or peaks with a valley or strip of earth between them. While this sign could depict two individual peaks in any mountain range, it approximated the mountain ranges which rose on either side of the Nile Valley and also had a deeper cosmic significance. The Egyptians visualized a universal mountain split into a western peak (Manu) and an eastern peak (Bakhu) which served as the supports for heaven. The ends of this great earth mountain were guarded by lion deities who protected the rising and setting sun and were sometimes portrayed as part of the cosmic mountain itself.[27]

I think it is very clear that this definition of the djew is also an excellent description of what was going on in the sky above Egypt during the 10,400 BCE period, even down to the lion deities (Leo) guarding these "mountains" and "protecting the rising and setting sun" as the Leo constellation travels from east to west. It shows at this ancient time the sky was an ideal mirror for Egypt and the Great Pyramid on Earth. This concept can even extend to the theory of two triangular tablets of the Ten Commandments, which were noted earlier as giving the laws of how to act with God and how to act with fellow humans. In this stellar case the northern triangle of imperishable stars would represent the God tablet and the southern triangle of setting stars would represent the humankind tablet.

A curious paralleling between the Maya and Egyptian astronomy seems to be implied here also. These starry triangles would fit author John Major Jenkins hypothesis that the Maya, besides having a trinity of stars, consisting of three stars from the Orion constellation (one from the belt and one from each leg) on the south horizon representing the hearth and the annual birth and resurrection of the agricultural Maya maize god, that there should also be a northern triangle of stars representing the greater eternal cosmic birth. The circumpolar triangle of stars of the summer triangle meets that criterion.[28]

Now I wonder, how many more of these "coincidences" that point to the period around 10,400 BCE need to occur before a deeper look is taken of the civilizations in this ancient time period?

The Tables and Turquoise

Now consider the possibility that the Tables of the Law could have been carved from turquoise-laden stones from the mountainous region of Serabit el-Khadim in the shape of two triangular tablets. In Judaic tradition, there is a tale that Moses was given the commandments on a sapphire-like stone.

> Jewish folklore records that Moses kept forgetting his lessons, a common experience for anyone going through a mystical experience. However, he was reassured that *the Teaching was deeply embedded within the spiritual levels of his nature*. At the completion of his celestial training course *he was given two tablets made of a strange sapphire-like stone* [Author's emphasis] that could be rolled up like a scroll. On to these had been engraved the Ten Commandments in such a way that they could be perceived from both sides. Moreover, between each line were written all the particulars of the precepts. This instrument, written by the Divine finger, was to form the basis of the Bible as we know it.
>
> . . . All the foregoing, when seen on the level of the individual, is the experience of the deepest realization. In such a moment what was, what is, and what shall be for oneself is revealed in a profound illumination in which all the apparently unconnected events in life fuse into the recognition that one has been trained to fulfill a certain destiny.[1]

The previous quote: "However, he was reassured that the Teaching was deeply embedded within the spiritual levels of his nature." with the translation of "luah" as tablet and house of the soul acquires a deeper meaning, meshing the spiritual with the physical.

The text in the Cayce reading 5276-1 mirrors this comment of Moses' difficulty and the embedding of such knowledge in his spiritual nature:

> So the entity, as in Moses, finds itself slow in making comprehension; until he had been through those experiences of even being in the presence of the divine, having given to man the outline of the law, and of how man in his relationship to God, in His relationship to his fellow man, in his relationship to himself could say, as must the entity learn, "Say not who will descend from heaven to bring a message, for lo! The whole law is expressed, is manifested, is indicated within one's own consciousness." For the body is indeed the temple of the living God and He hath promised to meet thee there. Open thy consciousness and let it ever be as, not merely in words but in purposes, of hopes, of desires: . . .

The question here is directed to the other italicized quotation from Judaic folklore of a "sapphire-like stone" that the two tablets were made of. Sapphire is as a blue to blue-green gemstone and the root word is *sappir* from Hebrew meaning a precious stone, hence enters the turquoise and Serabit el-Khadim and the "Golden Calf,"[2] particularly because there is evidence that the ancient Hebrew word *sappir* is misconstrued and that it was actually referring to turquoise. This conclusion comes from how turquoise got its name and where it is found. The name comes from a French word *Turquie* which means stone of Turkey from where Persian trade goods passed on their way to Europe.

The name turquoise may have come from the word *Turquie* because of the early belief that the mineral came from that country (the turquoise most likely came from Alimersai Mountain in Persia [now Iran] or the Sinai Peninsula in Egypt, two of the world's oldest-known turquoise mining areas.)

Another possibility could be the name came from the French description of the gemstone *pierre turquin*, meaning dark blue stone.[3] This could have caused the confusion and accounts for the mislabeling of *sappir* as sapphire rather than turquoise, turquoise being "sapphire-like." Hebrews and Egyptians in the Middle East would have been much more familiar with turquoise as a gem than sapphire because turquoise is considerably more prevalent in the area. This notion is supported by author Cyril Aldred as he writes about the great value ancient Egyptians had for turquoise, carnelian, and lapis lazuli. He states that turquoise was mined from the Sinai area but that lapis lazuli was not found within the confines of Egypt and needed to be "imported from the Euphrates area whither (sic) it had been traded from Badakhshan in Afghanistan."[4]

Evidence for the use of turquoise mounts with information from the book *Edgar Cayce Guide to Gemstones, Minerals, Metals, and More* by Shelley Kaehr. From her research she believes that the stone spoken of in the Cayce readings as "Lapis Linguis" could very well be turquoise.[5] The readings go on to describe them as singing or talking stones. What I noted in another reading I find even more fascinating as to the stone's attributes.[6]

> (Q) Of what value is it? (Lapis Linguis)
> (A) Of particular value to those who are interested in things psychic! Read what was in the first effort that was made, as to all those that used the stones as settings to induce the influences from without that would aid an individual in its contact with the higher sources of activity!   440-2

There is some discussion over seeming ambiguity in the Cayce readings as to the nature of Lapis Linguis and whether it could be azurite or turquoise. I believe the geologic formation of turquoise holds the answer. Turquoise is considered a secondary mineral that can be formed from deposits in the earth that include azurite and malachite. This being the case, these minerals are closely related and could share the properties described in the Cayce readings.

The tables of the Ten Commandments were placed in the Ark of the Covenant that was used to communicate with God (the higher sources of activity) by the Hebrews. The mountains of Serabit el-Khadim were filled with turquoise, and with Cayce's reading on turquoise (Lapis Linguis), what better mountain for Moses to go up to communicate with God? This certainly all seems to tantalizingly tie in together.

Accordingly this reading imbues turquoise with the ability to psychically talk and assist one in getting in touch with "higher sources." It also certainly compares to the Cayce description of the Tuaoi stone of the Atlanteans. A comparison can be seen in the spelling **turquoise**. Turquoise is a stone that also is believed to protect one's health and from falls, particularly falls from horses. I find this a curious connection with the fall of humankind from God's grace and the possibility that Moses may have had turquoise tablets to help humankind with its fall. Dr. Kaehr writes in reference to turquoise: " . . . I believe it connects you with the heavens while healing the physical body here on earth."[7] A similar concept to "as above, so below," bringing heaven to earth, and such is a concept symbolized in the vesica pisces, which will be discussed in Chapter 6.

A tractate from the Nag Hammadi Library, which is popularly known as the Gnostic gospels and consists of early Christian texts discovered near the town of Nag Hammadi, Egypt in 1945, gives credence to support the concept of turquoise tablets. The tractate entitled, "The Discourse on the Eighth and Ninth," is introduced as describing the beginnings of the divine realm and states that the eighth and ninth spheres can be stages of advanced spiritual development. The excerpt says:

"My <son> write the language of the book on *steles of turquoise*, in hieroglyphic characters . . . that this teaching be carved on stone . . . This is the oath I will make him *swear by heaven and earth and fire and water and seven rulers of substance and the creating spirit in them*[8] [Author's emphasis]

The last section of the quote is the oath's significance and will become apparent later with its use of the four elements and seven rulers when comparing them to the four hermetic symbols of the ancient elements, which create a six-pointed star and to the seven chakras (spiritual centers of the body) aligned with the spine.

Further support for the symbolism and use of turquoise in Moses' time comes from the writing and research of Drs. Lora and Greg Little and John Van Auken in their book, *Secrets of the Ancient World*. In a chapter discussing the Urim and Thummim of the ancient Hebrews, they state that the Urim and Thummim were special tools for attunement, possibly stones, likely used as a type of oracle to receive divine guidance.[9] Their research continues with the possibility of the Urim and Thummim stones being made of sapphire (See the earlier discussion of sapphire/sappir actually being turquoise in Middle East texts). They relate that sapphire/sappir in Hebrew literature had unusual powers and that

Moses' staff was made of sapphire/sappir and engraved with the name of God. This research ties in well with the idea of the symbolic importance of turquoise that has been put forth here. Could these two stones have been triangularly shaped symbols of the Tetragrammaton *representing* God's name and how to act with and bring together heaven and earth?

A final curious note on the Urim and Thummim comes from writings about Joseph Smith, the founder of the Latter Day Saint Movement. In a book written about Smith by his mother, she describes his creation of the Urim and Thummmim to interpret golden tablets given to him by an angel what were triangularly shaped.

> "On the morning of September 22, after Joseph had returned from the hill, he placed the article [the Nephite interpreters] of which he spoke into my hands, and, upon examination, I found that it consisted of two smooth *three-cornered* diamonds set in glass, and the glasses were set in silver bows, which were connected with each other in much the same way as old fashioned spectacles. . . "[10] [Author's emphasis]

An interesting note on turquoise is that it has crypto–crystalline properties. Its crystalline nature is not obvious in the mineral, and the crystalline structure, with rare exception, becomes apparent only under a microscope. Its crystalline structure is hidden within its rounded surface. Another intriguing fact is the shape of these crystals, which is described as triclinic pinacoid bar 1. (See color Fig. 7.)

The full description of the turquoise crystal system is as follows:

> The bar stands for the center, a symmetrical inversion through the crystallographic center of the crystal. Faces on one side of the crystal are inverted on the other side. The inversion switches everything about the individual faces; *what is left is right and what is up is down.* [Author's emphasis] The 1 refers to the one full rotation required to repeat a face or edge about each crystallographic axis. In other words, there is no rotational repeating of faces or edges.
>
> The lack of symmetry gives rise to the thought that the triclinic system is the closest system to amorphism, having no form or order. It is actually the other way around. *Triclinic*

minerals have a more sophisticated ordering of the atoms in their structure than other minerals. [Author's emphasis] Ordering is a way of saying that the atoms are precisely placed into specific sites and these sites, in the case of triclinic minerals, are not symmetrically arranged.[11]

This is a crystalline mineral, not easily recognized as such; its pyramidal crystals have a single center point. The crystal's shape reverses, as in flipping one triangle over on top of another, and creates a six-pointed star. They have a more sophisticated ordering of the atoms in their structure than other minerals which creates a more ordered structure. Until 1911 this crystal was also thought to be amorphous, meaning without shape, specifically without crystalline structure. It is a stone that appears to be one mass, yet made of many. Its three axes will be shown later to compare with the symbols of the cube in the hexagram, the axis mundi, and the chi–rho.

Portions of the Cayce readings describe Atlantis, the Atlantean beings, and their influx into Egypt due to the destruction of Atlantis. (See the Cayce 364 series of readings for more information on Atlantis.) This destruction occurred in increments until the final demise of Atlantis, this mysterious land described by Plato. One of the keys to the destruction of Atlantis and the subsequent Atlantean exodus, according to the Cayce readings, was the misuse of the Tuaoi stone and the conflict between the inhabitants who had split into two factions: those that followed the Law of One and the followers of the Sons of Belial. Those that followed the Law of One can be seen as highly spiritually, ethically minded, and monotheistic. The sons of Belial can be viewed as materialistic and carnally driven. "The word Belial means literally, 'not profitable.' Something that is Belial is empty; 'children of Belial' are people whose views and opinions are worthless and empty, and therefore not to be listened to."[12]

The aforementioned Tuaoi stone was described by Cayce as being in the temple or powerhouse and that originally it gave the Atlanteans the ability to communicate with the "saints" or where the finite could contact the infinite. The Tuaoi stone description and purpose subtly describes and brings together the ultimate symbol of Oneness in a similar way as the Sri Yantra, the Axis Mundi, and other symbols representing the uniting of heaven and earth. (Detailed in Chapter 6) This application degraded into a use as a physical power source and purportedly led to the destruction of Atlantis. The Cayce readings describe the Atlanteans as originally more like thought forms, but as desire for gratification in the material occurred, they became hardened or set in material form. The Atlantean injection into Egypt was apparently very early, before 10,000 BCE. " . . . of which later we find that peoples who entered into the black or mixed peoples, in what later became the Egyptian dynasty." (364-4)[13]

In the Cayce readings, along with its use and misuse, what caught my attention was the physical description of the stone. It is a six-sided crystal that in the beginning was the source from which there was the spiritual and mental contact, and it apparently radiated energy. If one pictures this six-sided crystal and its energy radiating from each side, one can easily visualize a six-pointed star, Solomon's Seal, or a Magen David (Shield/Star of David). This possibility is strengthened by the authors Lora Little and John Van Auken when they present evidence from the Mayans in Piedras Negras that the six-pointed star may be a sign of the lost Atlantean records and a symbol of the Tuaoi stone.[14] In addition they present this six-pointed star which was also discovered in the ancient Mayan city of Uxmal in a sun disc.

Fig. 4.1–Six-Pointed Star in Sun Disc

The Finite Communicating
with the Infinite

The beginning of the symbolism of uniting the infinite with the finite, the heavens with earth through the fusion of triangles is starting to be evidenced. Following this hypothesis or this thought experiment, let us continue on to the Magen David (the Star or Shield of David), also known as the Seal of Solomon, Creator's Star, or in geometry a hexagram. Here is a six-pointed star/shield or two triangles where one is inverted and the two are placed on top of each other. On the Israeli flag this symbol/shape can be seen in a blue color very similar to the turquoise of Serabit el-Khadim. If the Tables of the Law are, as surmised, triangular and made of turquoise and even if it is turquoise powdered on scrolls, which are inverted and laid on top of each other, the comparison is evident.

Besides this evidence and the arguments for such triangular tablets, there is a metaphysical interpretation of a six-pointed star as being representative of the spiritual man's seven chakras, with the seventh being hidden in the center. Again we are drawn back to the tables representing the "house of the soul."

P.D. Ouspensky describes the six-pointed star as:

> (That) which represented the world on ancient symbolism is
> in reality the representation of space-time or the "period of
> dimension," i.e. of the three space-dimensions and the three
> time-dimensions in their perfect union, where every point of
> space includes the whole of time and every moment of time
> includes the whole of space, when *everything is everywhere
> and always*.[1]

This perfect union in the six-pointed star and its spiritual symbolism is noted in a somewhat similar fashion by Robert Krajenke in his series of books about the Bible using the Edgar Cayce readings. In Genesis interpreting the days of creation, he says: "The Sixth Day brought forth the creation of Man, and the soul partook of both spiritual and physical awareness. The sixth state is the level of the god-man."[2]

It should be noted that the six-pointed star can not only be created with two triangles, but also with three overlapping diamonds.◊ This comes into significance with the Tibetan mantra "Om Mani Padme Hum." Though many argue this cannot be truly translated, some attempts to convert it are: "Behold the Jewel in the Lotus" or "Hail to the Jewel in the Lotus." Others transliterate it as Om, the oneness of all, which is found in the crown chakra. Mani Padme is the jewel in the lotus while Hum is limitless compassion and is found in the heart chakra. This central core Buddhist mantra with its six syllables is often depicted on a six-petal lotus, comparable to the six-petal flower of life symbol.

Fig. 5.1—Om Mani Padme Hum lotus

Buddhism also has the three-fold jewel—the enlightened ideal, the teachings, and the enlightened community. As noted, the overlapping of the three diamonds creates the six-pointed star, the jewel in the lotus, the flower. The flower of life in each of its petal has the jewels to create this. It is where the infinite and the finite meet.

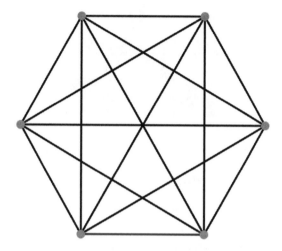

Fig. 5.2–Cube and Star in Hexagram

This is an apt description of what "houses of the soul" (luah) would mean and one that also appears to be embraced by the merkaba/ mercavah, a Hebrew word for chariot or vehicle, probably best known in Ezekiel's vision in the Old Testament of the Bible. The ancient source of information on Merkavah mysticism comes from Judaic writings entitled Hekahlot (Palaces/Temples) and apparently pre-dates Kabbalism. This mysticism explains basically that through long periods of preparation, prayer, and meditation, the initiate journeys through seven stages of mystical ascent. Again the number 7 appears, and the journey is sometimes described as a descent into the Mercaba/Merkavah achieving the vision of Ezekiel. I find this comparable to going to the temple within.

In New Age esotericism, the Mercaba is depicted as a three–dimensional Star of David created out of light using tetrahedrons (3–sided pyramids).

Even in the Ancient Americas, similar symbolic comparisons can be found. Author John Major Jenkins notes:

> Alnitak, the southernmost star in Orion's belt, combines with the 2 leg stars to make a cosmic triangle. Schele pointed out

Fig. 5.3—The Mercaba

that the Maya called this triangle the hearth, and identify it
with the 3 stones used in their hearths. They are thought of as
the 3 stones of creation.[3]

The Mayan three hearth stones make a good association to the Buddhist three-fold jewel and the ancient flower of life which will be discussed later.

It is a curious synchronicity that the Maya would compare the universe both to a table and a house reflecting the Hebrew meaning of
luah that can be translated as both a table and a house, with both
cultures sharing them with similar meanings.

Jenkins explains: "For the Tzotzil Maya, the universe was like a house
or a *table*. Furthermore, in the social life of the house is the domain of
the woman, who owns the hearth . . . "[4] [Author's emphasis]

In addition there is one more reference to the housing of the soul or,
as in this case, the tomb. An excerpt from writings of Richard Henry
Drummond highlights the importance of Egypt and the meaning of the
Great Pyramid:

as indicated oft through this channel, the unifying of the
teachings of many lands was brought together in Egypt, for
that was the center from which there was to be the radial
activity of influence in the earth (no. 2067-7) . . . The initiation of Jesus in Egypt is said to have involved a literal passage

through the chamber in the pyramid—evidently the Great
Pyramid on the Giza plateau (no. 5748-5; no. 5749-2)—*symbolic of the tomb of the soul.* [5] [Author's emphasis]

Is the symbolic description of Great Pyramid as the tomb of the soul
just coincidental to the Hebrew meaning of table/tablet in references to
the Tablets being houses of the soul? One definition of tomb, as a verb,
is "to place or enclose in."[6] This is similar as to the definition "to house"
something. For the spiritually minded it can be said our physicality
houses or entombs our soul.

Also along those lines is the " . . . radial activity of influence" which is
merely coincidental to the description of the function of the Atlantis
Tuaoi stone according to the Cayce readings:

It was in the form of a six-sided figure, in which the Light
appeared as the means of communication between infinity
and the finite; or the means whereby there were the communications with those forces from the outside. Later this came
to mean that from which the energies radiated, as of the center from which there were the *radial activities* guiding
[Author's italics] the various forms of transition or travel
through those periods of activity of the Atlanteans. 2072-10

This description of the finite communicating with the infinite will
have greater significance shortly when the modern–day term of fractal
from Chaos theory is reviewed. It follows quite well the definition of a
fractal—infinite perimeter within a finite area. For that matter it would
seem to answer what appears to be an expanding universe for cosmologists, a fractalizing universe.

In researching the use of ancient symbolism of the triangle along
with the six–pointed star, it appears to me that there is potential evidence that the ancients had greater scientific and esoteric knowledge
than they may have been given credit for. This can be seen in the modern science of Chaos and the study of fractals. Chaos theory puts forth
basically, though many events may seem chaotic and unrelated, that
there is actually very little randomness in the universe and that patterns invariably emerge. This is a very Pythagorean and spiritual belief.
Pictured on the following page are phases of the Koch Snowflake, including a six–pointed star, an example of a fractal developed from Chaos

theory. Now, what is a fractal or, for that matter, a Koch Snowflake? Following are the representations and definitions:

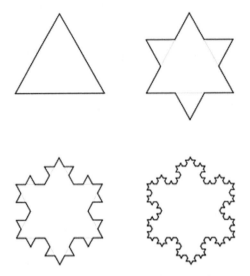

Fig. 5.4–Koch Snowflake Fractal

A *fractal* is a *geometric* object which can be divided into parts, each of which is similar to the original object. Fractals are said to possess infinite detail, and are generally *self-similar* and independent of scale.

A *Koch snowflake* is the result of infinite additions of triangles to the perimeter of a starting triangle. Each time new triangles are added (an *iteration*), the perimeter grows, and eventually approaches infinity. In this way, *the fractal encloses a finite area within an infinite perimeter.*[7] [Author's emphasis]

And finally what is self-similarity?

A *self-similar* object is exactly or approximately *similar* to a part of itself. A *curve* is said to be self-similar if, for every piece of the curve, there is a smaller piece that is *similar* to it. For instance, a side of the *Koch snowflake* is self-similar; it can be divided into two halves, each of which is similar to the whole.

Many objects in the real world, such as *coastlines*, are statistically self–similar: parts of them show the same statistical properties at many scales. Self–similarity is a typical property of *fractals*.[8] [Author's emphasis]

Looking at the second phase of Koch snowflake, a six–pointed star, and the fact that fractals enclose a finite area within an infinite perimeter, the Judaic "house of the soul" and the phrase that the Kingdom of God is within certainly take on more significance.

All this evidence from the Bible, through the shared symbolism of several ancient mystery schools, and modern science have led to this conclusion that the tablets of the Ten Commandments are triangular in shape and that their shape is as significant to humankind's spiritual development as the words themselves on the tablets. They incorporate the macrocosm and the microcosm, heaven and earth. The words inscribed for unity with others, the symbolic shapes for unity within us.

> And remember that thy body is indeed a shadow of that tabernacle . . . thy body is indeed the temple where he has promised to meet thee.   1595-1

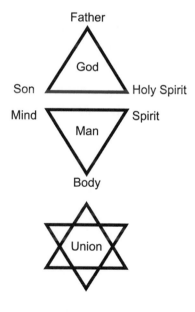

Fig. 5.5–Symbolic Unity of Spirit and Matter

Looking back on the earlier description of turquoise, it can be seen to meet much of the definition of a fractal. (Faces on one side of the crystal are inverted on the other side. The inversion switches everything about the individual faces; *what is left is right and what is up is down.* [Author's emphasis] The 1 refers to the one full rotation required to repeat a face or edge about each crystallographic axis.)

The importance of the scientific research into fractals goes beyond the mathematical curiosity of their geometric structure. Author James Gleick notes that theoretical biologists are discovering that structural system throughout the body such as blood vessels, bronchial networks, heart muscle cells, and other anatomical systems have fractal organizations as a controlling factor. Gleick continues on this avenue with the functioning of DNA averring that our vast and complicated biological systems could not be completely coded in DNA, "but it can specify a repeating process of bifurcation and development."[9] He concludes by commenting that "theoretical biologists began to speculate that fractal scaling was not just common but universal in morphogenesis."[10] Morphogenesis pertains to the biological process that causes any life form to develop its shape.

These statements about DNA and its theorized fractal organization, for that matter such arrangements in all life, will certainly seem prophetic when we proceed to the geometry of DNA itself in Chapter 15.

There is on-going debate over the age of the six-pointed star symbol. Some think the Magen David (Seal of Solomon) is a relatively recent symbol; others think it is much more ancient. In other esoteric fields, as noted, the six-pointed star is a hermetic symbol combining the four ancient elements: fire, water, earth, and wind.

Sacred Symbols and Sacred Geometry

Up to now many of the physical manifestations of triangular-type archetypes have been shown and more are to come, but first let us pause to begin the tracing from where these physical representations gather their creative energy to be birthed. What are the geometric archetypes that show us an echoing of the Oneness, the infinite materializing in the finite? Where is the divine eternal womb with the umbilicus linking heaven and earth? Let's start this journey in the East with the Hindu symbol of the *Sri Yantra*. The Sri Yantra is used as a focal point, an archetypal mandala, for meditation. The Sri Yantra is a symbol of the entire cosmos both in macrocosm and microcosm in its unity and creation. "Sri" translates as holy, light, or illumination; "Yantra" literally means loom or instrument. So then there is a holy instrument or the creative loom of light, appropriate for weaving together the unity that is found in all beings written about here. An example on the following page shows that it consists of nine overlapping triangles, four pointing upward and five pointing downward, and the bindu point in the center. It is surrounded by a circle representing eternity and wholeness, while the bindu point represents manifested creation. Notice that these nine triangles and the bindu point in the middle also gives a total of ten. This is not at all dissimilar to the earlier discussion of triangular tablets with ten utterances, Hebrew letters, or Pythagorean commas. This also coincides with the earlier description in Chapter 2 by John Anthony West of the Egyptian Ennead with its 9 Neters (principles rather than triangles). These emanate from the central fire, bindu point, unity of many repetitions in one. This should also sound familiar as to the fractals discussed in the previous chapter.

A fascinating coincidence of these triangles is their correlation to the

Great Pyramid. The curious relations of the number 51 discussed in Chapter 3 comes into enigmatic play again in the Indian Hindu tantric symbol of the Sri Yantra.

> There is, however, a curious fact about all the correctly constructed *sriyantras*, whether enclosed in circles or in squares. In all such cases the base angle of the largest triangles is about 51°. The monument that comes to mind when this angle is mentioned is the Great Pyramid at Gizeh in Egypt . . . The slope of the face to the base (or the angle of inclination) of the Great Pyramid is 51°50'35".
>
> The largest isosceles triangle of the *sriyantra* design is one of the face triangles of the Great Pyramid in miniature, showing almost exactly the same relationship between pi and phi as in its larger counterpart.[1]

Fig. 6.1–Sri Yantra

The Sri Yantra is another example of how many diverse spiritual philosophies are drawn to the same geometric shapes incorporating aspects of triangles and arcs to express similar meanings of Godhead and creation, the infinite and finite. The Edgar Cayce readings appear to knit humankind's eternal and temporal aspects with the house of the soul and the number 51 also. In reading 443–6 Cayce is asked: "Has the human body a numbering system? If so, what is it?" His answer is: "Those fall into the natural sequence of certain influences. As the male, is either from or to those sequences of 23; while the female—the natural sequences of 28. Or one the perfect whole number, . . . " As can be seen if the masculine and the feminine are incorporated, this also adds up to 51 and reflects back to the masculine/feminine god aspects previously discussed in relationship of Horeb and Sinai, joining the sun and the moon.

Axis Mundi, Chi-Rho, Vesica Pisces, and the Cube in the Hexagram

Such types of curious circumstances continue. Remembering the previous diagram of the turquoise axis, it is not difficult to see the axis mundi symbol, a symbol shown in many fashions representing the center of the universe/world, the joining of heaven and earth through its umbilicus. Mountains also quite often represented this link in many cultures; even the tekhenu/obelisk of ancient Egypt can represent this. The chi rho (a Christian symbol depicting the first two letters in Christ in Greek) can be derived from the axis mundi symbol showing the meeting and connection of heaven and earth through Jesus Christ, known as both the son of God and son of man.

By closing in the sides of the axis mundi and by connecting each point, the cube in the hexagon is created.

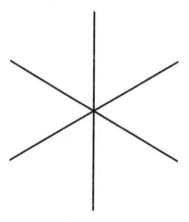

Fig. 6.2—Axis Mundi

Geometrically a hexagon is a six-sided polygon with the core shape of a hexagram being a six-pointed star. If lines are drawn from oppos-

ing vertices, such as an axis mundi, it divides the hexagon into six triangles and unfolding those six triangles creates a six-pointed star. The
lined hexagon also gives the illusion of a cube. The cube is a model of
the New Jerusalem dimensions in the biblical Revelations twelve thousand stadia by twelve thousand stadia by twelve thousand stadia, and
the holiest site of Islam at Mecca is the Kaaba, meaning cube. The cube
is also found to be important to the Freemasons as to symbolically
shaping themselves towards spiritual perfection. It was also noted earlier that the white altar where the two golden delta tablets were placed
by Enoch was a cube. The Buddhist three-fold jewel discussed in Chapter 5 and its accompanying illustration also show this. A hexagon also
fits the described six-sided Taoui stone from the Cayce readings. This is
a stone according to the Cayce readings that allowed the people to commune with the saints, to connect to heaven from earth.

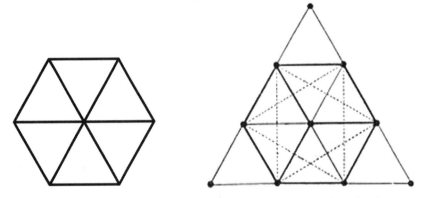

Fig. 6.3—Hexagon/cube and the axis mundi/hexagram/cube/triangle

Fig. 6.4—Chi Rho I

Fig. 6.5–Chi Rho II

Fig. 6.6–Chi Rho III

In all these examples from different venues the same meaning is shared—that is in the connecting, the joining, the communion, and the union with both heaven and earth in perfect harmony.

It does not stop there. If you examine the crystalline structure of turquoise and compare it to the Platonic and Archimedean solids, more curiosities show up. The turquoise crystal compares to the octahedron.

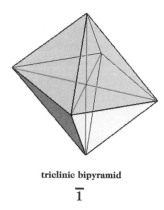

triclinic bipyramid

$\bar{1}$

Fig. 6.7–Turquoise crystal system

The *octahedron* has four special orthogonal projections, centered, on an edge, vertex, face, and normal to a face. The second and third correspond to the B_2 and A_2 Coxeter planes.

Fig. 6.8–Orthogonal Projections

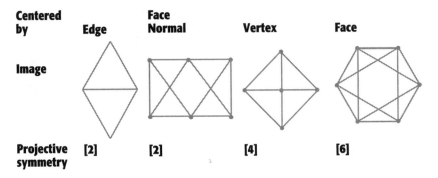

Centered by	Edge	Face Normal	Vertex	Face
Image				
Projective symmetry	[2]	[2]	[4]	[6]

Plato sees the octahedron as symbolic of air, thus the breath, and the intermediary between water and fire, which fits in well with the symbolism of John the Baptist baptizing in water and telling of baptism by fire respectively and the spirit (breath) as their intermediary. It has been shown already that the symbol for fire is an upright triangle and that the symbol for water is an inverted triangle, one hundred and eighty degrees opposites of each other. Interesting to note that there is a similar juxtaposition not only in the baptisms of John and Jesus, but also in their births. John's birth is celebrated on June 24 by the Catholic Church and Jesus' is celebrated six months apart on December 25, more subtle clues of the fulfillment of the "laws," the unification of heaven and earth.

Viewing the geometric examples given in spherical/circular form, the axis mundi connection of heaven and earth can be seen in the flower of life. It is from here we begin to discover the infinite Creative Forces of the universe.

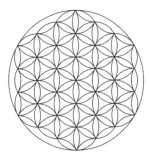

Fig. 6.9–Flower of Life

The **Flower of Life** is a geometrical figure composed of multiple evenly-spaced, overlapping circles that are arranged so that they form a flower-like pattern with a six–fold symmetry.

The Flower of Life contains the patterns of creation for ancient civilizations.

Fig. 6.10—Seed of Life

It can be seen that they form a relation to a single six-petalled flower of life. There are six vertices, six petals, six sides to two triangles—the similarities of the houses of the soul to the pattern of creation. From one petal of the flower of life the vesica pisces (bladder of the fish) is seen. This is an ancient symbol adopted by Christians, though this point is debated, and is called the ichthys.

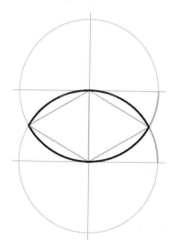

Fig. 6.11—Vesica Pisces/Ichthys

It has been the subject of mystical speculation at several periods of history, perhaps first among the Pythagoreans, who considered it a holy figure. The mathematical ratio of its width (measured to the endpoints

of the "body," not including the "tail") to its height was reportedly believed by them to be 265:153. This ratio, equal to 1.73203, was thought
of as a holy number, called *the measure of the fish*. The geometric ratio of
these dimensions is actually the square root of 3, or 1.73205 . . . (since if
you draw straight lines connecting the centers of the two circles with
each other, and with the two points where the circles intersect, then you
get two equilateral triangles joined along an edge, as shown in light red
in the diagram).[2]

Essentially the intersection of two overlapping spheres, the vesica
pisces (including the interior portion of it and/or the more common
two dimensional versions) represents, among other things:

1) The joining of God and Goddess to create an offspring,
2) A symbol for Jesus Christ,
3) In art a pointed oval used as an aureole in medieval sculpture
   and painting,
4) The vagina of the female goddess,
5) The basic motif in the Flower of Life,
6) An overlay of the Tree of Life,
7) The formative power of polygons,
8) A geometrical description of square roots and harmonic proportions, and/or
9) A source of immense power and energy[3]

This symbol not only represents the joining of the god and goddess
in creation (sun and moon; heaven and earth); but please note from the
previous list #7 which says it has the formative power of polygons. The
vesica pisces is a form generator; from its waves or arcs the family of
polygons are created. This form generation is comparable to how physicists wrestle with light having both a wave and a particle nature. The
sacred geometry of arcs and triangles is their meaning of manifested
creation; the particles of light, the fabric of materiality, are now seen to
be birthed from the waves or the arcs of the vesica pisces' creative energy. The infinite energy of arc and wave forms is the precursor of the
physical universe. These waves are the arcs of the vesica pisces, and the
particles are the triangles and higher polygons that have the potential
to be created from the vesica pisces' waves. This is where the infinity of
waves meets the finiteness of closed forms (wave collapse). Author Kevin
Todeschi not only notes the discovery in science of this wave-to-par-
ticle phenomenon but also that the particles, at the subatomic level,

themselves emit vibrations (waves) which in turn confirms the Cayce readings of seventy years ago describing all being vibration.

> Twentieth century experiments in physics gave rise to the wave—particle duality, which simply means that light waves of energy experiments behave like particles, and particles of matter in some experiments behave like waves of energy. Therefore, quantum theory contends that all matter is in motion because particles of *matter fundamentally behave as a wave*, and waves are essentially vibrations that repeat continuously. Everything is vibration.[4] [Author's emphasis]

The latest science has taken this even farther into the makeup of the material plane.

> Current scientific theory holds that *all* particles *also* have a wave nature (and vice versa). *This phenomenon has been verified not only for elementary particles, but also for compound particles like atoms and even molecules.*[5] [Author's emphasis]

So not only does light have a nature both as a wave and particle, but even molecules, thus confirming the statement: all is vibration.

To be clear about the idea that when you are discussing vibrations, you are also discussing waves, the following is the physics' definition of a wave:

> A *vibration* which moves through a substance—Each individual molecule undergoes SHM . . . (Simple Harmonic Motion)— . . . but energy moves from molecule to molecule. SHM: Periodic balanced motion, i.e. a pendulum[6]

Author Lawrence Blair points out that the vesica pisces is a geometric form generator.

> once a circle or "sphere-point," has moved at least one radius distant from itself, it produces an archetypal symbol: the vagina-shaped "vesica pisces" —the feminine principle of generation from which spring all other geometrical forms, such as the triangles, squares, and "golden mean" rectangles which abound in sacred architecture.[7]

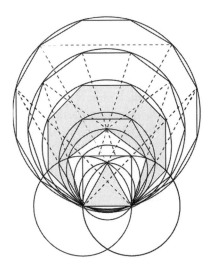

Fig. 6.12–Vesica Pisces Form Generator

In the vesica pisces can be seen the octahedron; two-dimensionally this is viewed as the two triangles, diamond shaped. The vesica pisces is one petal of the flower of life. When the entire six-petalled flower of life is created, and each petal has its diamond inscribed, it can be seen that a six-pointed star will be created from the base-to-base triangles connecting within each petal.

The vesica pisces is the symbolism of the Creative Forces. It is the circle, the All in eternity that moved, which can be seen as the circle overlapping itself. Picture this moving circle as waves, as vibrations that created the universe; God moved, the universal consciousness spoke, and in so doing creation occurred. This is a common theme of creation stories throughout the world. Whether God moved, spoke, or breathed over waters or another sacred sound of creation occurred, they are themes of vibrations bringing forth creation. A depiction of such a circle moving over itself is the vesica pisces, the womb of creation.

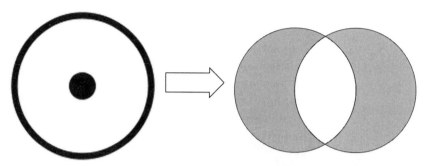

Fig. 6.13–Circumpunct/Ra symbol   **Fig. 6.14–Vesica Pisces**

A symbol representing God

A symbol of God moving, breathing, speaking; thus producing waves, vibrations, creation.

The Circle is the most common and universal signs, found in all cultures. It is the symbol of the sun in its limitless or boundless aspect. It has no beginning or end, and no divisions, making it the perfect symbol of completeness, eternity, and the soul.[8]

The circle with the center dot is an ancient symbol; it represents the sun and the Egyptian sun god Ra. This representation of god, then moving, creating humankind in its own image brings us back again to the creation in the vesica pisces. Viewing this from a scientific symbolism, the dot is the singularity of Oneness at the beginning of the creation of the universe. The circle is the "Big Bang" cosmological theory of creation expanding outward, moving with overlapping waves and vibrations. Through quantum physics, science also tells us of the unity of everything, through the singularity, when all was one, unmanifested. This Oneness was not lost with the Big Bang, the manifestation, or the moving of God. The science also shows and proves, through Bell's theorem, that everything is connected and what affects one, affects the other. It is called entanglement. The theorem confirms that the universe is nonlocal, meaning that in the physics of quantum mechanics, particles that had previously been in each other's fields (entangled) can now be moved light years apart, and if one of the particles is influenced, the other is instantly affected in apparent violation of the laws of the time and the speed of light. So with our original essence, our particles, being with the first cause, a singularity, even in the later expansion we are entangled, connected, remaining one at some level.

Fig. 6.15–Vesica Pisces in ripples

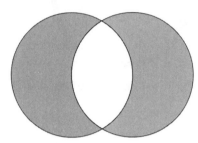

Fig. 6.16–Vesica Pisces

What has been presented with the descriptions of various shapes and patterns in all these chapters and the chapters to come is what is called Sacred Geometry in its many different manifestations. Sacred geometry involves sacred universal patterns used in the design of everything in our reality and is most often seen in sacred architecture and sacred art. The basic tenet is that geometry as well as mathematical ratios, harmonics, and proportion are also found in music, light, and cosmology. Sacred Geometry is expansive and has many levels. A library could be filled with the volumes written about it. Here will be examined only the two basic core universal archetypes that can be considered to generate the rest: arcs and triangles. This system of sacred geometry can be seen as widespread, even in prehistory, and has an apparent shared consciousness of symbols which are universal to the human condition. In the Hermetic tradition of "as above, so below," they reflect each other in the macrocosm and the microcosm. They reflect the fabric of the universe and the very fabric of our beings. The Cayce readings refer to them as patterns or models.

> . . . for to begin from the first we have in that as has been given in the material plane, we have the counterpart, pattern or model through which all may be understood in the etheric or in the celestial, terrestrial plane.   900-348

Galileo, considered the father of modern science and physics states it this way:

> Philosophy is written in this grand book, the universe, which stands continually open to our gaze . . . It is written in the language of mathematics, and its characters are triangles, circles, and other geometric figures without which it is humanly impossible to understand a single word of it; without these one is wandering in a dark labyrinth.[9]

Sacred Geometry is the joining of spirituality and science, created at a time when the scientists were also philosophers and high priests. What is incredible is that this sacred geometry reflects in spiritual symbolism, attained through intuition thousands of years ago, what science is now confirming about the fabric of the universe in science's own geometry.

Much that has been written here so far has been about the physicality, the particle aspects of the universe, but what of the Creative Forces behind this materiality? As of yet the wave aspect of the particle, the waves and vibrations of the "Big Bang" of creation have been touched upon only lightly. The following will begin to remove the curtain between the wave and the particle and address where our physical universe began—in vibrations!

This creation from vibrations is also found in the Cayce readings.

> As is understood, Life-God-in its essence is vibration . . .
>
> 281-4

And in reading 699-1

> . . . everything that has taken on materiality as to become expressive in any kingdom in the material world, is *by the vibrations* that are the motions . . . *all vibration must eventually, as it materializes into matter,* pass through a stage of evolution and out. For it rises in its emanations and descends also. *Hence the cycle, or circle, or arc, that is as a description of all influence in the experience of man.* And very few do they come at angles! [Author's emphasis]

This Cayce reading put it in a nutshell:

> . . . everything is vibratory—is—
> (A) Absolutely correct!   195-54

This may seem like a dramatic, mystical observation at its time in 1929, a time when the greatest physicists of the era were just beginning to grasp the wave particle implication and codify quantum physics. Now, eighty years later, science is confirming what the Cayce readings stated about vibration and what is depicted in the vesica pisces and the seed and flowers of life, those still life symbols of vibrations and waves representing the creation of the universe.

Scientists describe a universe created from vibrations:

> *The early universe rang with the sound of countless cosmic bells,* which filled the primordial darkness with ripples like the surface of a pond pounded by stones. *The wave fronts later served as spawning grounds for galaxies,* astronomers announced Tuesday.
>
> "The whole thing sits there and rings like a bell," Eisenstein said. The thick hot soup would transmit sound waves in the same manner that air or water do. When the fog cleared, *the sound waves would have remained as countless ripples of material.*
>
> Think of a rock dropped into a pond, Eisenstein suggested. The ripples are areas where extra water is piled up. In the early cosmos, *the sound ripples would have been areas where extra matter piled up, and more galaxies should have formed along these ripples than elsewhere.*
>
> "The twist is, [the extra matter represented by] the rock also helped formed galaxies," he said.
>
> The effect is subtle in another way, because the ringing cosmic bells (the rocks in our analogy) were ubiquitous. So instead of one rock tossed into the pond, "It's more like a handful of gravel," Eisenstein said. "*You get overlapping ripples.*"
>
> *And the results confirm other methods that have found the universe is composed of just 4 percent regular matter* (the atoms that make everything from people to clouds to stars), 25

percent dark matter (mysterious stuff that must be there but can't be seen), and the rest dark energy, an even more mysterious force that is driving the universe to expand at an ever-increasing pace.[10] [Author's emphasis]

Science is confirming the Cayce readings that all is vibration!

This picture of multiple waves in water is a visible analogy of what the flower of life represents and that the scientists are describing:

The effect is subtle in another way, because the ringing cosmic bells (the rocks in our analogy) were ubiquitous. So instead of one rock tossed into the pond, "It's more like a handful of gravel," Eisenstein said. *"You get overlapping ripples."*[10] [Author's emphasis]

This creation by vibration is depicted in the same fashion symbolically in the sacred geometry of the flower of life, showing wave over overlapping wave, ripple over ripple.

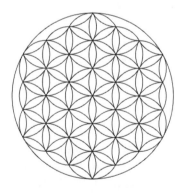

Fig. 6.17—Flower of Life

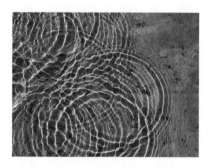

**Fig. 6.18–
Flower of Life in Wave Ripples**

The science describes these wave fronts as overlapping ripples and as the places where extra matter would pile up and thus being a place for the birth site of galaxies more than anywhere else. As an analogy, one may think of weed lines floating in the ocean. Anyone who has ever gone out in the ocean to fish comes to realize that some of the best places to find life exist at the weed lines which have been collected together on the surface of the ocean by wind and wave action. This pattern can also be seen while just walking along the beach at low tide. In this case wavy lines of this seaweed can be seen collected and washed up on the shore in intervals. It appears just the same as described by science for the sites of matter in the universe.

Fig. 6.19–Weed Lines from Wave Actions

How is this occurrence in life depicted in sacred geometry? It is displayed by the polygons created in the waves of the vesica pisces, the diamond shape or back–to–back triangles in the midst of this petal. A petal of the seed of life and the six petals of this seed creation in its physical form becomes clearly manifest.

Below is depicted the vesica pisces, and in its wave/arcs of creative energies the diamond or gemstone particle is formed. As these vesica pisces petals multiply, overlap, or reiterate themselves in their movement and vibration, the six–petal seed of life blossoms. In this blossom of the seed of life comes the six–pointed star, the Creator's Star which is the physical manifestation of life. (See color Fig. 6.) Heaven and earth have joined time and time again in the vesica pisces, expanding out in the seed of life and continuing to expand in the flower of life. That potential of the perfect unison of heaven and earth is shown in the six–pointed star.

Science has confirmed in its methods what spiritual philosophies have intuited for thousands of years and expressed in the symbols of sacred geometry and their faiths, whether it be in the Eastern traditions

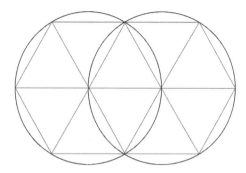

Fig. 6.20—Hexagrams in Vesica Pisces

of *Om Mani Padme Hum* (behold the jewel in the lotus) or from the Christian traditions in 1 Peter 2:5 *(New International Version)* "you also, like living stones, are being built into a spiritual house to be a holy priesthood . . . "

The spiritual house or the lotus of the Creative Forces makes life manifest as living gemstones in the physical and thus represent the tabernacle, the "ark." Then within us can be seen the laws "imbedded" in our nature through the Creator's Star.

And remember as stated in Cayce reading 587-6:

> . . . the understanding that the law was written in the *hearts* of men, rather than upon tables of stone; that the temple, that the holy of holies was to be within.

Is it coincidental that the ancient school of Hermetic mysteries places

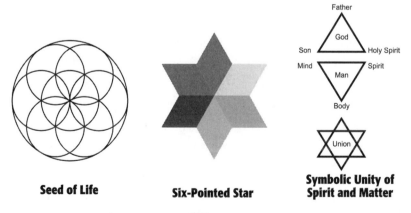

Seed of Life　　**Six-Pointed Star**　　**Symbolic Unity of Spirit and Matter**

Fig. 6.21—
Six-Pointed Star from the Seed of Life and Symbolic Unity of Spirit and Matter

such significance to the triangle? Is it coincidental that the Cayce readings describe the Tuaoi stone as six-sided along with it uses? Is it coincidental that Serabit el-Khadim was home to the worship of the "golden
calf" and that the surrounding mountains were mined for turquoise? Is
it coincidental that turquoise has the properties described earlier and
that Judaic folklore describes the tablets of the Law as being written on
magical blue stones? Is it coincidental that the Hebrew word for tablet/
table has the literal translation of the house of the soul and the general
esoteric symbol that it does? Are the shape and meaning of the
Pythagoreans' Tetracyst or the Qabbalists' Tetragammaton coincidental?
Is it coincidental that the Ark of the Covenant, where the Tables of the
Law were kept, would fit inside the coffer of the Great Pyramid? Is it
coincidental that multiple different faiths share geometric spiritual symbolism with the same meanings and that these same meanings are
shared in the geometry used in science?

There are too many "random" coincidences and that is part of the
reason for putting forth the hypotheses presented here. Yes, it seems
fantastic and farfetched, but the weave of the thread is there, the loom
of light is still shuttling to and fro, but of course, this is a decision each
individual reader will have to make.

Before continuing, a quote from Bill Bryson may aid in keeping in
perspective this hypothesis versus the accepted "facts" of our universe.
It is basically in reference to today's study of both the heavens and the
earth by physicists of cosmology and quantum physics.

> The upshot of all this is that we live in a universe whose age
> we can't quite compute, surrounded by stars whose distances
> we don't altogether know, filled with matter we can't identify,
> operating in conformance with physical laws whose proper-
> ties we don't truly understand.
>
> And on that rather unsettling note, let's return to the Planet
> Earth and consider something we do understand—though by
> now you perhaps won't be surprised to hear that we don't un-
> derstand it completely and what we do understand we haven't
> understood for long.[11]

To paraphrase Shakespeare who was correct so many years ago, there
certainly is more in heaven and earth than we have dreamt of in *any*
philosophies.

The further ramifications of this spiritual and scientific geometry will be discussed in more depth in later chapters.

Obelisks, the Benben Stone, and the Baptism of Jesus

It appears the ancient Egyptians also tried to capture the symbolism of such wave/particle duality—where the infinite meets the finite. They put this symbolism in their monuments; it was a symbolism they saw echoed celestially. The Cayce readings and researchers of Atlantis state that the turmoil and destruction of Atlantis began a migration into Egypt. It was during this influx, according to the readings, that Egypt accelerated its rise to considerable heights in prosperity, science, and construction. This construction included the building of the pyramids of Giza, and particularly the Great Pyramid. The Cayce readings describe the Great Pyramid as a timeline and a place of initiation and that the secrets of the Pyramid were sealed with the clanging of the metal capstone located at its peak. This metal apex is equivalent to what Egyptologists describe as a Benben stone, a "miniature four-sided pyramid."

Some aspects of the Benben stone have been already shown in Chapter 3. This stone is best recognized as the apex of an obelisk. The background of the Benben stone is an important aspect. The name is derived from the Benu bird described often as either a gray heron or a yellow wagtail. As noted earlier, the Benu bird is the precursor to the better-known Greek phoenix. The phoenix was a mythological bird that burst into flames when it died and from its own ashes was resurrected and came back to life. The ancient Egyptian word Benben has been translated to mean to copulate or to create. Copulate's root word meaning is to link or join together. It has also been translated "as related to the verb *weben*(wbn) which means 'to rise, rise in brilliance, or shine' as well as ben–ben, the up thrust sacred stone of *Heliopolis* . . . "[1] Perhaps this linking or joining together represents the wave and particle duality of not only light, but also, as science has recently discovered, the wave and particle aspects of all matter, the joining of heaven and earth, the finite to the infinite.

The Benben stone can be seen as a symbol of resurrection where one rose in brilliance and completed oneself. The Great Pyramid itself could be viewed as a great Benben stone capped with a Benben stone. It is a place for an ultimate rebirth and resurrection.

The word *obelisk* was Greek for the four-sided vertical freestanding stone column that tapered to a pyramidal point at the top. (See color Fig. 11.) The Egyptians term for what we call an obelisk is *tekhenu* or *tekhen* meaning bodily emission; [*tekhen*] is shown as an upside down bowl (or geometrically, a paraboloid—a three-dimensional arc which creates a bowl shape) over a circle with slanted lines next to a pillar on a base with a pyramidal shape on top.[2] There are interpretations of the Egyptian obelisks both as phallic symbols and as representations of beams of light from the sun, specifically the first rays of light to fall on earth or fell on the Egyptian primordial mound, surrounded by water, from which the world was created. This latter interpretation will gain significance in Chapter 15 with discussions of the 2012 alignment of Earth with the center of our galaxy. This center alignment by the galactic bulge or mound of the Milky Way centered with the constellations Cygnus and Sagittarius will have Earth receiving cosmic rays from our galactic center. Remembering the Hermetic adage, "as above, as below," the primordial mound of the galactic center with its shaft of light – Sagittarius A* which is abbreviated as Sgr A*. Sgr A* is believed to be a super massive black hole at the center of our galaxy which emits cosmic radio waves. Thus this shaft of rays, signifying the obelisk and the benu bird, becomes Cygnus!!! This idea fits in smoothly with the discussions in Chapter 3 about the astronomical and symbolic significance of the polar "summer triangle" and Cygnus with the Great Pyramid and Benben stone. "The obelisk is also thought to resemble the rays of the sun, phrased in the saying *Ubenek em Benben* which means: 'You shine in the Benben stone.' "[3]

The background of the term *tekhen* also known as *tekhenu* or *tekenu* is interesting and convoluted in itself. Hieroglyphs are difficult to translate because they have multiple meanings and interpretations. The following description is such an example.

Tekh stands for the Thoth or the symbol for Thoth, the ibis. Ralph Ellis traces back the Greek word *tekton*, meaning master builder, to the Egyptian tekh both as Thoth the sacred scribe or weigher of the heart. There is an additional Egyptian meaning for the word which is bread and wine mixed together, reminiscent of Christian communion.[4]

The second part of the tekenu—*enu* or *henu*—has its own roots. Author Ernest Moyer states:

> Perhaps An or On come from an earlier linguistic form. Hebrew ayin is a basic root word which, through inflectional variations, led to Aan and or Aon, but its origin is unknown. Its meaning as a feminine noun is the eye. It also means spring, as in water. The Assyrian form is enu, or inu. Importantly, it has a figurative meaning of mental and spiritual faculties, acts, and states.[5]

This possible root word *ayin* comes into play again in Chapter 11 in reference to the Great Pyramid's architecture and the possibility of it being a site of initiation to open one's third-eye chakra.

In Kabbalah traditions ayin is the first *sefirot* (an emanation, an archetypical Pythagorean number being an attribute for God, the spiritual eye). Ayin symbolizes the undifferentiated God.[6]

There is also the hieroglyph henu, meaning praise, jubilation, or rejoicing. It is a figure of a person beating one's chest. (See color Fig. 8.)

So the compilation of the meanings for the stems of tekhenu/tekenu is the first light of the heavens striking the primordial mound of earth; Thoth, sacred scribe, weigher of the heart; the root for master builder, a mixture of bread and wine put together, spiritual praise, jubilation, eye, spring, emanation, mental and spiritual faculties, and God undifferentiated.

If this puzzle of meanings and purposes is not enough, there is another interpretation for tekenu.

> Early Egyptologists believed the ⌒ ⌒⟶◯ tekenu (teknu) was a representation of the human sacrifices that the 1st Dynasty rulers were buried with. It seems to be a figure of a man, in a fetal or sitting position, shrouded in a bag, hides or a sack that was placed on its own sledge during funeral processions. Current theories suggest that it contains the spare body parts that were left over during the mummification process, occasionally having a mask of the deceased where a face would be on the figure, and sometimes not

looking like a man at all."[7]

Egyptologist Greg Reeder shows a depiction in the tomb of Montuhirkhepeshef (Mentuherkhepshef) (18th Dynasty) at Waset (Thebes) that actually reveals a man lying on the sledge, being dragged along just as the tekenu was in the funeral procession. In the tomb of Rekhmire (18th Dynasty) the tekenu is finally placed in the tomb, on a chair or couch, with the head poking out of a bag. Then the man sits up on the couch in the "Opening of the Mouth" scene, shown to be wearing shroud-like wrapping, yet obviously human and alive:

> It is the Sem priest who is awakened from his trance at the beginning of that ceremony at the tomb of the deceased. The Sem states that he was "asleep" but had visited the deceased in the otherworld. The Sem then is a shaman undergoing a trance like dream state in the guise of the tekenu. As the tekenu he is transported to the tomb wrapped in a shroud to help facilitate his "death" so that he can be transported to the other world. Thus having visited the spirit world, the Sem was imbued with powers which enabled him to perform the succeeding "Opening of the Mouth" ceremony for the deceased. The tekenu was no more for he had been transformed into the Sem.[8]

It is significant to note that this description of the tekenu includes a figure both dead and asleep with the body, up to the neck, either wrapped and bound in bandages or tied in a sack. While attending a 2006 retreat seminar with Dr. Michael Mirdad, author of *The Seven Initiations of the Spiritual Path*, one of the issues discussed was how, in metaphysical schools of thought, the seven spiritual centers in the body, also known as chakras and identified with the endocrinal glands, described the four lower centers as being physically/materially based while the three highest, one in the throat and two in the head, were the spiritual trinity. The feeling was that it was necessary to subdue or put to symbolic death the four lower spiritual centers to reach the Godhead or the trinity of the three highest, though it is also believed that it should be truly an attunement of all seven centers balanced around the fourth, heart chakra. Perhaps this is the reason why the only organ left in the body of an Egyptian mummification was the heart, yet mainstream

Egyptology attributes it to the belief that one's essence was located in the heart, though these seem one and the same.

Dr. Mirdad's description of the symbolic death of the lower self to resurrect and spiritually enlighten one's higher self is a perfect description of this tekhenu figure bound or bagged and restrained. Here is the "death" or restraint of the lower, material spiritual centers, calming the water of physical creation and the elevation of the three upper spiritual centers, creating the resurrection of a spiritually perfected person. The concept of it as a human sacrifice or the spare parts of a mummification are on track, because it is a depiction of the previous sacrifice of the lower man, what could be considered spare body parts, and the raising of the higher self. Compare this to the symbolism within the Christian community where the bread and wine are symbolic of human sacrifice and consider the meaning of the host:

> Host: Lat., = [sacrificial victim], and its purpose of communion. Middle English communioun, Christian fellowship, Eucharist, from Old French communion, from Late Latin commūnionō, commūnionōn-, from Latin, *mutual participation*.[9]

So even in ancient Egyptian times this can be viewed as a symbolic sacrifice, whose purpose is to become resurrected and one with God. A common hieroglyph for god and king are depicted as beings in a sitting position, knees upright, covered over except for their necks and heads seem reflect this purpose of binding the lower body also:

king   **god, king**
                                    [10]

This situation of a tekenu being apparently dead and bound and then resurrected in perfection has its correlation in the New Testament, Luke 23:52-53:

This man went unto Pilate, and begged the body of Jesus. [**53**] And he took it down, and *wrapped it in linen* [Author's emphasis], and laid it in a sepulcher that was hewn in stone, wherein never man before was laid. (KJV) In Luke 24:12 "Peter, however went running to the tomb. He bent down and saw *the binding cloths* [Author's emphasis] but nothing else: he went back home, amazed at what had happened.[11]

A biblical New Testament parallel for the tekhenu as an obelisk representing a ray of light and a resurrecting bird is also found in all four canonical gospels. It is John the Baptist who advises that while he baptizes with water, the one coming (the Christ) will baptize with fire and the Holy Spirit. This baptizing in fire and the Holy Spirit, making one reborn, parallels the symbolic resurrection and rebirth represented in the obelisk. The descriptions of what occurred after His baptism describe the heavens opening with light and the Spirit descending upon him like a dove. The meanings of the tekhenu both as an obelisk symbolizing a ray of light and a dove-like bird with its resurrection and union representing a symbolic sacrifice as one reaches perfection seem apt. (See color Fig. 9.) This concept is also further strengthened by this research of Mr. Reeder:

In the tomb of Rekhmire, the words relating to the tekenu say: "Causing to come to the god Ra as a resting tekenu to calm the lake of Khepri."[12]

"To calm the lake of Khephir" put a question mark in my mind. Khephir was the patron god of creation, life, and resurrection. In the papyrus of Ani (*The Egyptian Book of the Dead*) he describes himself accordingly: "I came into being of myself in the midst of the Primeval Waters (Nu) in this my name of Khopri."[13] Readers note, Khopri is a variation of Khephir. So you have one coming to rebirth with God in the baptismal of fire and water, calming the same. Some might be familiar with Khephir by his symbol, the scarab which is the beetle that resurrected itself out of a ball of earth/dung.

This is presented as evidence that the interpretation of the obelisk being symbolic of the baptism of Jesus in the New Testament is actually assisted by the Catholic Church itself through a Pope. If one was asked where the most standing obelisks in the world are, one would think the answer would obviously be Egypt! This is not the case. The answer is Rome where there are thirteen standing obelisks, (seven from ancient Egypt and six made by ancient Rome) with seven of them in front of

Catholic basilicas. This raising of obelisks by the Popes began with Pope Sixtus VI after he had his Vatican librarian do exhaustive research on them. The public line of the Vatican was that the placement of the obelisks showed how the true religion had defeated paganism, and as such, these were spoils of spiritual war. The issue with this public party line is that all these obelisks, which had been brought to Italy by ancient Roman rulers when controlling Egypt, had toppled. Many of these monuments were broken, buried, and forgotten through the ages. The Church had to go to enormous lengths and expense to "resurrect" these in front of some of their holiest shrines. The epic saga involving the year it took to move an obelisk one thousand feet and erect it in front of the Vatican is testimony to this. Personally I believe they knew and understood the significance of the obelisk and how it related to Jesus the Christ.

Part of the intuition for this comes from the Catholic Church's spiritual pilgrimages to seven basilicas in Rome along the Appian Way during the Middle Ages. Some of these basilicas had obelisks placed by them. Taken from a travel brochure by the Catholic Pilgrim Office, we learn that:

> Throughout the Middle Ages, pilgrimages traced the seven churches. Through the years, however, pilgrims lost interest in all seven churches and only chose to visit the Four Basilicas of Rome. It is not until the Jubilee 2000, that Pope John Paul II encouraged Christian pilgrims to resume the visit of all seven churches as part of their spiritual journey. Christians now from all corners of the earth come to Rome to follow in the steps of Saint Philip. The Philippine Itinerary takes pilgrims to the Seven Churches on their quest to discover the true sense of Christian Spirituality. The Seven churches were all built under Emperor Constantine marking the presence of the first Christians in Rome. They comprise: Saint Peter's, Saint John in Lateran, Saint Mary Major, Saint Paul Outside the Walls, Saint Laurence Outside the Walls, The Holy Cross Church, Church of the Catacombs of Saint Sebastian. Finally, it is fitting to visit the Millennium Church which was commissioned by Pope John Paul II to celebrate Jubilee 2000.[14]

The Appian Way was the Roman name for the main thoroughfare of the city of Rome and the route that the spiritual pilgrims took to visit the seven churches. I believe this pilgrimage was analogous to the symbolism of the Egyptian tekhenu/tekenu representing the aligning and purification of the seven spiritual centers described within us. It also fits in with the Catholic Church's resurrection of such fallen obelisks in front of its sacred sites. Of note is that the Cayce readings (281-13) also mention the Appian Way; in the readings this way is the dissemination of the divine Creative Forces through the seven chakras. This dissemination described the process in meditation of purifying and attuning oneself with the divine Creative Forces both physically and spiritually. Again all these sources point to the same symbolism and (dare I say?) "lead to Rome."

Although tekhenu and tekenu are represented by different hieroglyphs, their transliterations and symbolic meanings are so similar that they give argument for representing the same purpose through different processes.

Another thought along the lines of these correlations is on the Egyptian word *ankh*. Three of the Gospels have John the Baptist stating that he is not worthy to undo the sandal of Jesus. The Egyptian ankh is not only representative of eternal life, but also of a sandal. Are we being told by John, using Egyptian symbolism, that Jesus brings eternal life?

The Tekenu

Fig. 7.1—Benben Stone from Pyramid of Amenemhet III—Cairo Museum

Fig. 7.2–The Tekenu

The strangeness of the tekhenu (obelisk) symbols continues. I can note a personal experience I had with the remains of the obelisk mounted on its side. (See color Fig. 10.) I had read that if one slapped the side of this monument and someone else placed his ear on the tip at the top, a tone could be heard. While in Egypt in 2005 and again in 2012, I experienced this along with our guide and author John Van Auken and others in our group. By simply slapping with the side of the obelisk at one end and having someone else press his ear at the pyramidal (Benben stone) end, an emanating tone could be clearly heard. The possible purpose, a specific note, and the celestial correlations for such a tone will be explored in Chapter 14. Curiously a large statute of a scarab (Khephir), symbol of the patron god of creation, mentioned by researcher Greg Reeder as being related to the tekenu symbolism, was not ten paces away.

Arcs

From the triangle we go to another significant geometric symbol on this jour-ney—the arc. It was recently introduced as a portion of the flower of life and the vesica pisces. It is the symbol of the infinite Creative Forces, which has been seen to have far-reaching ties and implications of its own.

As you will see, the arc is all around us in life. What really brought this symbol to my attention was an October 2004 seminar presented by Dr. Mark Thurston in Deerfield Beach, Fl. Dr. Thurston used an arc/parabola on an x–y axis as an example of the journey of the soul from being un-individualized with God in the beginning. Un-individualized with God here means a type of oneness with a perfect universal consciousness or soul where there is no recognition of a unique consciousness or souls within the universal consciousness or a soul. It could also be viewed as a lack of individual "I am's" in the universal "I AM." The concept and gift of free will thus allow independent, unique consciousness within a universal consciousness. The difficulty is that free will then allows for mistakes and falls, but such falls are inevitable in the learning process. This is evident with anyone who has or does work with children. The final goal then is to learn and understand our oneness with God yet retain our unique consciousness, thus becoming friends, co-creators, peers with God. The path back from this fall is this journey to oneness with God, but now with individualization.

Un-individualized with God   **Individualized with God**

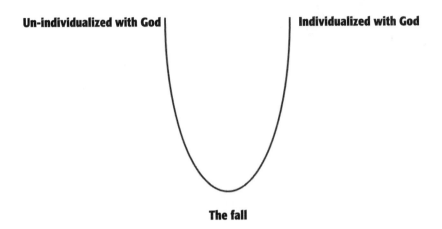

The fall

Listening to Dr. Thurston brought forth a memory of a passage from the New Testament that reflects a similar meaning: "I do not call you servants any longer, because a servant does not know what his master is doing. Instead, I call you friends, because I told you everything I heard from the Father." (John 15:15) The quote from John 15 has always struck me as appropriate for this analogy, because it represents the journey from unknowing, un-individualized servants in God to knowing, individualized, friends, and co-creators with God.

Dr. Thurston's example led my research deeper into the meaning of the word parabola and found that it was synonymous with the word parable—the choice of communication by Jesus to many in the New Testament. Further research led me to three-dimensional parabolas known as paraboloids. In today's civilization these paraboloids are an essential part of global communication, better known as satellite dishes. It is in the shape of a cup or dish that all have a shared meaning. When used spiritually, it is the communion with the Godhead, or it can also be communication with each other as these also create satellite dishes.

Herbert Silberer's book *Hidden Symbolism of Alchemy and the Occult Arts* addresses well many of the symbolic aspects of the arc or parabola. The first chapter of the book recounted a story found by the author entitled "The Parabola." This story came from *Geheime Figuren der Rosenkreuzer aus dem 16ten und 17ten* (*Secret Symbols of the Rosicrucians from the 16th and 17th Centuries*). Basically the author gives different interpretations of the parabola through different schools of thought, such as dream and myth, psychoanalytical and hermetic philosophical interpretation. The bottom line is that it is about the journey of mankind to perfection, alignment, and wholeness. In Dr. Silberer's words: "To be sure the final outcome of the work can be summed up in the three words: Union with God."[1] This is a conscious reunion to what is, similar to Dr. Thurston's interpretation, hence the arc/parabola and the scientific use for parabolic dishes. As in either the spiritual or science–based case, the parabola can be considered a symbol of clear communication between the heavens and earth, bringing both together. This is another example of where through the ages of spirit and science the same conclusions occur, one metaphysically and the other physically. It was something that the Rosicrucians seemed to have intuited in this case.

As noted earlier, we are surrounded by these symbols in our daily lives; they are better known as parabolic dishes or paraboloids for receiving or transmitting an assortment of energy waves such as television, radio, and microwaves. The description of paraboloids from the online encyclopedia Wikipedia definition includes: "a point light source at the focal point produces a parallel light beam. This also works the other way around: a parallel beam of light incident on the paraboloid is concentrated at the focal point."[2]

Another important point is that such a dish puts the waves in phase. When the two waves are in–phase, they interfere (combine) constructively, and the result has twice the amplitude of the individual waves. Essentially the waves are aligned and coordinated, magnifying the wave itself.

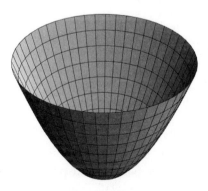

Fig. 8.1–Parabolic dish/cup

A parabolic dish microphone is essentially a mirror telescope for sound. A parabolic surface has the interesting property that all sound waves which propagate parallel to its central axis travel the same distance to get to its focus. That means that when you aim the dish at a distant sound source, all of the sound from that object bounces off the dish and converges toward the focus *in phase* with its pressure peaks and troughs synchronized so that they work together to make the loudest possible sound vibrations.[4]

This is important in the respect that it acts like a laser in putting waves in phase and synchronization. This is what allows lasers to create holographs which are amazing three-dimensional representations of complete information created through the use of lasers and a collection of curves and arcs. It is also vital in transmitting and receiving communications that the signals are in such phase.

How lasers function and create holographs through waves and vibrations make an important comparison to the waves and creation symbolized in the vesica pisces, itself a noted form generator and a depiction of waves and vibrations symbolizing the spiritual creation through the vibrations of God by speaking or moving, letting there be Light.

As physicists and cosmologists are able to probe deeper and deeper into the mysteries and the creation of the universe, it has been shown that they are catching up to what is found in the Cayce readings and the spiritual symbolism explaining the same concepts.

Michael Talbot's research has led him to believe that the universe may be one huge holograph. In Mr. Talbot's words:

> Put another way, there is evidence to suggest that our world and everything in it—from snowflakes to maple trees to falling stars and spinning electrons—are also only ghostly images, projections from a level of reality so beyond our own it is literally beyond both space and time.[5]

Most of us are familiar with and have been entertained by holographs, whether they are in science museums or amusement parks. But how many of us have ever paused and pondered how these three-dimensional figures that we can walk around, that float in the air, that can be seen from different perspectives as real objects, and that can even appear to be animated, are actually created?

So what is a holograph/hologram?

> A Hologram is a photographic emulsion in which information about a scene is recorded in a very special way. When the hologram is illuminated, you the viewer see, a realistic, three-dimensional representation of the scene . . . This is done in such a way that the information is *complete*, so that the scene can be made visible in all its true spatial 3-D aspects with shadows and varying intensities through the scene reproduced realistically, in fact, the word *holography* is derived from the Greek roots meaning 'complete writing.'[6]

Where did holograms come from? To answer this we will start with a brief history of the workings of a holograph. Dr. Denis Gabor put forth his theory in 1947 and received the Nobel Prize in 1971 for his work. The theory itself is based on the wave theory of light. That theory is, simply put, that all light acts and function like waves in an ocean rather than the individual particles of sand on a beach. Though he was able to make very basic holograms, their true existence came about when lasers (light amplification by stimulated emission of radiation) were invented and produced the necessary coherent light.

What is coherent light? It is that light which is parallel, traveling in the same direction, and its waves which are in direct correlation. This light could be considered to be aligned and attuned, to use the terminology that Cayce often did or was symbolized in the tekhenu (obelisk) frozen shaft of light of creation. With lasers the stunning results and impact of Gabor's work could be seen, literally! Since that time the field of holography, with its knowledge and application, has continued to expand and is now used for movies, computer data storage, a type of quantum remote viewing, and audio holophony (holographic sound).

There are many other facets to holography, but we will delve into only two in this chapter. The first deals with a laser having its beam split and being aimed at an object and on a special holographic plate that creates the holograph itself. This plate, similar to photographic film, records the interference waves created by the laser and object. When you developed the plate, there would be no visible picture of the object in question as would be expected on a photographic plate. It would appear apparently blank. Put under a microscope, one would see cloudy areas, wavy and squiggly lines, and ripples or arcs! It can be compared to looking down on a pond rippling from a hand full of pebbles just being thrown into it. These ripples are called interference waves which are being captured on the plate. This is the same analogy discussed earlier for the genesis of creation by both spiritual philosophies and science. When the laser apparatus is projected unto or through this plate, the three–dimensional, life–like image of the object appears.

The second point is that this holographic plate can be cut into pieces, and when a laser beam is applied, the entire holograph will still be projected. Albeit, depending on how many pieces, it may become fuzzy, but the entire object will still be projected. (See color Fig. 12.)

Fig. 8.2–Holographic swirls

> Close-up photograph of a hologram's surface. The object in the hologram is a toy van. It is no more possible to discern the subject of a hologram from this pattern than it is to identify what music has been recorded by looking at a CD surface. Note that the hologram is described by the speckle pattern, rather than the "wavy" line pattern.[7]

Michael Talbot then expands on this and the idea of a holographic universe with more recent concepts brought forth by two scientists: "University of London physicist David Bohm, a protégé of Einstein's and one of the world's most respected quantum physicists; and Karl Pribram, a neurophysiologist at Stanford University and author of the classic neuropsychological textbook *Languages of the Brain*."[8]

Dr. Pribram research led him to believe that a person's brain works as a holographic system, specifically that memory is non–local and is stored like a hologram, i.e. wavelike interference patterns through the brain. This was based on research of the ability of test animals and brain-injured human beings to retain memories despite removal of or damage to different portions of the brain. He believes that it is comparable to the ability of a piece of holographic plates to contain the whole image. Dr. Pribram expanded the holographic brain concept also to vision and beyond. The far-reaching potential of these ideas is best stated in Dr. Pribram's own words:

> It isn't that the world of appearances is wrong; it isn't that there aren't objects out there, at one level of reality. It's that if you penetrate through and look at the universe with a holographic system, you arrive at a different view, a different reality. And that other reality can explain things that have hitherto remained inexplicable scientifically: paranormal phenomena, synchronicities, the apparent meaningful coincidence of events.[9]

Bohm cautions that this does not mean the universe is a giant undifferentiated mass. "Things can be part of an undivided whole and still possess their own unique qualities"[10]

This last sentence in particular reminds me of what the Cayce readings meant when they stated that we are all part of the whole, the Oneness, and that this did not mean the loss of any individuality.

The idea that consciousness and life (and indeed all things) are ensembles enfolded throughout the universe has an equally dazzling flip side. Just as every portion of a hologram contains the image of the whole, every portion of the universe enfolds the whole. As Michael Talbot stated in his book that " . . . for in principle the whole past and implications for the whole future are also enfolded in each small region space and time. Every cell in our body enfolds the entire cosmos."[11]

Again the Cayce readings come to mind in reference to the creative force and a consciousness found in all creation. There is within each of us a microcosm of the universe, reflecting the "as above, so below" philosophy of Hermetic tradition.

These relatively short excerpts from the extensive study and research that Drs. Pribram and Bohm have done speak volumes in and of themselves. When correlated to the Cayce readings, their finds are even more impressive. What follows are some examples of the correlations be-

tween the Edgar Cayce readings and the scientific concept of a holographic universe.

The idea that our day-to-day level of reality is a projection, as the
holograph, comes to mind first. The Cayce readings of how life and the
human race came to be on earth are filled with provocative descriptions akin to the process terminology used in holography. Some of these
descriptions are that things take form through projection and that the
human race appears from these projections and pushes into material
form. The mind functioning as the creative force has the ability to build,
to project and knows itself as a portion of the whole—in it, through it,
and of it. A portion of Cayce reading 364-10 sums it up well:

> . . . *and their projections into the realms of fields of thought*
> *that pertain to a developing or evolving world of matter,* with
> the varied presentations about same, of the expressions or at-
> tributes in the various things about the entity or individual, or
> body, through which such science—as termed now, or such
> phenomena as would be termed—became manifest. [Author's
> emphasis]

How are these projections accomplished? For holographs, as we know
them, it is with coherent light waves. As for the universe, the scientists'
observations show comparable results and properties, but not the how
or with what. Mr. Talbot answers this with a scientific explanation that
makes many physicists uncomfortable. The evidence he cites is the hypothesis that since all waves have some energy and that the universe in
inundated with fields composed of waves, "they find that *every cubic cen-*
timeter of empty space contains more energy than the total energy of all the matter in
the known universe!"[12] [Author's italics] This is known as Zero Point
Energy(ZPE) or the Zero Point Field. The Soviet physicist Andrew
Sakharov stated:

> . . . that we should regard all matter as floating in a sea of
> energy. Modern physics tells us that the space between the
> stars and the space between the particles that which make up
> matter are filled with vast amounts of fluctuating energy: fluc-
> tuations that are fundamental to our view of the fabric of na-
> ture.[13]

Similar ideas and concepts are brought forth in Lynne McTaggart's book *The Field*. The field is described as: " . . . an ocean of microscopic vibrations in the space between things . . . The very underpinning of our universe was a heaving sea of energy—one vast quantum field."[14] Besides going into other depths and different arenas of the quantum basis of the universe, McTaggart delves into the implications which show that everything has a unity, a oneness. She also postulates that at our essence we are all energy, capable of sharing and exchanging information within all aspects of the universe. Her book describes this field as providing "the ultimate holographic blueprint of the world for all time, past, present, and future."[15] In the Cayce readings this description is analogous to the Akashic records which are the "record of all experiences since the beginning of time, believed by some metaphysical traditions to be stored on an indelible, nonphysical medium (akasha)."[16]

ZPE or the Field has the potential to answer the question of available energy or matter from the physics' point of view. Though ZPE may be controversial with physicists, another recent discovery, not fully understood by scientists, but accepted as a "reality," is dark matter and dark energy. This is in the latest studies by physicists and cosmologists who have identified, though one cannot say observed, this dark matter and dark energy. It is described as unseen matter and energy pervading the universe. It is a phenomenon which they cannot measure but can observe the effects of. They theorize that the universe is made approximately of 95% unseen matter and energy (30% dark matter, 65% dark energy). That leaves the visible universe consisting of only 5% of the whole. When I think of what goes into creating a holograph, the energy of a laser and the specially designed plate, or for that matter, in the creation of the images we enjoy washing across a movie screen, it seems that the 5% of the universe which is visible is equivalent to the rest being the process to create our visible universe in a holographic process. Perhaps a better understanding of the Creative Forces would be to categorize the 95% of the universe as the light energy and matter of a true underlying reality, while we live in the illusory shadows of the 5% physical universe consisting of its small portion of dark energy and matter with us being virtually like the prisoners in Plato's cave.

At this point we might want to revisit the definition of a wave, particularly as it pertains to the holographic concepts. "In physics a wave is a D'Artanian disturbance or oscillation that travels through spacetime, accompanied by a transfer of energy . . . They (waves) consist . . . of oscillations or **vibrations** around almost fixed locations."[17] [Author's boldface]

The key in this definition is the word **vibration**, not only for a wave and in the description of "the field" being made up of vibration, but particularly in correlation to the Cayce readings. Throughout the readings the description of materiality in the universe is explained as originating in vibration or vibratory force and that life takes form from and is a manifestation of such force. Matter is the result of this energy; the energy from a one, unified source came first and created our concept of matter. Light, the electro-magnetic spectrum, itself is where all such creation may be found. As mentioned earlier, the Cayce readings describe this succinctly: "everything is vibratory—is—(A) absolutely correct! 195-54"

How prophetic was this statement is revealed in Chapter 6. What is shown to be evident here is that such a scientific concept as a holographic universe was basically described in the Cayce readings forty years before eminent scholars in the scientific community did so! Though all the terminology was not available or would have been understood by those present at the readings, the following excerpts show it clearly. " . . . Their projections into the realms of fields of thought that pertain to a developing or evolving world of matter . . . (364-10) . . . projections that pushed itself into form . . . (364-7) . . . thought bodies gradually took form . . . (364-11) . . . all vibration [waves] must eventually, as it materializes into matter, pass through a stage of evolution and out. (699-1) . . . life in its manifestation is vibration . . . (1861-16) . . . everything is vibratory . . . (195-54) . . . there is no difference between anything such as electricity and, say iron, save in rate of effection . . . (195-70) . . . all matter is a form of vibration . . . (900-448) . . . What is light? That from which, through which, in which may be found all things, out of which all things come. (2533-8)"

The concepts and the ramifications of a holographic universe put forth by Talbot, McTaggart, Pribram, Bohm, and others helps explain the oneness, interconnectedness, and the synchronicities of our universe in today's science of physic-type terms. These scientific concepts aid in strengthening ideas found in the Cayce readings. As noted earlier, it is wave theory that not only makes holographs possible, but it also makes it possible for a portion of the holograph to contain the whole. The science that explains and makes the holograph a reality, along with the science that gives birth to the concept of a holographic universe, also strengthens the Cayce readings by adding pillars of today's physics to the pillars of spirituality. This premise is reiterated in *The Field*. "There need no longer be two truths, the truth of science and the truth of religion. There could be one unified vision of the world."[18]

These findings only scratch the surface of the investigation. The parabola led to the paraboloid, and the phase synchronization of waves also led to parabolic spirals. When these manifestations are examined as a whole, a fascinating picture begins to emerge.

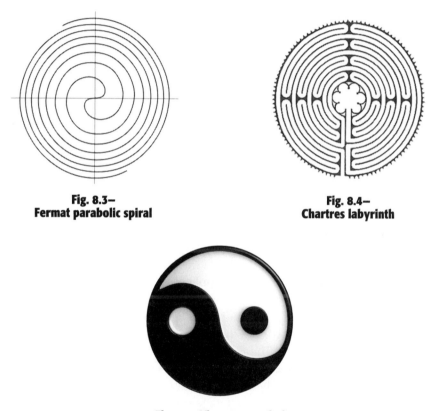

Fig. 8.3–
Fermat parabolic spiral

Fig. 8.4–
Chartres labyrinth

Fig. 8.5–Yin-yang symbol

As can be seen, the Fermat's parabolic spiral shows a close correlation to both the labyrinth design found in the floor of Chartres Cathedral in France and the yin–yang (taijitu) symbol of the Eastern religious philosophy of Taoism. The purpose of this labyrinth was to simulate a pilgrimage to Jerusalem within oneself. In a labyrinth you cannot get lost, as in a maze. The journey leads you out just as you came in with the only difference being that you come out spiritually aligned. In a similar way chaotic light goes into a parabolic dish and is aligned as it comes out. From Eastern traditions the Yin/Yang symbol clearly represents the perfect balance and alignment of everything spiritual and physical in unmanifested and manifested phases that lead to wholeness.

As one continues to delve into the aspects of both the parabola and the paraboloid, symbolic evidence of them can be found through the ages. There is the menorah holding seven candles which is the Judaic candelabra made with what can be described as three parabolas. This is considered one of the most ancient symbols of Judaism. (See color Fig. 13.) "The lamp stand in today's synagogues, called the ner tamid (lit. the continual light, usually translated as the eternal flame), symbolizes the menorah."[19]

Could the Menorah represent the seven chakras and the concurrent symbolism of the parabola? Is this symbolism of our souls, the continuous light, and our eternal flame? Like a parabolic solar oven, the arcs on the Menorah symbolize the focusing of energy to central light.

What of the Holy Grail with its paraboloid cup? The definition of the word grail which comes from Middle English greal, from Old French graal, and from Medieval Latin gradâlis, means flat dish. The flat dish is also known as a paten, which is a shallow dish or plate that is used to hold the host during the celebration of the Eucharist. Its definition as a flat dish even better describes a parabolic dish antennae.

Author Louis Charpentier discusses the etymology of the word grail, he states: "Its origin is not . . . certainly Celtic. It may well be very much earlier. I believe that this word derives from the root "Car' or 'Gar," which has the meaning of stone. The Gar–al, or Gar–el, the urn that contains the stone or the stone urn (Gar–al), say, the Stone of God (Gar–el)."[20] This correlates interestingly to the discussion in early chapters, such as the stone tablets fashioning the Creator's Star within the paraboloid (cup) or in this case depicted as a stone in the urn. It also parallels the Tibetan Buddhist gemstone in the lotus and the bindu gem stone symbol of manifested creation. I think it particularly resonates to the earlier biblical quote of 1 Peter 2:5 (New International Version) "you also, like living stones, are being built into a spiritual house . . . " To put this in terms of science, this is where the implicate, that is the potential present in wave creative energy, becomes explicate by collapsing into the form of matter. Could we be the stones of God? Are our bodies acting as houses of the souls? Are they the stones where our spirit has been poured in?

A significant point in reference to the Holy Grail is not only the spiritual perfection (necessary to have) represented the Grail, but the other symbolism with the Grail as well. In his book *The Secret Teachings of All Ages* Manly P. Hall writes that from the tale of *Parsifal and The Holy Grail*:

> . . . the key to the Grail Mysteries will be apparent if in the sacred spear is recognized the pineal gland with its peculiar pointlike projection and in the Holy Grail the pituitary body containing the Mysterious Water of Life, Mount Salvat is the human body; the domed temple upon its summit, the brain . . . "[21]

These last lines mention the domed temple of the brain. This reference plus the functioning of paraboloids and structures in the brain bring me to the Judaic yarmulke (Kippah)—a paraboloid skullcap. The word "Kippah" means dome.

The *Talmud* tells us that Rav Huna (a Palestinian sage who lived in the 4th century, CE) never walked four amot (approximately six feet) with his head uncovered. When asked why, he replied, "Because the shechinah (Divine Presence) rests above my head." From this, we derive the meaning of wearing a kippah—to remind us of God's presence and that there is something higher and greater than we.[22]

This leads into the significance of symbolic headwear in the next chapter.

Domes/Cups in Symbolic Headwear

It certainly appears that the kippah is a symbol representing the function of a parabolic dish in a spiritual manner. The references and symbolism of the parabola/paraboloid in this manner seems to be widespread. Is the conical hat of the wizard or the Wiccan derivatives of this the Pope's mitre? Was the conical dunce cap placed on the head of a slow student used not for punishment, but actually as an attempt to impart knowledge or wisdom and to attune the wearer to the infinite, akin to a parabolic receiver? This was its original intent when it was created by John Duns Scotus, a Franciscan monk and philosopher in the thirteenth century.[1] Could it be the same for the gold wizards caps found in Europe? Even the muu dancers in pre-dynastic Egypt, related to the tekenu ceremony, are shown with similar conical crowns made of reeds.

Fig. 9.1—Wizard's Hat

Fig. 9.2—Witch's Hat

Fig. 9.3— Dunce's Cap

Fig. 9.4–Gold Cone Hat 900 BCE

Just as interesting is how such a cap can be created, starting as a triangle and ending in a dome, conical shape!

To get a dunce hat, take a solid triangle and successively glue together all three sides with the indicated orientation.

In topology, the *dunce hat* is a compact space formed by taking a solid triangle and gluing all three sides together, with the orientation of one side reversed. Simply gluing two sides oriented in the same direction would yield a cone much like the layman's dunce cap, but the gluing of the third side results in a space that . . . is difficult to depict. The dunce hat has a number of interesting properties. Notably, the dunce hat is contractible, though this is very difficult to show explicitly.[2]

This can be seen through a different aspect.

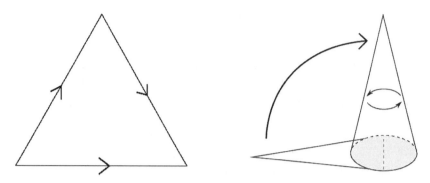

Fig. 9.5—Triangle to Cone

The mitre, worn by the Pope, cardinals, and bishops, also shows simi-larities. For that matter its early development looked much like the Egyptian hieroglyph called *amenta*, representative of the western hori-zon or the underworld.

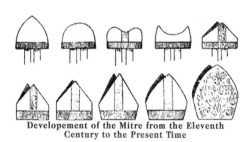

Developement of the Mitre from the Eleventh
Century to the Present Time

Fig. 9.6—Mitre Evolution

**Fig. 9.7—Egyptian
Hieroglyph Amenta; the
underworld/west horizon**

The mitre is a type of folding hat, basically created out of two trian-gular-shaped, reinforced pieces of cloth with two lappets hanging down in the back. Hermetically speaking, while we are on earth, we can be considered in the underworld. If Chapter 2 is remembered, these two triangles used to create the mitre can be seen as the wisdom of the Ten Commandments represented on triangular tablets sitting on the mind of the priest. This also incorporates the concept of conical headwear assisting in imparting wisdom. The mitre's original shape was derived from conical form.

Origin

The pontifical mitre is of Roman origin: it is derived from a non-liturgical head-covering distinctive of the pope, the *camelaucum*, to which also the tiara is to be traced. The camelaucum was worn as early as the beginning of the eighth century, as is shown by the biography of Pope Constantine I (708- 815) in the "Liber Pontificalis." The same head-covering is also mentioned in the so-called "Donation of Constantine." The Ninth Ordo states that the camelaucum was made of white stuff and shaped like a helmet. The coins of Sergius III (904-11) and of *Benedict VII* (974-83), on which St. Peter is portrayed wearing a camelaucum, *give the cap the form of a cone, the original shape of the mitre*. The camelaucum was worn by the pope principally during solemn processions. The mitre developed from the camelaucum in this way: in the course of the tenth century the pope began to wear this head-covering not merely during processions to the church, but also during the subsequent church service. Whether any influence was exerted by the recollection of the sacerdotal head-ornament of the *high-priest* of the Old Testament is not known, but probably not—at least there is no trace of any such influence. It was not until the mitre was universally worn by bishops that it was called an imitation of the Jewish sacerdotal head-ornament.[3] [Author's emphasis]

More Symbolic Arcs/Parabolas

The evidence of arcs in symbolic headgear or focused around the head does not stop there. Author John Van Auken describes the god Hermes, the moon:

> As the rays or godlings went forth, some lost their connectedness to the great Ra (the sun). They moved too far into darkness. Their light dimmed, darkness overcame them. Their faces turned away from the original light. All they saw were the shadows of life. They needed help. Some power needed to help them recall the original light, the original way, the original purpose. This was the power of the moon god Thoth, or

> Hermes in Greek. This power reflects the light of all things
> that have turned away from the direct light.[4]

This certainly fits the function of a paraboloid. Often above the heads
of Egyptian figures are images of the sun and the moon. The depiction
of the moon is that of a sickle shape with both ends of the sickle pointing straight up. This is a perfect example of a parabola.[5] This also reflects the significance of the two sacred "mountain" sites of Horeb and
Sinai, the Great Pyramid and Serabit el-Khadim also representing the
sun and the moon, the masculine and feminine of divine forces discussed in Chapter 3.

These depictions are not only wonderful examples of a parabolic
dish; they carry a second representation of its purpose with the moon
reflecting the light of the sun. The book *The Divine Pymander*, attributed to
Hermes Mercurius Trimegistus, also known as the Egyptian god Thoth,
notes the importance of the cup or paraboloid.

> . . . Filling a large Cup or Bowl therewith, he sent it down,
> giving also a Cryer or Proclaimer. And he commanded him to
> proclaim these things to the souls of men. Dip and wash thy-
> self, thou that art able, in this Cup or Bowl: Thou that
> believest, that thou shalt return to him that sent this Cup . . . "[6]

Can the human skull itself with it interior concave shape be seen
acting as a parabolic dish? Could there be focal points on the pineal
and/or pituitary gland? Did ancient man have the vestiges of memories
of such a function? The Hopi Indians speak of such a time:

> The first of these in man lay at the top of the head. Here,
> when he was born was the soft spot, ko'pavi, the "open door"
> through which he received his life and communicated with
> his creator. For every breath the soft spot moved up and down
> with a gentle vibration that was communicated to the Cre-
> ator. At the time of the red light, Talawva, the last phase of his
> creation, the soft spot was hardened and the door was closed.
> It remained closed until his death, opening then for his life to
> depart as it had come.[7]

Further potential evidence of such a function comes from author

Andrew Collins. Mr. Collins writes of purposely deformed skulls found at Tell Arpachiyah close to Mosul in the area of Iraqi Kurdistan during the Neolithic period. He elucidates on this practice in other cultures including the Mayans and the Chinook tribes of North America. Though there is no definitive answer to why cultures practiced the skull deformity, Mr. Collins asks: " . . . did they also purposely elongate their heads like serpents and wear feathered headdresses in honour, or in memory, of ancient wisdom-bringers who entered their world at the beginning of time?"[8] In ancient Egypt the Amarna period of the heretic pharaoh exposing a monotheistic belief was known for the depiction of different-shaped head.

Was this practice from a memory such as the Hopi had of being connected with the creator and is it an attempt to create a better parabolic receiver/transmitter to reconnect with the Creative Forces? Could the paraboloid shaping of heads or shaping of hats be an attempt to bring wisdom from such sources directly combining it with the eastern concept of the kundalini serpent spiritual energy to focus it in our higher selves rather than along the lines as suggested by Mr. Collins?

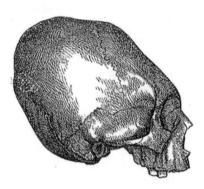

Fig. 9.8–Chinook Flathead Skull

The Great Pyramid as the Great
Receiver and a Holographic Universe

With all these thoughts and coincidences spiraling through our minds, let us
return to the plateau of Giza, coming back towards the beginnings of
this trek, towards completing the circle. At this point in time the Great
Pyramid still remains an unresolved mystery to all. With that said, perhaps we can still peek behind the veil. Thanks to photographs of the
original entrance to the pyramid on its north side and the view of the
stone-carved symbol (an arc shape) above the entrance along with the
picture of the inscriptions on the symbol, some interpretations will be
presented.

Could the Great Pyramid's chamber represent the pineal and pituitary glands and could the Pyramid act as a parabolic dish to focus on
the chambers? Could it be symbolic of the human skull and tissues? Or,
for that matter, could the human skull and its multiple arc and paraboloid aspects function in such as manner? This question again harkens to
the reasons of the previously mentioned skull shaping of some cultures
and the pineal and pituitary in the grail mystery Manly P. Hall described earlier.

The *Gray's Anatomy 1918* edition describes the pituitary body (hypo-
physis) as "a small reddish-gray body."[1] Is it just more coincidences that
the Great Pyramid's King's Chamber is made of reddish-gray rose granite? Is it also a coincidence that the pineal body, though also reddish
gray, is described as being:

> . . . attached by a stalk or peduncle of *white substance*. The
> **stalk** of the pineal body divides anteriorly into two laminæ, a
> dorsal and a ventral, *separated from one another by the pineal
> recess* of the third ventricle. These follicles contain a variable

quantity of gritty material, composed of phosphate and *carbonate of calcium*, phosphate of magnesium and ammonia, and a little animal matter.[2] [Author's emphasis]

There are even more coincidences when considering that the Queen's Chamber in the Great Pyramid is made of white limestone, limestone also known as calcium carbonate and that the chamber's "niche" seems similar to the pineal recess. Another curious point is that phosphate and phosphate of magnesium are in the phosphate mineral class, as is turquoise, the possible stone of the Ten Commandments with its potential use to contact the ethereal. If one pictures a person lying down with his head face up, the comparative positions of the pituitary and pineal glands to the King's and Queen's Chambers in the Great Pyramid are evident. This recalls an earlier chapter quoting the pyramid texts:

Utt. 442
The king becomes a star
Truly, this Great One has fallen on his side, He who is in Nedyt was cast down. Your hand is grasped by Re, Your head is raised by the Two Enneads . . . Who lives by the gods' command, You shall live! You shall rise with Orion in the eastern sky; You shall set with Orion in the western sky . . . "[3]

As described, the king has fallen and his head is being raised by the two enneads, comparable to the two triangular tablets of "god's commands" representing the union of the wisdom of heaven and earth. This observation along with the relationship to the glands and the position of the chamber leads to a connection that can be seen as a way to become a celestial, imperishable being.

To continue on with the aspects of the Great Pyramid and its potential relationship to a paraboloid, possibly focusing vibrations towards specific areas of the human body, I was struck by other visual similarities. Could the Great Pyramid function as a transmitter or receiver or both? Many people mention the amazing sound wave resonance that occurs even today in the Great Pyramid. (I have experienced it myself both in the Grand Gallery and the coffer of the King's Chamber.) In addition there are many numerous haphazard theories. It brings to mind the Cayce reading 378-14 where the capstone of the Great Pyramid was struck and rang throughout the countryside, sealing other area pyramids. One wonders what would occur if the Great Pyramid was returned to its original condition. Is there more to the theorized initiation rites and passages than already imagined?

Included below are examples and the functions of a parabolic dish. It is not that great a stretch of the imagination to compare the Great Pyramid composed of the King's Chamber, Queen's Chamber, and other subterranean chamber with these representations.

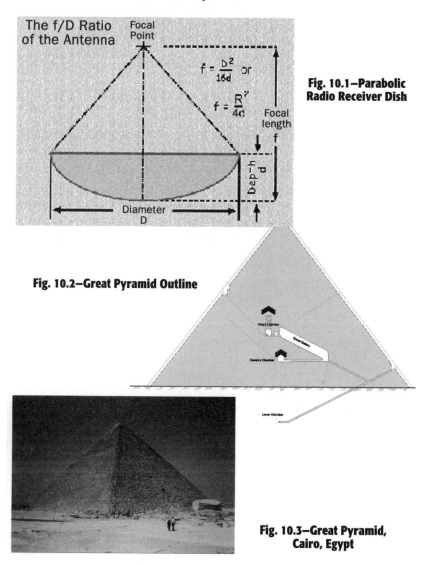

The f/D Ratio of the Antenna

Focal Point

$$f = \frac{D^2}{16d} \text{ or}$$

$$f = \frac{R^2}{4d}$$

Focal length f

Depth d

Diameter D

Fig. 10.1–Parabolic Radio Receiver Dish

Fig. 10.2–Great Pyramid Outline

Fig. 10.3–Great Pyramid, Cairo, Egypt

Fig. 10.4 - Radio Receiver Dish Array

Fig. 10.5–Bindu and Raif symbol

Fig. 10.6–Radio Receiver Dish

Aren't these shapes an interesting similarity?

This brings us to the inscription carved in the arc over the entrance of the Great Pyramid itself. (See color Fig. 14.) To my knowledge there is no definitive translation of its meaning. Could the divining of the pyramid parabola and the four symbols inscribed on it answer the mystery of why it was built and for what use, excluding what the Cayce readings state?

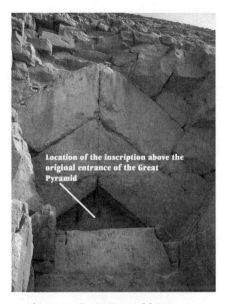

Location of the inscription above the original entrance of the Great Pyramid

Fig. 10.7–Great Pyramid Entrance

If we keep in mind that the function of an arc/parabola is either to direct waves to a focal point or to transmit waves in parallel alignment, I think that two similar interpretations come forward. The first symbol, the inverted triangle with the open topside, signifies the ability of the Great Pyramid to receive communications from the heavens. The second symbol, a circle with a horizontal line through the center, symbolizes the material man who is whole in mind and in body but still in duality with his higher and lower self. The third symbol, three horizontal lines, signify the three–dimensional universe and the triune aspects of man in spirit, mind, and body in it. The fourth symbol, a circle with two parallel vertical lines dividing it, signifies earth man becoming the cosmic man through the three–dimensional universe and aligning all three aspects of his nature with the divine forces. A second interpretation is that the initiate opens his life forces which have been purified in mind and body beyond the three–dimensional realm to become attuned to direct communication with the Creative Forces of the whole. Would this not be akin to those abilities described for the Tuaoi stone?

Along similar lines could these symbols inside the parabola be representing with the V–like symbol the parting of the veil of the Holy of

Holies from top to bottom? Does the next symbol, similar the hieroglyph believed to depict a placenta, mean one's rebirth through the initiation? Does the third symbol, consisting of three wavy lines—which in hieroglyphs can mean cleansing or water—and of three carved lines mean the cleansing or purification of spirit, body, and soul? Does the last symbol signify the mind, body, and soul aligned with and attuned to God?

To reiterate the functions of a parabolic dish stated previously:

> . . . the sound from that object bounces off the dish and con-
> verges toward the focus *in phase*—with its pressure peaks and
> troughs synchronized so that they work together [4]

In relationship to light this type of in phase alignment is called co-herent light.

> Coherent light are light waves that are "in phase" with one
> another. For example, two waves are coherent if the crests of
> one wave are aligned with the crests of the other and the
> troughs of one wave are aligned with the troughs of the other.
> Otherwise, these light waves are considered incoherent.[5]

The similarities to how a parabolic dish acts are evident. Is it that far of a stretch to revisit and relate the concepts put forth by Michael Talbot in Chapter 8 to the concepts and symbolism of multiple religions and thinkers through the ages?

In Mr. Talbot's book he expands on ideas put forth by Drs. Karl Pribram and David Bohm that our universe functions as a hologram in wave theory. Akin to many spiritual systems which assert that the reality we see around us is an illusion or shadow play as described by Plato's cave, or echoes and reflections of Divine reality as put forth by Aldous Huxley in *The Perennial Philosophy*.

> Put another way, there is evidence to suggest that our world
> and everything in it—are also only ghostly images, projections
> from a level of reality so beyond our own it is literally beyond
> both space and time.[6]

The aforementioned deeper order of existence, comparable to

1. Mount Ta Dehent

2. Copper Ore

3. Original Entrance of the Great Pyramid

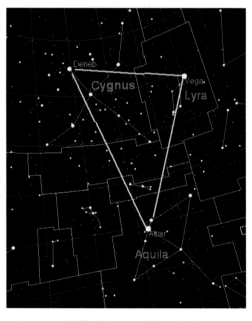

4. The Summer Triangle

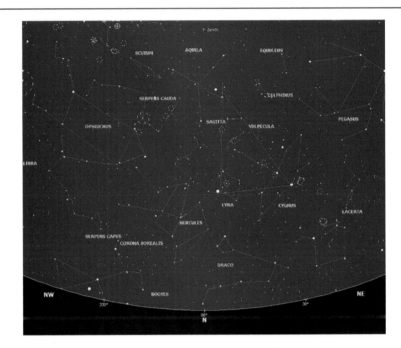

5. Egyptian Skies 10,400 BCE

6. Six-Pointed Star

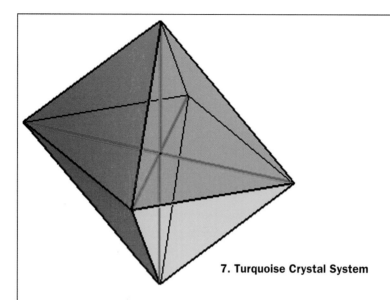

7. Turquoise Crystal System

triclinic bipyramid

$$\overline{1}$$

8. Tekhenu Hieroglyph Depiction

9. Baptism of Jesus

10. The obelisk that emits a tone! Karnak, Egypt (obelisk on side)

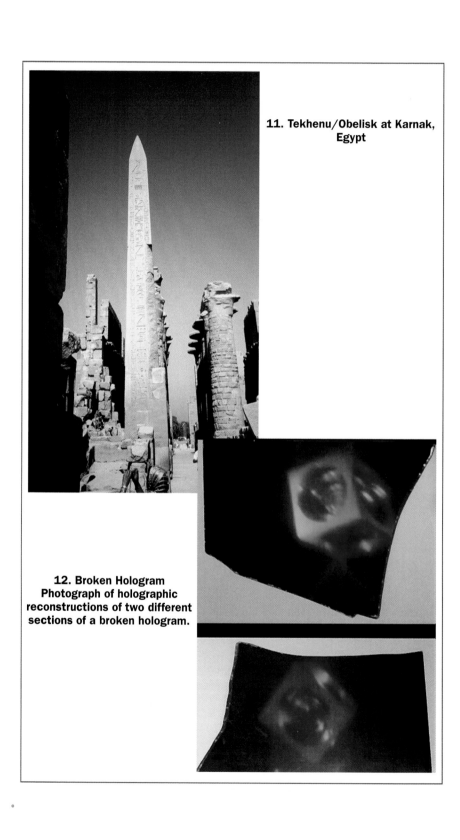

11. Tekhenu/Obelisk at Karnak, Egypt

12. Broken Hologram
Photograph of holographic
reconstructions of two different
sections of a broken hologram.

13. Menorah

14. Great Pyramid Entrance Inscription

15. Great Pyramid and Sphinx

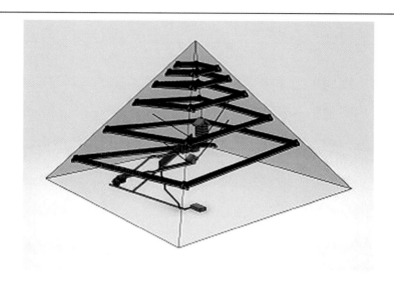

16. Predicted Pyramid Shafts

17. Djed Hieroglyph

18. Mayan Kukulcan Pyramid

19. Kukulcan Pyramid "Serpent of Light"

20. Maya Serpent Bar

21. Raising the Djed

22. Stonehenge

23. Djed on a Pillar at the Philae Temple, Egypt

24. Djed with Serpent

25. Egyptian Crook and Flail

26. Sycamore Figs

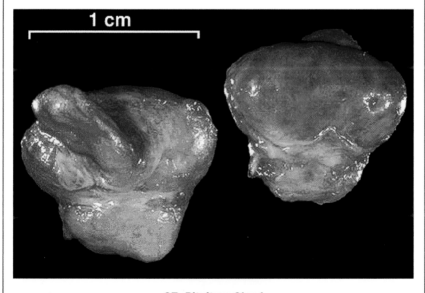

1 cm

27. Pituitary Gland

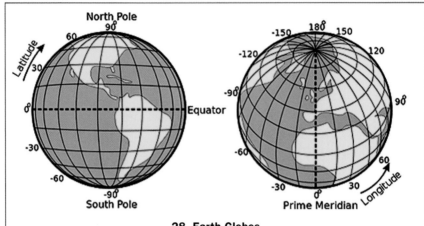

28. Earth Globes

29. Kukulcan
Pyramid Staircase

30. Dream Stelae—
    Sphinx

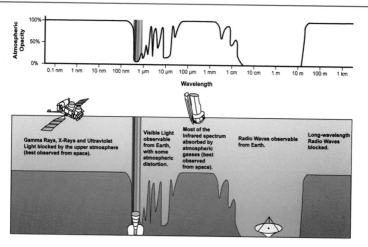

31. Electro-Magnetic Spectrum

32. Milky Way

33. Super Nova Sound Waves

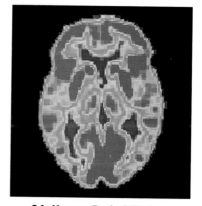

34. Human Brain PET Scan

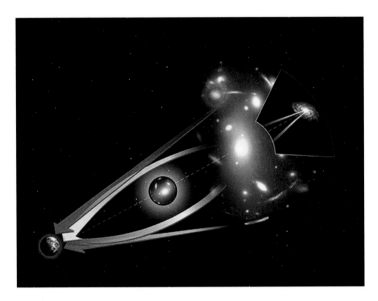

35. Gravity Lens Depiction

36. DNA-Star

Huxley's divine level of reality that gives birth to all the objects and appearances of our physical world described by Pribram, also reflects the creation found within the waves of the vesica pisces—the unmanifested becoming manifest, God moving. Again, this is what Bohm calls the *implicate* (which means "enfolded") order, and he refers to our own level of existence as the *explicate* or unfolded order. He uses these terms because he sees the manifestation of all forms in the universe as the result of countless enfolding and unfolding between these two orders.[7] Through the spiritual lens this can be seen as the multiple ripples of the vesica pisces, through the flower of life manifesting creation wave upon wave. Chapter 6 has shown how science, in its own interpretation, has come to the same conclusion about the creation of the universe.

Why the inclusion of a concept of a holographic universe is pertinent in this discussion is found in the creation of holographs by lasers through coherent light and the functioning of a parabolic dish. I propose that the Great Pyramid functioned in a similar manner. It acted as a source of alignment and attunement, a focusing with the implicate and explicate life forces which make up our universe. It was a place where the infinite could meet with the finite and communion could take place. This is in alliance with the meaning of the raif and bindu as with the Tuaoi stone.

Sacred Initiation Sites, Sacred Serpents, and Sacred Geometry

To substantiate the claim that the Great Pyramid may be an initiation site and the explanation of the possible meanings of the four symbols of the inscription over the entrance, I add the words of author Jeffrey Furst:

> The key to this symbolic interpretation came about initially from a question we had often entertained, but had never found a suitable explanation. Namely, "Why did Jesus have to be baptized?" If we consider the story of Creation from the beginning, this baptism (which was necessary according to Cayce) could be the symbolic third Baptism of Man in a series of Four Baptisms—Earth, Air, Water, Fire. These four, as elements are well documented and oft repeated both within and outside the readings; In the Zodiac, the Four Seasons, the four corners of the earth and sides of the square, the base of the pyramid, *the four lower centers of the body*, the Four Gospels, etc.

Briefly, the Four Baptisms could be conceived as follows:

> **Earth**—The "Fall of the Angels." Spirits became so enmeshed in materiality that they totally lose their identity and awareness with God.
>
> **Air**—Amilius, as Adam leads the "Sons of God" to earth in order to help entrapped "Sons of Man" back to awareness. Then God breathes air (spirit) into Adam and he comes aware of God, though in a material flesh body.

Water—The practice of Baptism preceded Jesus (possibly through Zoroastrianism) as a symbolic means of purification—(again Spirit) washing away the original sin of Adam. When the actual Adam was to be purified by John the Baptist, God's voice was heard to proclaim, "This is my first begotten Son, in whom I am well pleased." (Matt. 3:17) Then to, the fact that Jesus required baptism may further substantiate his role as Adam, since there, He had sinned.

Fire—The promise of The Pentecost is the final baptism. There the disciples received the baptism of *The Holy Spirit, which came as tongues of flame from the heavens.* Afterward they were able to perform miracles as The Master had throughout the balance of their lives in Palestine."[1] [Author's emphasis]

Mr. Furst's interpretation correlates to P.D. Ouspensky's previously mentioned four aspects of God's name in the pyramid–shaped Tetragrammaton and creates the six–pointed star amalgam of the ancient elements. The upright vesica pisces would depict a perfect "tongue of flame." Mr. Furst also notes the four elements represent the four lower centers of the body that need to be purified or bound. This was discussed in Chapter 7 as part of the meaning of the tekhenu/obelisk.

The *Divine Pymander* offers possible correlations of baptism along with the cup for the Great Pyramid:

The Workman made this Universal World, not with his Hands, but with his Word. Therefore thus think of him, as present everywhere, and being always, and making all things; and one above, that by his Will hath framed the things that are. For that is his Body, not tangible, or visible, nor measurable, nor extensible, nor like any other body. *For it is neither Fire, nor Water, nor Air, nor Wind, but all these things are of him; for being Good, he hath dedicated that name unto himself alone. But he would also adorn the Earth, but with the Ornament of a Divine Body.* And he sent man, an Immortal, and Mortal wight. And had more than all living Creatures, and the World; because of his Speech, and Mind. For Man became the spectator of the Works of God, and wondered, and acknowledge the

Maker. For he divided Speech among all men, but not Mind, and yet he envied not any; for Envy comes not thither, but is of abode here below in the Souls of men, that have not the Mind. Tat. But wherefore, Father, did not God distribute the Mind to all men? Herm. Because it pleased him, O Son, to set that in the middle among all souls, as a reward to strive for. Tat. And where hath he set it? Herm. Filling a large Cup or Bowl therewith, he sent it down, giving also a Cryer or Proclaimer. And he commanded him to proclaim these things to the souls of men. Dip and wash thyself, thou that art able, in this Cup or Bowl: *Thou that believest, that thou shalt return to him that sent this Cup; thou that acknowledgest whereunto thou wert made.* As many therefore as understood the Proclaimation, and were baptized or dowsed into the Mind, these were made partakers of Knowledge, and became perfect men receiving the Mind."[2] [Author's emphasis]

There is a similarity of the elements and a cup or bowl is identified. It also includes a baptism or initiation. The cup or bowl also compares similarly in its stated use to a parabolic dish. Those, who use the bowl received, will be able to transmit back to the source that sent it; Communion is then made possible. This is the completion of the parabolic/arc journey, a true co-creative mutual participation, and is equivalent to unifying or bringing together the aspects of heaven and earth, the divine and the material and can be seen as being "in phase."

As to the initiate or initiates themselves, the research leads to the belief that this was done in pairs whereby two went into the Great Pyramid together—one went to the King's Chamber and the other to the Queen's Chamber. This is based on the following evidence: The Djew symbol over the Pyramid's original entrance not only translates as mountain, but two mountains, as noted in an earlier chapter, which were often symbolized by lions. The dream stele depicts two sphinxes or human-headed lions. The two chambers in the Pyramid called the King's and Queen's Chambers could represent the yin and yang or feminine and masculine, the positive and negative, the sun and the moon, just as the Great Pyramid could represent the sun and Serabit el-Khadim could be the moon, if you will. These are all representations of pairings. Along with this evidence of the Great Pyramid representing the Holy Mountain, the Bible states, or at the very least infers, that Moses took

Joshua onto the mount with him one time and Aaron another. The Cayce readings state that Jesus and John the Baptist both went to Egypt to get initiated, and Cayce in his trance state for readings recommended a facilitator of what he termed reverse polarity for the process, reminiscent of Jesus and John the Baptist birthdays being six months apart, as noted in Chapter 6. All are examples of more pairings for enlightenment.

Also note that in the Magen David itself, the six-pointed star, the juxtaposed triangles representing opposite poles are brought together in unison as are the two overlapping circles of the vesica pisces. The Mayan pyramid of Kukulcan at Chichen Itza has also been found to have at least one chamber accessible underneath the north stairs of the pyramid, and I would not be surprised if a second chamber is found. Is Jesus giving us a clue in the New Testament? "For where two or three are gathered together in my name, there am I in the midst of them." (Matt. 18:20 KJV)

To recap earlier research, such curious correlations do not end there, if anything they become curiouser and curiouser. The angle of the Great Pyramid has been measured at 51 degrees and 51 minutes. When the sine is determined for 51 degrees, the result is 0.777. The sine of an angle is the ratio of the length of the opposite side to the hypotenuse. This is an interesting, perhaps coincidental, result with the significance of the number seven in many cultures (total days in the creation of the universe, chakras, etc.) and the aforementioned menorah with seven candles. Such curiosities continue, as earlier noted, in a word search of the King James version of the Bible for Horeb and Sinai, both purportedly identifying the Holy Mount of God, bring a result of Horeb being found 17 times and Sinai being found 34 times for a total of 51. Word translations for Horeb and Sinai are sword and thorny respectively. As noted earlier, author Ralph Ellis postulated that the Great Pyramid may well have been God's Mount, and I elaborated on the fact that there may have been actually two, both the Great Pyramid and a mount near Serabit el-Khadim. Was this a sign left to signify same? Some of the aspects of the hieroglyph djew have been mentioned; here it will be touched upon in more detail, along with a closely related hieroglyph. The hieroglyph djew, which consists of two mountains or a split peaked mountain, also creates a parabolic arc.

The djew glyph is depicted as two rounded hills or peaks with a valley or strip of earth between them. While this sign could depict two individual peaks in any mountain range, it approximated the mountain ranges which rose on either side of the Nile valley, and also had a deeper cosmic significance. The Egyptians visualized a universal mountain split into a western peak (Manu) and an eastern peak (Bakhu) which served as the supports for heaven. The ends of this great earth mountain were guarded by *lion deities* who protected the rising and setting sun and were sometimes portrayed as part of the cosmic mountain itself.[3] [Author's emphasis]

So, this universal single mountain spilt into two peaks, perhaps the Great Pyramid and a peak at Serabit el-Khadim, explains why the Holy Mountain in the Biblical texts is known both as Sinai and Horeb. Then there is Akhet, the symbol when the sun disc is sitting between these two mountains, the home of the sun-god, perhaps in communion. This research and background brings up some other aspects to explain the reasoning of two holy mountains. It is possible that the Great Pyramid, as a holy mountain, represented the sun and masculine aspects of the Creative Forces while Sinai, when translated from the Babylonian language rather than the Hebrew, comes from Sin, a moon goddess. In this case then both the masculine and the feminine aspects of Creative Forces are being represented. In this way the akhet can represent also the crescent moon peaks of the mountains of Serabit el-Khadim with the sun, the Great Pyramid, nestled between them. This was pointed out in an earlier chapter that horns with the sun sitting between them in the headdress of Hathor can have the same representative meaning.

The Symbol Akhet

The hieroglyph sign *akhet* 𓈌 is composed of the Sun disk and the hieroglyph for mountain. The akhet symbol was previously translated as "horizon," which I believe was in error since the ancient Egyptians had a different conception of the horizon. The sign first appeared in recent times (as related to other Egyptian hieroglyphs) since it never occurred in the Pyramid Texts. In the Pyramid Texts the sign that corresponds to the word akhet is the hieroglyph of a sandy island. The ideogram is connected to the root akh, "to shine." The dualistic nature of the sign (used also as 'tomb') is made by the symbolic portrayal in which two human or mummified figures are placed on the two slopes of the sign. The sign akhet is also interpreted as a schematic depiction of the mountains between which the Sun rose and was the regarded as the home of the Sun-god. The akhet was also protected by the Aker, a god depicted as a pair of lions. Sometimes the mountains are replaced by the pair of lions. Also in the Egyptian myths the God Shu and the Goddess Tefnut are depicted as a pair of lions lifting the akhet. The akhet is also a metaphor for a temple and the royal palace.[4]

Are these mountains where man can commune with God? Can they represent outwardly a tomb and inwardly a palace? Do they represent the finite area versus the infinite perimeter of a fractal? Are they places where initiations or baptisms took place to become one with God or perhaps to become a God–man on earth? Are they the home of God where one can commune? Is the outward physical body the tomb and the kingdom within while the eternal soul, the palace? I find it fascinating that the Christian Eucharist, the cup and the host, in cross section view are similar to the akhet symbol and comparable in meaning, where the sun meets the earth and humans can commune with God.

Fig. 11.1–Satellite Dish

Fig. 11.2–Eucharist Communion

Additionally the number 7 was important not only in Egypt and other cultures, but also in early Eucharistic traditions and was incorporated in the rite. It is similar to the significance of 7 in chakras and the sine (.777) of the Great Pyramid and its meaning of the cross to the Coptic Gnostics.

> In this, as in all Eucharistic frescoes, the symbol of Communion appears in close proximity with a *baptismal* symbol . . . The number of guests in all symbolical repasts of the Eucharist is invariably seven, a peculiarity which Wilpert regards as due to the early *Christian* fondness for the symbolism of numbers. According to St. Augustine (Tract. cxxiii, in Joan.), the number seven represented the totality of the *Christian world.*[5]

At such a site of initiation, such as the Great Pyramid, a place both for a spiritual baptism and to commune with God through one's higher self, it could be expected that its entire design and symbolism would be made to invoke its exact purpose. This would include not only its symbolic shape but also the units of measurement and numbers used in its construction where such symbolic numbers would be derived. The units of measures used could be expected to have significance in their derivation.

The Cayce readings relating to Egypt that deal with some of its temples and pyramids indicate a specific unit of measurement used in their design and construction. This unit of measurement was identified as having a length as 27.5 inches (69.85 centimeters).

> . . . what journey is meant. As indicated, it, the globe within the pyramid without, was four forty and four cubits (twenty-seven and one-half inches was a cubit then, or a mir [?] then). [GD's note: The pronunciation was MYRRH.] The height was four and twenty and forty and four mir [?], making then that in the form of the ova, or the egg in its ovate form.   281-25

Through the ages in the study of ancient metrology (measurements), the accepted cubit length has varied between 18 and 28 inches. Most Egyptologists consider the royal cubit, the measurement used to construct the Pyramid, equal to 20.61 inches—smaller than Mr. Cayce's 27.5 inches (69.85 cm)—and only recognize the length of one other Egyptian cubit, the "little cubit" of 17.5 inches.

Historically, measurements often related to the human body, such as hands measured the height of a horse; a cubit equaled the length from the elbow to fingertip; a yard began from the center of the chest to the end of an outstretched arm, and a foot was, well, a foot.

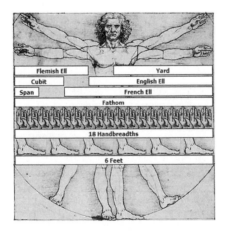

Fig. 11.3–Da Vinci's Vitruvian Man

The classic drawing by Leonardo da Vinci, the Vitruvian man, was a depiction of such measurements and proportions derived from the human body. This drawing was named after Vitruvius, a Roman engineer and architect, who wrote a ten-volume treatise entitled *On Architecture* around 50 BCE. In it he described the human figure as being the primary source of proportion among the classic orders of architecture. He felt that the body was ideal since it was a Divine creation.

Pondering about the length of 27.5 inches and researching what body segment and proportion this might come from started the formulation of an idea that the Cayce cubit might be related to the human spinal column. This especially resonated when recalling the importance of the ancient kundalini and the serpent symbol. The Cayce reading 3481-3 describes the kundalini as "the source of life-giving forces in the body." The Cayce readings further state that the kundalini rises along and reacts to centers along the cerebrospinal system. (2329-2 and 2334-1)

Kundalini is a Sanskrit word, meaning coiled-up, which often specifically refers to a snake or serpent energy. Many have addressed raising the kundalini energy along the path of the spinal canal as a way to open the seven chakras during meditation. Awakening, elevating, and properly channeling this energy has a rich history in many cultures— more obvious in some than others. The Buddhist and Hindu religions have the serpent symbolism and energy as core aspects. The tale of the enlightenment of the Buddha under the Bodhi tree includes his protection by Mucalinda, the king of the serpent gods (nagas) who wrapped the Buddha in seven coils of his body and shielded him with a seven-headed cobra hood during his enlightenment. The Mayans and Aztecs had Kukulcan and Quetzalcoatl, the winged serpent god. In the Mayan culture Kukulcan has been identified, in the post classic period, with the Maya vision serpent. The vision serpent served as the gateway to the spirit realm where they could communicate with their gods and spirits. Australian aborigines have their rainbow serpent of creation. The ancient Egyptians had the Uraeus (Wadjet), the cobra emanating from the forehead of their crowns and was also shown winged. In all these spiritual beliefs the serpent was seen as positive and good. These cultures recognized the positive energy of the serpent but also warned of the negative aspects. This can be considered much like electricity, a vital and important part of technology that has been integral to the advancement of civilization. Electricity and its uses have been a technological boon, when used properly; when used improperly, it can do serious damage.

In Christianity, on the surface, the serpent seems to be relegated to negative aspects. Many of us have been raised on the story of the evil serpent in the Garden of Eden that caused the fall of Adam and Eve from grace. What are often overlooked are the positive, constructive stories of serpents in the Bible:

> *Genesis 3 (King James Version)* [13]And the LORD God said unto the woman, What is this that thou hast done? And the woman said, The serpent beguiled me, and I did eat . . . [15]And I will put enmity between thee and the woman, and between thy seed and her seed; it shall bruise thy head, and thou shalt bruise his heel.

> *Exodus 4 (King James Version)* [2]And the LORD said unto him, What is that in thine hand? And he said, A rod. [3]And he said, Cast it on the ground. And he cast it on the ground, and it became a serpent; and Moses fled from before it. [4]And the LORD said unto Moses, Put forth thine hand, and take it by the tail. And he put forth his hand, and caught it, and it became a rod in his hand:

> *Exodus 7 (King James Version)* [9]When Pharaoh shall speak unto you, saying, Shew a miracle for you: then thou shalt say unto Aaron, Take thy rod, and cast it before Pharaoh, and it shall become a serpent. [10]And Moses and Aaron went in unto Pharaoh, and they did so as the LORD had commanded: and Aaron cast down his rod before Pharaoh, and before his servants, and it became a serpent.

> *Numbers 21 (King James Version)* [6]And the LORD sent fiery serpents among the people, and they bit the people; and much people of Israel died . . . [8]And the LORD said unto Moses, Make thee a fiery serpent, and set it upon a pole: and it shall come to pass, that every one that is bitten, when he looketh upon it, shall live.

> *John 3:14-21 (King James Version)* [14]And as Moses lifted up the serpent in the wilderness, even so must the Son of man be lifted up: [15]That whosoever believeth in him should not perish, but have eternal life.

Matthew 10:16 King James Version (KJV) [16]Behold, I send you forth as sheep in the midst of wolves: be ye therefore wise as serpents, and harmless as doves.

In the first three of these examples after Genesis, God shows how to turn his rod or staff into a "risen/standing" serpent for positive forces and results. In the fifth example it is Jesus using the example of Moses raising the serpent in the desert as analogous to the Son of Man being lifted up. In the final example Jesus is telling his disciples to maintain the positive aspect of the serpent—wisdom combined with the gentleness of the dove or the Holy Spirit. These examples clearly show that there are many positive connotations to serpent symbolism in Christianity, but unfortunately the most press has gone to the negative side.

Even the Hebrew translation of "seraph," the Christian highest order of angel at the throne of God, literally translates as "burning ones" and is considered synonymous in the Hebrew bible for serpent! What all of these spiritual beliefs warn us is that it is the lower self, the snake in the grass, which causes the trouble and not the risen, upright, or winged serpent representing our higher spiritual self. It seemed to me that the length of the spine representing this spiritual energy pathway would be a perfect body proportion and measurement unit for sacred sites and structures to be based upon, but was there validating evidence for the Cayce cubit, let alone this theory of ancient sacred sites? The answer is a definitive Yes!

Fig. 11.4–Moses and Aaron with Pharaoh

Fig. 11.5–Moses Raising the Serpent

First examine the linear dimensions of the spine itself. According to *Gray's Anatomy* the average length of a human male's spine is approximately 71 cm (27.9")—very close to Cayce's cubit of 27.5 inches, within a two percent variation.[6] An earlier edition of *Gray's Anatomy* presents another surprise with the description of the spine. The 1901 edition describes the spines as: "Viewed in front, it presents two pyramids joined together at their bases . . . when examined more closely, the upper pyramid is seen to be formed of three smaller pyramids."[7] If such visual observations and descriptions of the spine could be seen in 1901, there is no reason not to believe ancient Egyptian and other cultures could make the same observations. Interestingly, the spinal canal, found within the spinal column, rises from a hollow triangular–shaped portion through a circular or tubular section and then ends with a hollow triangle–shaped segment at the top.

This observation makes it possible to symbolically depict the individual parts of the spinal column or vertebrae as a triangle in a circle, an oft used symbol today and one with ancient roots connected to the general meaning of the Trinity embraced by God. Also with the three canal segments making shapes of a circle and two individual triangles, these shapes return us to the messages of the six–pointed star, the house of the soul, and the Koch snowflake to bring the infinite inside the finite. The lumbar vertebrae by itself are very similar to the Egyptian ankh hieroglyph. Beyond all this is the striking visible resemblance of the spine to a serpent! (See the following page.) This resemblance is absolutely uncanny and would not be lost on any observer.

As noted earlier the Bible itself shows many examples of serpent symbolism and the raising of such energy. If examined closely, we find that its meaning is not only to raise one's consciousness, but also to identify the spine as the avenue for this serpent energy. Another clue that the spine is a pathway can be found in Genesis 3:

> [15]And I will put enmity between thee and the woman, and between thy seed and her seed; it shall bruise thy head, and thou shalt bruise his heel.[8]

Earlier in this chapter it was shown how similar the shape of the spine is to the body of a serpent. The serpent's tail would be up at the head or neck of a human being while its tail would be the pelvic area and be part of the pelvic girdle of humans.

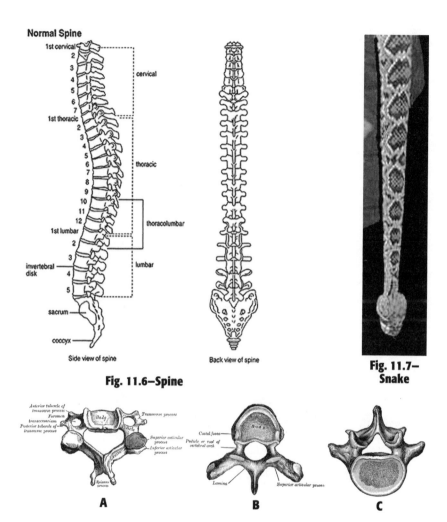

Normal Spine

1st cervical
2
3
4
5
6
7
1st thoracic
2
3
4
5
6
7
8
9
10
11
12
1st lumbar
2
3
4
5

cervical

thoracic

thoracolumbar

lumbar

invertebral disk

sacrum

coccyx

Side view of spine

Back view of spine

Fig. 11.6–Spine

Fig. 11.7– Snake

A   B   C

Fig. 11.8–Vertebrae

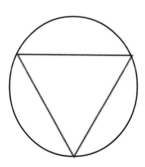

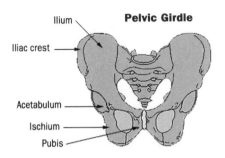

Fig. 11.9–Pelvic Girdle

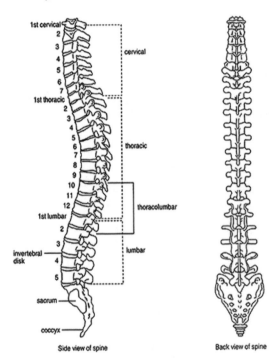

Fig. 11.10–Spine

In women this pelvic girdle surrounds the reproductive area—the womb, and it is the same place where the spinal sacrum, the head of the serpent, is located. In later stages of pregnancy the fetus' head aligns inside the pelvis girdle. During this time, as the birth nears, joints of bones soften due to the effect of pregnancy hormones. As the end of pregnancy approaches, the ligaments of the sacroiliac joint stretch and loosen, allowing the pelvis outlet to widen somewhat to help the birthing process. The stretching and loosening of ligaments is commonly called a sprain which is generally defined as causing pain, swelling, and bruising. This is the birth of the woman's seed bruising the head of the serpent. It is also not uncommon for the newborn child to have a very red torso and bluish extremities as the first breaths begin. This is particularly visible in the lower extremities such as the heel, thus giving it a bluish or bruised appearance. So, as stated in the Bible, the head of the serpent is bruised by the seed of man and woman and the newborn's heel is bruised.

Up to now we have delved into the spiritual side of this discussion, but there is independent academic support for the Cayce cubit which comes from the work of Livio C. Stecchini, a Harvard PhD science historian, who focused on ancient weights and measures. In his treatise *A History of Measures, Part II*, he states:

> More recently one has come to realize that a number of documents indicate the use of a unit equal to 1-1/3 royal cubit. In my opinion this mysterious unit is a cubit of two hybrid feet, that is, 37-1/3 natural basic fingers, 700mm. The name of this unit is nb, nebiu, which means "carrying" indicates that the original unit of length was the carrying yoke; the term for cubit in Semitic languages and in Greek(-) means the arm of the carrying yoke, that is, the half of it. On Egyptian cubit rules, the position of the hybrid foot it indicated by the sign of the forearm rmn; the term means "cubit," but it corresponds to the idea of "to carry" and it also means "half," indicating that essentially it signifies the half of the carrying yoke.
>
> My explanation of the unit nebiu is supported by a neglected specimen of the Metropolitan Museum of New York. This object is listed in the catalog as a cubit of 27-1/2 American inches (698.6mm or 69.86cm). It is a double hybrid foot (rmn) or a "carrying yoke" of 700mm. It consists of a simple round rod of plain wood divided by lines cut with a saw into 7 parts; the seventh at the meddle (sic) is further divided into two parts, so that the rod is divided at the center in two halves of 3-1/2 sevenths.[9]

Dr. Stecchini's conclusion is that there is a mysterious Egyptian cubit equaling 27.5 inches (The same as the Edgar Cayce's measurement).

The significance of the serpent was briefly noted earlier with the uraeus symbol emanating from the forehead of the Pharaohs, and throughout their ancient culture the symbolism of the serpent can be found. Ancient Egyptian spirituality also presents evidence for the serpent/kundalini connection. This connection is in the pre–dynastic Egyptian God, Nehebkau (Nehebu–Kau, Nehebkhau). His name comes from the ancient Egyptian word for "yoke together" or "unite," *nhb*, the same root word for the mysterious cubit Dr. Stecchinni had discovered. Nehebkau or "He Who Unites the Kas" was a benevolent snake god whom the Egyptians believed was one of the original primeval gods. The Ka was one of the aspects of the Egyptian soul and represented the divine spark, the divine spirit. Nehebkau was linked to the sun god, swimming around in the primeval waters before creation, and then bound to the sun god when time began. He was a god of protection who watched over the pharaoh and all Egyptians, both in life and the afterlife. It was believed he gained his power after swallowing seven cobras, and he was the one who gave each Egyptian his true name and fed him with the milk of light. He was occasionally depicted with a head at each end of the body. He could also cure snake bites, similar to what the risen "bronze serpent" of Moses did for the Hebrews in the Exodus, saving them from the poison of their lower selves. Jesus alluded to this risen, higher self in the New Testament.

What may be noticed in many of these examples is the reoccurrence of the number 7: 7 coils, 7 heads, and 7 cobras. The example of this 27.5 inch cubit discovered by Dr. Stechinni was also divided into 7 sections. This 7 also has an application in determining its use in the Great Pyramid. His research regarding the Egyptian use of multiples of 7 fortifies this conclusion:

> Following Newton's method I presume that the height (re the Great Pyramid) was expressed by a round figure. The method followed by the Egyptians in calculating angles indicates that the height was calculated by multiples of 7. (Units of Length: The Dimensions of the Great Pyramid)[10] (See color Fig. 15.)

Converting the original measurements of the Great Pyramid from a side base of 756 feet results in 330 (329.89) cubits. The height of 481 feet results in 210 (209.89) cubits—a multiple of 7 (7 X 30 or 70 X 3). These meet the criteria of round figures and a height divisible by 7 per Newton's method. Another "coincidence" is that the original Great Pyramid possibly totaled 210 courses (70 times 3). I also correlated the side base length of 330 Cayce cubits to the spine with its 33 vertebrae. These results are curiously mathematically significant in other ways also. The height of 210 is also the result of multiplying the first four prime numbers. (2x3x5x7 = 210) Prime numbers are considered unique by mathematicians as they are divisible only by one and themselves to result in a whole number. It also can be noted that adding these prime numbers gives you a sum of 17, the number discussed in Chapter 3 and used to identify the Great Pyramid as the biblical Mount Horeb. The side length of 330 is also the result of multiplying the first three prime numbers, skipping 7, the fourth prime number used for the height, and using the fifth prime number 11. (2x3x5x11 = 330). The height and width share the primes of 2, 3, and 5; then the height uses the prime of 7 and the width the prime of 11. Proportionally the height over the width 210/330 = 7/11! The ancient Egyptians certainly seem to be encoding this cubit length in the Great Pyramid.

If that seems farfetched to some, let's present a modern day example. In 1974 at a ceremony to mark the remodeling of the Arecibo radio telescope, the world's largest radio telescope, a radio message was transmitted to globular star cluster M13 for the ceremonial purpose of transmitting a message to potential extraterrestrial intelligent life. The determination of how to send a message that would be understood was decided upon by using semi-prime and primes numbers, due to their uniqueness, so that such intelligent life would understand that this was not random radio "noise" and that the prime and semi-prime numbers would guide such intelligences to translate the graphic message sent.

Even other ancient numerical symbolism of numbers guides us. The number 70 in Hebrew Gematria (a system of assigning numbers to words or phrases) is "ayin," meaning spiritual eye. Could this symbolize wisdom and insight through the "Third Eye" or the pineal gland, located behind and between the eyes? The "gimal" is the Hebrew word for the number 3. It also means "staff," reinforcing the connection between the spine and the path of the kundalini. The number 3 times 70 gives us the height of the Great Pyramid. The symbolic significance of the number 70 can be seen elsewhere. Looking in the Bible, Moses went up the Holy Mountain to speak with God with 70 elders (spiritual eye). In setting up the tabernacle in the wilderness for the Ark of the Covenant he brought 70 priests. Jesus in the New Testament sent out 70 disciples to preach. The biblical Septuagint, which means 70 in Greek, according to Judaic tradition, got its name from how it was translated into Greek. King Ptolemy reportedly gathered 70 Rabbis to get a Greek translation of the Hebrew Bible. He isolated each one in separate rooms and told them to write it. Upon its completion he compared all 70 copies and found them to be identical. The number 70 was of vital important in Egypt also. The journey of Isis and Osiris through the underworld took 70 days. The mummification process to prepare for the afterlife and rebirth was 70 days. The star Sirius, which was used to measure the inundations from the Nile, set below the horizon for 70 days. These examples exhibit why the number 70 would be found incorporated into the Great Pyramid.

There are also clues left in the geometry of the Great Pyramid with its measurements and 51 degree angled sides. For the angle á, the sine function gives the ratio of the length of the opposite side to the length of the hypotenuse.

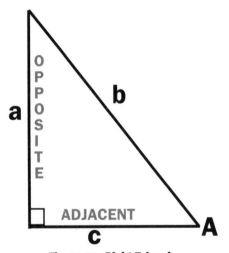

Fig. 11.11–Right Triangle

The sine; ratio from 51 degree angle (a) is .777
7+7+7 = 21 re: height of 210

John Van Auken's research of an Egyptian Gnostic community with Judaic influences using cabbalists' numbering quantified the heart chakra as 777 and signified this as the cross.[11] This fits nicely into the observation that the site of the Great Pyramid can be considered at the cross or the heart of Earth's land masses.

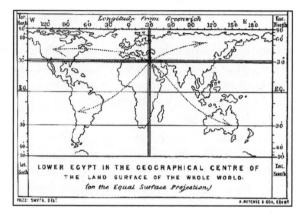

Fig. 11.12–Smyth map

Fig. 11.13–Hebrew Lamed

Coincidently the remaining shared prime numbers of the Great Pyramid's height (2x3x5x7) and width (2x3x5x11) are 2x3x5 which give a product result of 30. In reviewing Hebrew gematria for the number 30, the result is the Hebrew letter "Lamed." (Shown above) Lamed is the tallest Hebrew letter found in the center of their alphabet and is called the "king of kings." It is an acronym for *lev mevin daat* (a heart that understands wisdom). That's pretty appropriate for a believed sacred initiation site that was the tallest manmade structure, for at least 4,500 years, until the 1880s. In looking at how the letter lamed is written, its resem-

blance to the image of a serpent is clearly evident. This fits in well with
the serpent symbolism that is being discussed in this chapter and in the
particular case of the Great Pyramid. Finally, this result of 30 being
shared by the Great Pyramid's height and width may be akin to a modern day GPS coordinate notation identifying its geographical location.
The location of the Great Pyramid coincides closely with the 30 degree
longitude and 30 degree latitude markings of this world land mass center as considered by the map from Charles Piazza Smyth. The longitude
is actually off one degree (at 31) or approximately 70 miles. This is very
accurate considering a 25,000 mile circumference of the earth, making it
off by less than one half of one percent.

Then there are the hints in the hieroglyphs. Cayce not only called
this length a cubit, but also referred to it as a *mir*, pronounced myrrh.
The vocal pronunciation of *mir* (myrrh) could well have been written as
mer. Upon examining Budge's *An Egyptian Hieroglyphic Dictionary, Volume 1*,
it does **not** have a *mir*, but there is an ancient Egyptian word *mer* with
several translations, one of these translates as "a sacred serpent kept at
Edfu."[12]

Another intriguing connection of the Cayce cubit to the Great Pyramid is that one of Budge's dictionary alternative translations of *mer* is
"pyramid."[13] These translations give an apparent significant connection
to this unit of measure of 27.5 inches with serpent symbolism and pyramids. It is even more fascinating that *mer* translates as both sacred serpent and pyramid particularly with the following research of others.
Tony Bushby writes: "That ancient Sumerian documentation provided a
direct link to the Great Pyramid for it was originally called by Mystery
School initiates, 'The house of the Serpent.'"[14] Author C. Staniland Wake,
the first director of the England and Ireland Archeological society wrote:
"The Great Pyramid is thus a monument not only of Sabaism, but of
serpent worship . . . "[15] Author Andrew Collins writes of local Arab lore
that speaks of a snake spirit (el-Hanash) that guards the underground
passages of Giza.[16] In Chapter 3 the pyramidal mountain "The Peak" was
described and theorized by the archaeologist to represent a pyramid for
the burial tombs of the New Kingdom pharaohs in the Valley of the
Kings. This peak also had a tradition of being called "Meret Seger," she
who loves silence. Meret Seger was a benevolent Egyptian serpent goddess that protected the area and was believed to live in this pyramidal
mountain. Following the thought process of the archaeologist that this
area was chosen because of its pyramid-shaped peak reflecting the pyra-

mids of Giza, then it may well be mirroring the serpent symbolism of the Great Pyramid.

Further evidence of this serpent of light unit of measurement is found in Dr. Schoch's book where he describes the remains of a bronze instrument that had a double hook on the end like a serpent's tongue and in the etymology of the word "pyramid," one translation literally meant light measurements.[17]

Recent research in the possible construction process of the Great Pyramid also gives us a possible reason for it to be associated with serpent symbolism. This research comes from Mr. Houdin, an architect from France, whose theory and compelling evidence has brought around him a team of archaeologists and an engineering company, that has even created an hour-long 3D movie describing the theory. Color Fig. 16 shows the basic theory that a spiral tunnel is concealed beneath the surface of the Great Pyramid and was used for moving the blocks during its construction. Like the kundalini "coiled serpent" of Eastern philosophy, the symbolic coiled serpent can be seen in this possibly hidden coiled shaft of the Great Pyramid and would fit in with the evidence already shown here tying the Great Pyramid to sacred serpent concepts.[18]

Even the Egyptian hieroglyphs for cubits tantalize us with a little known or seldom described *aakhu meh* cubit. As noted earlier, mainstream Egyptologists recognize only two Egyptian cubits, but there are three Egyptian cubits identified in the hieroglyphic records. The third cubit is the *aakhu meh* cubit— *meh* meaning cubit and *aakhu (akh, khu)* meaning the soul mind, which is the glorious effective spirit that links the *ba* or the individual soul with the *ka* or the life force. This *aakhu meh* cubit is easily comparable to the Eastern traditions kundalini which raises one's higher consciousness and links human beings to God. This matches with the *nebiu* cubit, the linking yoke of he who unites the *ka*'s cubit found by Dr. Stecchini.

Hints in the Hieroglyphics

Meh = cubit

Meh Nesu = Royal Cubit ...	*nesu* = royal/king
Meh Netches = Little Cubit ...	*netches* = to protect
Aakhu Meh (the name of a cubit)	*Aakhu* = spirit/light
(Light pole/staff)	(Stecchini's "mystery cubit"?)[19]

Finally and dramatically in Egypt is the djed, the symbol of the god
Osiris. (See color Fig. 17.) Osiris became the god and protector of many
cult places, including the site of the pyramids on the Giza plateau. His
symbol, the djed, is also known as Osiris's spine. A ceremony known as
"raising the djed" served as a metaphor for the stability of the monarch
but also symbolized the resurrection (rebirth) of Osiris. As I have pointed
out, this is analogous to raising our higher self through spiritual energy.

It is the conclusion here that the ancient Egyptians planned to aid
future civilizations understand the meaning and significance of the
Great Pyramid by leaving multiple clues in the structure of the Great
Pyramid which are explained by the mathematics, esoteric numbers,
and astronomical alignments of the monument. Language and knowledge may be lost, but numbers and mathematics are a universal language that survives the ages and acts as a key to the meanings.

The "Cayce cubit" and its use in sacred structures can be found in
other cultures and places such as South America. It has been discovered
there that the Mayans had a similar measurement for their pyramids
called a *zapal*. Civil engineers Craig Smith and Kelly Parmenter found
an overview of the Mayan measurement system in the article entitled
"An Ancient Maya Measurement System" from the January 1986 issue of
America Antiquity. The article was focusing primarily on the principal
dimensions of ten buildings at three ancient Mayan sites including
Chichen Itza. By looking at common dimensions of the Mayan structures, the authors calculated a standard unit of measurement of 1.47m
(147cm), with a variance of ±5 cm, called a zapal.

As a test for the hypothesis, several principal dimensions of the
Kukulcan Pyramid were converted into the zapal equivalents using the
above unit of measure and are listed in the following table:

Width	Meters	Zapal	Conversion Factor
Top	19.52	13	1.50
Base	55.30	37	1.49
Temple	13.42	9	1.49
Stairs	8.85	6	1.48

Using their calculations for the zapal, the researchers' findings resulted in the numbers 9 and 13, significant numbers for the Maya. The number 13 was associated with the levels of paradise and the number 9 referred to the levels of the underworld. As can be seen, these researchers also used results in meaningful numbers to validate a proposed unit of measurement.[20]

Taking the variance of ±5cm (142cm) of a Mayan zapal and the comparison to one Cayce cubits (69.85cm), it is clear that two Cayce cubits (139.7cm) are approximate to a Mayan zapal. To use Dr. Stecchini's terms, the Mayans used the measurement of a full yoke rather than the Egyptian half yoke. I note that 142cm is exactly the lengths of the average spinal column documented earlier.

The Kukulcan Pyramid was dedicated to their god of the same name meaning: "The Plumed Serpent." (See color Fig. 18.) Interestingly, Mayan hieroglyphs depict a double-headed serpent bar, perhaps illustrating the double Cayce cubit. (See color Fig. 20.) This double-headed serpent sounds similar to the Egyptian serpent god Nehebkau who would also be depicted as having two heads, cited earlier in Chapter 3. Author John Major Jenkins notes that some classic Mayan stelae show the double-headed serpent bar held at an angle.[21] He compares this angle to the ecliptic across the Milky Way. Could this angled serpent bar relate to the raising of the Egyptian djed stelae? The djed stelae, a hieroglyphic often found on Egyptian temple walls, is depicted at an angle and is thought to symbolize Osiris' spine. (See color Fig. 21.) Is this more evidence of a connection between these two cultures? It will be shown that such evidence is available.

Color Fig. 19 is a picture of the Kukulcan period when, during the spring and autumn equinoxes, a *serpent of light* is created descending the north stairs.

As can be seen in that picture, a serpent of light is created connecting to the carved serpent head at the base of the stairs. This stone serpent of light is also made of 7 triangular coils showing similarities to the Egyptian serpent god Nehebkau, who had swallowed 7 cobras and fed the people with the milk of light. The possible name of the Cayce cubit in Egyptian hieroglyphs, the *aakhu meh*, described as the light, brilliant cubit, fits into the importance of the purpose of the light serpent and its initiation. It also reminds one of the Hindu serpent god king who protected Buddha during his enlightenment with his 7 coils and 7 hooded heads. The number 7 even comes back into play again. The name of the site, Chichen Itza, is translated as "mouth of the well of the Itza" or "mouth of the well of the enchanter," but researchers have found evidence in the Maya books of *Chilam Balam* of an earlier name for this site. The *Chilam Balam* "Jaguar Priest" writings date back to the 1500s, preserving earlier traditional Maya knowledge. In these books the evidence names the Chichen Itza site as the 7 great rulers, the 7 bushy places, or the 7 lines of Abnal.[22] The one thing the translations concur on is the translation of 7 in its earlier name. This helps to solidify more links with the importance of the number 7 and with the creation of a light serpent on the pyramid representing the unifying of heaven and earth.

The Edgar Cayce readings themselves make interesting note of the meaning of light upon the altar stones of the Maya.

RE: Mayas
The altars upon which there were the cleansings of the bodies of individuals (not human sacrifice; for this came much later with the injection of the Mosaic, and those activities of that area), these were *later the altars upon which individual activities* - that would today be termed hate, malice, selfishness, self-indulgence—*were cleansed from the body through the ceremony, through the rise of initiates from the sources of light, that came from the stones upon which the angels of light during the periods gave their expression to the peoples.*
[Author's emphasis]   5750-1

Important to realize in the reading describing the play of light upon the stones of the Maya altars is that this reading was given in 1933. At that time archaeologists were not aware of the equinox light serpent created on the Kukulcan Pyramid, and when realized, was not published about until the 1970s!

In other parts of the world is found yet another correlation. The measurements at Stonehenge, in England, intrigue us because they are represented by this cubit, as do the Cayce readings which are possibly hinting at Stonehenge. Stonehenge, an enigmatic megalithic site located in England, has its origins traced backed by archaeologists to around 8,000 BCE with it upright stone circles believed to have been erected at approximately 2,500 BCE. (See Fig. 22.) The site is believed to have been used for not only religious and spiritual purposes but also for astronomical ones. When approaching Stonehenge, it appears dramatically out of apparently nowhere in the English countryside, keeping its secrets to itself. There are the remains of two megalithic stone horseshoe shapes surrounded by similar remains of two stone circles. Archaeologists have also found remains of more concentric circles emanating out from the center up to the circular berm that encloses the site.

As Stonehenge is also an ancient sacred site and is considered a place of initiation by many, the question is, as compared to pyramidal structures, how would such a site of concentric circles be measured? The answer came spectacularly with circle diameters.

The first inner blue circle has been estimated at diameters of approximately 75 to 76.1 feet. Using the mean of these measurements, 75.51 feet, it represents almost exactly 33 Cayce cubits (32.95). This was a very promising start considering the earlier results and importance of the number 33, as in one example representing the spine's 33 vertebrae, hence the kundalini path. The next Stonehenge circle (the Sarsen stones) has a mean diameter of 100.80 feet, equaling 44 Cayce cubits. Continuing on the multiple circle measurements at Stonehenge, the Z-postholes with a diameter of 127.87 feet translate to 55 Cayce cubits (55.8) and the Y-postholes with a diameter of 177.16 feet translate to 77 Cayce cubits (77.3). These results are absolutely incredible and are results that will occur only when using a unit measure of 27.5 inches, which has already been demonstrated to have amazing numerical results at the Great Pyramid with academic evidence and support from Dr. Stecchini and the Mayan unit of measurement that is equivalent to a double Cayce spinal cubit or full yoke. This is a Mayan unit of measurement put forth by Maya academic researchers themselves. Now, here at Stonehenge, the results yield concentric expanding circles, measured by the Cayce cubit, of 33, 44, 55, and 77. These results are straightforward and dramatic and go beyond what anyone could call coincidence. There is even an answer to the potential question of what happen to the missing sequence diameter of 66? If the following diagram of the Stonehenge site is examined, it can be seen that there is marked a circle of unexcavated post holes halfway between the 55 Cayce cubit diameter of the z–postholes and the 77 Cayce cubit diameter of the y–postholes. I believe that this unexcavated circle of postholes between the Z and Y holes will, if examined, equal 66 Cayce cubits. The results are clearly and obviously staggering and beyond coincidence. The diagram on the following page illustrates concentric circles at Stonehenge with Cayce cubits of 33, 44, 55, 66, and 77. Finding exact measurements of the Stonehenge circles is difficult and varies according to the use of the inside, outside, or mean diameters. The age and condition of remains at the site also hinder exact measurement of the original diameters. The only remaining wood or stone postholes at Stonehenge are found in the furthest ring from the center; these are the Aubrey postholes, with an approximate diameter of 123.7 Cayce cubits (approx. 86.4m). Intriguingly, and within the realm of possibility, if the original builders' aim was to construct an outside ring to act as a key for the inner rings, using the Cayce (spinal) cubit, a diameter of 86.2345 meters would result in a Cayce cubit diameter of 123.4567 (1-2-3-4-5-6-7).

The diagram illustrates concentric circles at Stonehenge with Cayce Cubits of: 33, 44, 55, 66, and 77.

Blue Circle   =   33 Cayce cubits
Sarsen Cir.   =   44 Cayce cubits
Z post Cir.   =   55 Cayce cubits
Unexcav.Cir. =   66 Cayce Cubits?
Y post Cir.   =   77 Cayce cubits

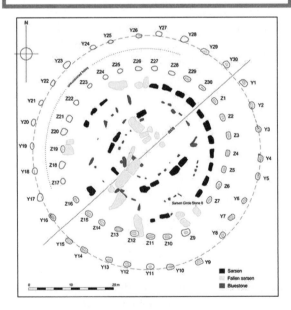

Fig. 11.14—Stonehenge Diagram Plan of the Y and Z holes at Stonehenge showing their relationship with the stone structure

Author John Michell demonstrates in his book *The Dimensions of Paradise* how the sacred geometry of the New Jerusalem and the six-pointed star are incorporated in the design of Stonehenge. His depictions link the significance of the sacred geometry to the triangles and arcs discussed in earlier chapters and even to Stonehenge.[23]

**Fig. 11.15–Star in the Stonehenge Depiction–
a graphic version of Michell depiction**

Cayce reading quotes and Stonehenge

The Edgar Cayce readings offer a very curious and unique possible connection to Stonehenge and its purpose. Though the readings do not specifically state Stonehenge itself, they talk about an exodus to England from the Middle East Holy Land due to persecution and turmoil. The readings describe how the children and grandchildren of Hezekiah during that time period left and sailed by boat to the shores of England so that they could continue to worship the living God and the laws of One. The readings state that these exiles both built altars and worshipped at present altars in England for this purpose—some near the plains of Salisbury, which are about ten miles from Stonehenge. The notes on Stonehenge in these readings were added at a later date by Gladys Davis, the stenographer of the readings.

> Before that the entity was in the English land during those periods when there were those journeyings into that land from the Holy Land, when *the children of Hezekiah* prompted many

of those even in authority to leave the Holy Land because of
Nebuchadnezzar's activities.

   The entity was young in years when it came into the coasts
of England where altars [*Stonehenge?*] were set up to tie up
the meanings of "The Lord thy God is one." The building up
of this thought makes no bonds, no slaves among any peoples.
[Author's emphasis]   3581-1

Before that the entity was in the English land during those
periods when there was the *breaking up of the tribes of Israel*
[Zedekiah period? 2nd Chron. 36:10?].

   The entity was a *granddaughter of Hezekiah the king*, and
among those who set sail to escape when the activities brought
the rest of the people into servitude in the Persian land.

   Then the entity was among those who landed and set up
the seat of customs as indicated in the altars built near what
is now Salisbury, England [*Stonehenge?*]. These were the early
traditions carried into those activities.   3590-1

Before that the entity was in the Holy Land when there were
those breakings up in the periods when the land was being
sacked by the Chaldeans and Persians.

   The entity was among those groups who escaped in the
ships that settled in portions of the English land near what is
now Salisbury, and there builded those altars that were to represent the dedications of individuals to a service of a living
God. [See 3645-1, Par. R5.] [*Stonehenge?*]   3645-1

Before that we find the entity was in the English land in the
early settlings [*Stonehenge?*] of *the children of Israel who were
foregathered with the daughters of Hezekiah* in what is now
Somerland, Somerhill or Somerset. *There the entity saw group
organization for the preservation of tenets and truths of the living God*, just as those admonitions would be for the entity in
the present as it begins that social service with children.
[Author's emphasis]   5384-1

   Now these readings, on the surface, may not seem as much of a connection to the other sites of the Great Pyramid and the Kukulcan Pyra-

mid, though the measurement results using the Cayce cubit are very compelling. There is another connection to the serpent symbolism imbedded in these Cayce readings. There are many biblical kings to choose from and many much better known than Hezekiah, yet this was the Hebrew king noted in the readings. It begs the question, why? In researching the biblical Hezekiah the serpent link becomes evident.

Hezekiah, Biblical King of Judah

Hezekiah introduced substantial religious reforms. The worship of Yahweh was concentrated at Jerusalem, suppressing the shrines to him that had existed till then elsewhere in Judea. *Idolatry*, which had resumed under his father's reign, was banned.

Hezekiah abolished the shrines and smashed the pillars and cut down the *sacred posts*. He also smashed the *Bronze Serpent* which Moses had made, "for until that time the Israelites had been offering sacrifices to it." (2 Kings 18:4)[24] [Author's emphasis]

In 2 Kings 18:4, a bronze serpent was set up in the Jerusalem Temple sanctuary.

The Masoretic text says that "he [Hezekiah] called it Nehushtan." According to Young's Literal Translation, *Nehushtan* means "piece of brass" (2 Kings 18:4).

When Hezekiah had become King, he tore down the Nehushtan. *It has been suggested that Hezekiah's destruction of the Nehushtan was a result of the balance of power moving towards Assyria, which permitted him to remain on the throne of Judah as a puppet ruler.* Hezekiah demonstrated his loyalty to the new regime by the destruction of an important symbol with Egyptian associations.[25] [Author's emphasis]

As can be seen the Bronze Serpent of Moses that was raised in the desert and its meaning and symbolic purpose discussed in detail earlier give probable explanatory evidence as to why the exodus to England occurred as described in the Cayce readings. This goes beyond coincidence and adds more solidifying evidence both psychically and academically to the connections at these multiple sacred sites. Some may argue that there are too many discrepancies in the dates of these sites and occurrences, but the information and research provide here the evidence of international serpent symbolism and a shared unit of measurement that has survived through the ages, cultures, and continents.

Further connections to the stone circles of Great Britain and serpent symbolism is provided by author and researcher Andrew Collins when he quotes William Stukeley on his research of the Avebury stone ring (twenty miles from Stonehenge) as a symbol of a sun disk and "its winding avenue symbolizing a winged serpent."[26]

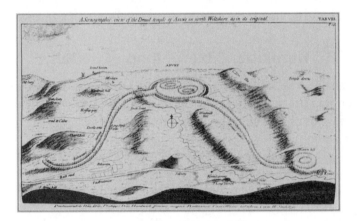

Fig. 11.16—Avebury Serpent

Even with all this research and the evidence that these three sacred sites were used as places of initiation—places to raise one's spiritual, kundalini energy, to commune through one's higher self to God, Stonehenge still amazes one with such evidence of purpose. Recent acoustic (sound) studies with Stonehenge and models have found that certain chanting and drumming at the site would be able to put the participants in theta and alpha brainwave patterns which in turn heighten and induce meditative states.

> These low frequencies are very similar to the brainwave frequencies of alpha and beta types of activity. It is possible that those *around the edge of the stone circle would have chanted* at the speed of the percussive sounds, or sung long notes with a vibrato wobbling at 5.2Hz, in time with the music, *in order to entrain their brainwaves to the music, to make the dominant frequency of their brain activity slow to a theta pattern, typical of deep meditation, hypnosis or trance.*
> *In the centre a different frequency* could have been produced by modal vibration and echoes, one of 10.4Hz, *still associated*

with closed eyes and meditation, and to some with healing.
10.4Hz is associated with alpha wave brain activity, a more
active state.[27] [Author's emphasis]

The researchers believe, from their results, that initiates would be
around the edge of the stone circle, where a deeper theta meditative
state would be reached, guided by a high priest facilitator in the center
who was experiencing a lighter alpha meditative state.

Let's return once again to a look at a summary of the physical measurements of each of the sacred sites we have explored in this chapter:

Great Pyramid

- **Height** . . . 210 Cayce Cubits

  Great Pyramid believed to originally having 210 courses

  2x3x5x7 (the first 4 primes numbers multiplied) = 210

- **Width** (side) . . . 330 Cayce Cubits

- Giza Plateau is dedicated to Osiris; Osiris' symbol the djed is
  known as the spine of Osiris. Human spine has 33 vertebrae.

- 2x3x5x11 (4 primes, skipping 7 multiplied) = 330

- Pyramid height over width = 210/330 = 7/11

- The sine of the 51 degree of Pyramid is .777. This is the proportion
  of the height to the hypotenuse. 7+7+7 = 21

Mayan Kukulcan Pyramid

- Archaeologically validated Mayan measurement called a zapal is
  equal to 2 Cayce Cubits.

- Mayan Pyramid top platform width = 13 zapals and Temple on
  platform is 9 zapals wide.

- This is considered significant to the 9 underworlds and 13 paradises in Mayan religion.

- Note: Mayan statues of gods and kings often holding double serpent bar.

Stonehenge: Circle Diameters

Blue Stone circle	33 Cayce cubits
Sarsen Stone Circle	44 Cayce cubits
Z—Posthole circle	55 Cayce cubits
Unexcavated posthole circle	66 Cayce cubits (projected)
Y - Posthole circle	77 Cayce cubits
Aubrey posthole circle	123.4567 Cayce cubits

They say extraordinary claims require extraordinary evidence. Let me check these off below.

Archaeological measurement validation methodology

Historic evidence of body proportions used: ✔, through ancient metrology and Vitruvius

Historic evidence of such a cubit measurement: ✔, through Dr. Livio Stecchini

Significant numerical results at sites: ✔ shown time and again here and by scientists at Chichen Itza

Historical evidence of spine/serpent symbolism ✔, in multiple cultures

Fact that Cayce cubit works remarkably on 3 different continents at 3 different sites with 3 different cultures: ✔ ✔ ✔, *Extraordinary!*

All three sites, the Great Pyramid, the Pyramid of Kukulcan, and Stonehenge are considered places of initiation, centers to raise up spiritual forces or kundalini energy. The evidence linking the Cayce cubit to the length of the spine is strengthened by the measurements found in these vastly separate sites, exhibiting this cubit as a shared international unit of measurement. The Cayce readings have again left us a trail—the length of a cubit leads us on a path towards our higher self and of unity and Oneness, of uniting heaven and earth across time, cultures, and three continents presenting tantalizing proof of a greater design.

These three sacred sites can be seen as representing the concept of bringing Heaven and Earth together in another fashion as well. This can be found in the axiom of squaring the circle. The phrase of squaring the circle has meant to try to do the impossible. This comes from a longtime mathematical conundrum of squaring the circle using a compass and straight rule. A solution to this problem was attempted for hundreds of years and was finally proven to be impossible. Though this is impossible in mathematics, in spiritual philosophies squaring the circle can characterize bringing heaven and earth together. What is considered impossible for humans is not considered impossible for God. The square represents earth and the circle represents heaven. This message can be intuited from the already discussed uses of these sites and how they were designed. The Great Pyramid's square perimeter divided by its height results in 44/7 or two pi. Two pi is an essential component in determining the circumference (perimeter) of a circle. The formula is 2 pi times the radius to determine the circumference of a circle. Now if we substitute perimeter for circumference, we can see that in the square-like base of the Great Pyramid over its height there appears the necessary constant to determine the perimeter of a circle. The Kukulcan Pyramid has the noted significance of its top dimensions representing the paradises and underworlds of the Maya belief, which can be seen as the bringing of heaven and earth together. Stonehenge, in its circle has been shown by John Michell to incorporate the six-pointed star, which in turn, has the cube (three-dimensional square) at its center. In many different ways each of these sites gives the clues to their purposes of doing the "impossible" and joining heaven and earth within oneself.[28]

It is essential to remember that while these external validations and evidence are important, they are just signposts to the real journey within.

More on the Spine

Along this hypothesis that the human spine or spinal cord was used to deter–mine the royal cubit, for the preceding elaborated reason, let us step out a little further on this limb or vertebrae, as the case may be, and see what we can see. It doesn't take much imagination to see the similarities of the Egyptian crown of the upper and lower Nile and the C1 and C2 spinal vertebrae, also known as the axis and atlas respectively.

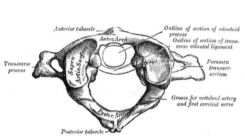

Fig. 12.1–Cervical Vertebra

Fig. 12.2– Osiris with Crown

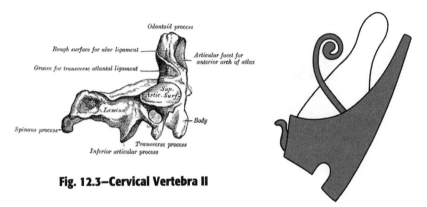

Fig. 12.3–Cervical Vertebra II

Fig. 12.4–Egyptian Peschent Crown

Added to this concept is the following Cayce reading. In 1928, however, he gave a reading in which he discussed the pineal as a functioning gland and pinned down its neural connections. Here's what he said, in part: " . . . also that of the pineal gland's connection with the brain forces in the 1st and 2nd cervical . . . "   (5691-2)

From the texts, one finds that anatomical studies have shown that the pineal gland, although lying in close proximity to the brain, almost surrounded by the brain tissue, has no connection to the brain except through the superior cervical ganglion of the autonomic nervous system—the ganglion paralleling the first three cervical segments of the spinal cord. It is the little items like this that impress me most dramatically about Cayce's clairvoyance and his insight into the human body.[1]

The importance given to the two top cervical vertebrae was also noted by author Shirley Andrews who researches customs of Atlantis. She documents this as a rite–of–passage initiation where the priests wore a bull costume. The bull would be ritually killed; then the carcass was stripped down to the hide and skull, including the top two vertebrae, to be worn by the priest for the ceremony.[2]

This again brings us back to the Egyptian djed and the Maya double-headed serpent bar. The book *The Orion Mystery* makes an argument tying the Great Pyramid to the Egyptian god Osiris. After extensive research Bauval and Gilbert concluded that Rostau, the place where Sokar–Osiris dwells, was the Giza plateau. It is further stated: "I at last understood that we were being told in plain language, that the pyramid constructions were to be considered Osiris."³ These tie-ins lend support to the cubit being measured from the spine. The hieroglyph djed is also known as the *spine of Osiris* and was found commonly on the inside of many Egyptian coffins. (See color Fig. 23.) There was also a ceremony of "Raising the DJED."

> Ptah, the national god known best as the patron deity of Memphis is sometimes described as "the noble Djed." However, the djed pillar was quickly associated with the god Sokar, and Sokar's association with Osiris, god of the dead, eventually led to the Djed being symbolic of that great god.
>
> As theology progressed in Egypt, we see more definitive concepts of the djed pillar. In the *Book of the Dead*, the djed pillar is said to represent *Osiris' backbone* and there are many other references in Egyptian literature to this association. Wallis Budge believed that it was the oldest symbol of Osiris, representing his body as well. However, there are many other tales from Egyptian mythology that explain the origin and meaning of the djed pillar.
>
> One such example, explaining the djed pillar's association with trees, comes directly from one of ancient Egypt's most famous accounts, the murder of Osiris.
>
> It was probably at Memphis that kings first performed a ceremony known as "raising the djed pillar," which not only served as a metaphor for the stability of the monarch, but also symbolized the resurrection of Osiris.⁴ [Author's emphasis]

Could the "raising of the djed" mean coming to spiritual enlightenment and perfection? Far Eastern cultures talk of raising the kundalini, the spiritual force through the spinal cord connecting the seven spiritual chakras.

Color Fig. 24 shows the djed pillar with arms on the right side. It is holding above it a snake/serpentine-like figure surrounded by an aura. Is this raising of the djed symbolizing spiritual enlightenment? Is this linked to the angled serpent bar of the Mayan?

The Egyptians' symbolic use of the crook and the flail appears to be another clue to their recognition of the kundalini and its avenue through the spine and spinal cord. (See color Fig. 25.)

These were important symbols of power representing leadership and a powerful ruler. They were generally associated with Osiris, but on occasion could also be linked to other gods and the kings. Mainstream Egyptologists considered them to represent the king's power to help his people—with the flail, he was a provider of food and with the crook, a shepherd for his people. The spinal symbolism brought forth here can show that they have other purposes—to represent the kundalini and the spinal cord. Author John Van Auken points out that: "The crook is the mystical symbol of the kundalini pathway," and that the flail represents "the control over one's urges and senses."[5]

Esoterically, the crook can be easily seen to be the kundalini pathway, as pointed out by Mr. Van Auken, and the fact that these symbols are primarily associated with Osiris should clearly point their symbolic purpose toward the spine. The flail as a symbol of the control of one's lower urges or lower chakras is also appropriate from the two other aspects. First Egyptologists believe that the flail as a harvesting tool representing the king providing food can also seem to be an instrument to collect the gummy excretions of plants to be used for incense.[6] John Van Auken has also pointed out Egyptian scenes showing the pharaoh inhaling the scent of the lotus in order to calm and quiet the lower self. Finally the flail is a very straightforward and clear depiction of the lower part of the spinal cord and central nervous system (representing the lower urges), called the cauda equina.

The central nervous system is considered the brain and spinal cord. The spinal cord connects to the base of the brain and travels down through the spinal column. The cauda equina is the set of fleshy cords of nerves that fan out from the spinal cord towards its terminus. The term *cauda equina* translates as "horse's tail" due to the considered visual similarity.

It has been demonstrated with the evidence presented here that multiple cultures recognized the concept of the kundalini and its spiritual energy and that a primary representation of it was through serpent symbolism. There is also a second major style of symbolism of representing this that should be touched upon. That is tree symbolism which many cultures used to represent the spinal cord and this spiritual energy. This tree symbolism was also noted earlier in this chapter with the djed pillar's "association with trees."

The spinal column, the core of the stability framework of the human body, is also the protective encasement of the central nervous system along with the skull. The central nervous system (CNS) consists of the spinal cord and brain. The comparison of the CNS to a tree system is

Fig. 12.5–Cauda Equina

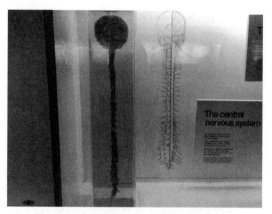

Fig. 12.6–Spinal Cord and Cauda Equina

Fig. 12.7–Tree System

self–evident from the spinal roots of the cauda equina through the trunk of the spinal cord to the crown of the brain. It also helps to explain why the djed would be associated with trees. As Lawrence Blair puts it, "It is the spine, of course, which is the 'tree of life' in the physical frame, the trellis upon which man rises upright from the biological world to walk erect in the direction of consciousness."[7]

The significance of this statement can be seen in the sacred tree lore found in cultures all over the world. The Norse had the Yggdrasil, literally the "terrible horse," similar to the spinal cord base root system called cauda equina, "horse tail." A Chinese tree of life shows a phoenix and a dragon, the dragon being comparable to the serpent spinal cord and

phoenix to the head cap, which is very analogous to the Egyptian obelisk and Benben stone discussed earlier. There is also the Qabbalic tree
of life. Trees of life or enlightenment are found in Islamic, Judaic, and
Christian tradition in the Koran and the Bible. The Mayans had a sacred
tree that also represented the cosmic cross of the Milky Way and the
ecliptic.[8] The ancient Egyptians revered the sycamore fig tree, having
two such trees of *turquoise* on the east horizon where their sun-god Ra
rose every morning. Again Hathor comes into play as she did at Serabit
el-Khadim where she is known as the "Mistress of the Sycamores."[9] In
addition, Buddhists have the Bodhi Tree, another fig tree, under which
Siddhartha gained enlightenment and became the Buddha.

It is of interest that the fig tree is specifically mentioned by Egyptians
and Buddhists and that many biblical scholars believe it was a fig tree
in the Garden of Eden and not an apple tree as is common in Christian
lore.[10] If one looks at the ripening fig fruit, it has a definite similarity to
the reddish pituitary gland. (See color Figs. 26 and 27.)

The biblical Old Testament presents numerous incidences where the
Israelites are directed by God to destroy and cut down the sacred poles
of other religions. The sacred poles in Hebrew are *asherim* which also
translates as sacred grove or tree.[11] Could the significance be that raising the kundalini or the life forces through the spinal cord in any other
way than by a sacred, monotheistic way towards Oneness was an im-
proper and abhorrent approach to communion with higher forces or God?

Multiple examples of the fig tree tied to raising one's consciousness
can be seen in the New Testament.

Let's visit Luke 19:1–10 (NKJV) when Jesus comes to Zacchaeus' house:

> 19 [1]Then Jesus entered and passed through Jericho. [2]Now
> behold, there was a man named Zacchaeus who was a chief
> tax collector, and he was rich. [3]And he sought to see who Jesus
> was, but could not because of the crowd, for he was of short
> stature. [4]So he ran ahead and climbed up into a sycamore tree
> to see Him, for He was going to pass that way. [5]And when
> Jesus came to the place, He looked up and saw him, and said
> to him, "Zacchaeus, make haste and come down, for today I
> must stay at your house." [6]So he made haste and came down,
> and received Him joyfully. [7]But when they saw it, they all com-
> plained, saying, "He has gone to be a guest with a man who is
> a sinner."

⁸Then Zacchaeus stood and said to the Lord, "Look, Lord, I give half of my goods to the poor; and if I have taken anything from anyone by false accusation, I restore fourfold."

⁹And Jesus said to him, "Today salvation has come to this house, because he also is a son of Abraham; ¹⁰for the Son of Man has come to seek and to save that which was lost."

Could this passage symbolize a person being short in stature, not having raised his consciousness, then raising his kundalini to his pituitary, up in the fig tree, and found salvation?

Then there is Matthew 21:18-22, (KJV):

¹⁸Now in the morning as he returned into the city, he hungered.

¹⁹And when he saw a fig tree in the way, he came to it, and found nothing thereon, but leaves only, and said unto it, Let no fruit grow on thee henceforward forever. And presently the fig tree withered away.

²⁰And when the disciples saw it, they marveled, saying, how soon is the fig tree withered away!

²¹Jesus answered and said unto them, Verily I say unto you, If ye have faith, and doubt not, ye shall not only do this which is done to the fig tree, but also if ye shall say unto this mountain, Be thou removed, and be thou cast into the sea; it shall be done.

²²And all things, whatsoever ye shall ask in prayer, believing, ye shall receive.

Is this example symbolizing what happens to a person if he does not raise his spiritual consciousness?

Finally in John 1:43-51 (KJV) when Jesus calls Philip and Nathanael

⁴³The day following Jesus would go forth into Galilee, and findeth Philip, and saith unto him, Follow me.

⁴⁴Now Philip was of Bethsaida, the city of Andrew and Peter.

⁴⁵Philip findeth Nathanael, and saith unto him, We have found him, of whom Moses in the law, and the prophets, did write, Jesus of Nazareth, the son of Joseph.

⁴⁶And Nathanael said unto him, Can there any good thing come out of Nazareth? Philip saith unto him, Come and see.

⁴⁷Jesus saw Nathanael coming to him, and saith of him, Behold an Israelite indeed, in whom is no guile!

⁴⁸Nathanael saith unto him, Whence knowest thou me? Jesus answered and said unto him, Before that Philip called thee, when thou wast under the fig tree, I saw thee.

⁴⁹Nathanael answered and saith unto him, Rabbi, thou art the Son of God; thou art the King of Israel.

⁵⁰Jesus answered and said unto him, Because I said unto thee, I saw thee under the fig tree, believest thou? thou shalt see greater things than these.

⁵¹And he saith unto him, Verily, verily, I say unto you, Hereafter ye shall see heaven open, and the angels of God ascending and descending upon the Son of man.

Nathanael becomes one of the apostles with Jesus saying he saw him under the fig tree. Again a symbolic representation of raising one's consciousness and (interestingly in Judaic tradition) of being under the fig tree is an idiom for studying and meditating on the sacred words of the Torah.¹² You may remember, noted earlier, it was under the fig (bodhi) tree where Buddha reached enlightenment.

The Cayce Cubit and Geodesy

This Cayce Egyptian/spinal cubit has been demonstrated to be, with extraordi-nary and compelling evidence, an example of an international unit of measurement shared at three different sacred sites, on three different continents, at least. This substantiation alludes to the fact that such a shared unit of measurement would have to come from an advanced culture that could travel worldwide, by sea or otherwise. Obviously this is verified in numerous Cayce readings. Unfortunately such a source is considered unacceptable by mainstream archaeology and science.

On the other hand, science is continuingly pushing back further the dates of the existence of civilizations and global travel by different groups. Example after example can be given of this. The existence in North America of the "Clovis" people, believed to be the first settlers, has been moved back recently by at least 3,000 years.[1] Evidence of an advanced civilization has been found at Gobekli Tepe, in Turkey, where people were carving and raising stone pillars and edifices from ten to twenty tons dating back to at least 9,000 BCE.[2] The oldest primitive stone tools that had been dated in the past to one and a half million years ago have now been overshadowed by stone tools dating an additional three hundred thousand years in the past.[3] Almost prophetically evidence is being found for the North American continent and the New World that human beings from Europe came to these shores at least as far back as 17,000 BCE and possibly as far back as 24,000 BCE.[4] Suddenly postulating a globally shared measuring unit comes well into the realm of possibility. Why cannot the evidence provided here be accepted as proof of such international sharing and unity of purpose in ancient times?

If the scientific community can reach beyond the hubris that we must be the most advanced society the earth has seen, and therefore, the further one goes back in history, the more primitive the culture must be, imagine the discoveries that could be found. Such self-induced blinders only limit us. Perhaps that last observation is too strong, but there does appear to be a bias towards the idea of an advanced ancient civilization that could travel between continents and share its wisdom and technology, thousands, if not tens of thousands of years ago. Add on top of that the fact that the initial evidence came from psychic information as provided by Edgar Cayce, and many simply stop listening at all. That is truly a shame. I understand merely stating it as fact is not enough; evidence needs to be provided, but that should not preclude researchers from using psychic information as a springboard for further investigation to the possibilities. Remember the "mythical" city of Troy from Homer's *Iliad* was actually found.

This research is now showing evidence that the "Cayce Cubit" could well be an even greater verification of a worldwide advanced culture, with an ancient international system of measurements, for a shared spiritual purpose in what would be considered prehistoric times. Obviously the evidence is already there as earlier presented with this same cubit being used at three sites, but is there any other precedent for such an international unit of measure? The answer is Yes, in what could be considered a subsequent system proof; it is in our modern day metric system (I.S.).

To really appreciate history repeating itself here, a brief record of the creation of the meter is needed. It started in the late 1600s with several scientists of the time who began calling for the need of international units of measure. Their initial suggestion for this unit of measurement was to use the length of a pendulum where half of its to-and-fro swing would equal one second. This became known as a "seconds pendulum." From the 1600s to 1930, pendulum timepieces were considered the most accurate chronometers in the world. The length suggested for this international unit of measurement was 39¼ inches (997mm). The rationale behind this length was that a pendulum with such a span, when swung at an approximate angle/amplitude of 7 or 8 degrees would give one a "seconds pendulum" which could be easily transported and recreated anywhere in the world. It would take over another one hundred years before the suggestion for an international standard would really begin to move forward.

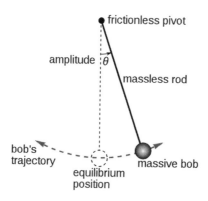

Fig. 13.1–Pendulum

While the French Revolution was going on struggling for its age of enlightenment, the push for an international unit of measure began once again. This time the scientists had come down to a final debate over two different methodologies to create an international unit of linear measurement. The discussion was to use the pendulum length as a unit of measure or a fraction of the length of the distance along a meridian from the Equator through Paris to the North Pole. As noted earlier the pendulum was considered a good choice because of its portability and ease to re-create all over the world. Think of the metronome used in keeping time for music or a grandfather clock; they used the same principle. It was argued that due to gravitational discrepancies in different places on the earth that the pendulum would not be accurate enough. It was finally decided to use one ten millionth of the distance from equator to pole, and this would constitute the meter. This decision then took another seven years, once started, to complete a survey of the distance at an average sea level from the equator to the North Pole. It could be argued that in reality its resulting measurement was no better or worse than if the pendulum solution had been used. The meter's fascinating history continues down a long convoluted journey and is now evolved to be the distance light travels in a vacuum in 1/299792459 of a second.[5]

Posited here is that the "Cayce Cubit" of 27. 5 inches was used in a similar manner as today's meter for an international unit of measurement in what is considered prehistoric time. Besides the structures themselves that provided standing evidence of its use in Egypt, Great

Britain, and Mexico, there is further evidence provided in the history of these ancient cultures and the history of the modern meter.

As noted above the way to determine the length of the meter boiled down to two final choices. The choices being a tiny fractional measurement of the earth's surface, which took another seven years of expeditions to get a very close measurement of, or the length of a "seconds pendulum." Each recommendation had its own drawbacks, but to think about which one would be easier to share and re-create among other varying cultures and could be passed on even if a civilization fails. I believe the answer is clear—it would be the pendulum. The next question deals with about their suggested length of 39.25 inches for the "seconds pendulum." That still doesn't fit! That is correct, for a pendulum that is swung only 7 or 8 degrees. Using mathematic software programs to test this theory gave a correct pendulum length of 27.5 inches, if the pendulum swing was started at a 90 degree amplitude/angle. This provides a simple and elegant solution of placing the apparatus in the ground, then bringing the pendulum up to the horizontal (90 degrees) and letting it swing. Even the amplitude is simple; just bring it to level, easily determined by a cup holding water, no protractor necessary. Just as in the suggestion of creating the international unit of the meter, this also creates such a measuring unit. (The Cayce Cubit)

The following are the results of other pendulum lengths compared to the Cayce cubit and a synopsis of the aspects of this research.

Summary
Egyptian Royal cubit (20.61 in): 1.7069 seconds
Megalithic Yard (32.64 in): 2.1503 seconds
Cayce cubit (27.5): 1.9748 seconds—less than 3/100ths of a second's difference.[6]

Please note there are different sets of calculations to be used whether a large amplitude swing pendulum (more than 22 degrees) or a small amplitude swing pendulum (less than 22 degrees) is used. Due to using a swing of 90 degrees, the large swing calculator was used. In addition I would like to recognize the authors Christopher Knight and Alan Butler of *Before the Pyramids* for giving me the inspiration from their book to pursue this line of investigation and thus include the megalithic yard of Scottish engineer and professor Alexander Thom in the results. In an interesting aside, Alexander Thom studied and surveyed over 200 megalithic stone circles, such as Stonehenge, in the area of the British Isles and came to the conclusion the builders used a unit of measure of 32.64 inches. Curiously he determined a megalithic rod was 81.66 inches, almost exactly (less than 2% difference) to 3 Cayce cubits.

As to the importance of this Cayce cubit length for universal understanding of spirituality, already with the preponderance of evidence linking it to the spine and path of the kundalini, the link to one's higher self, and communion with God, I will add this quote from other researchers in this field: "We can probably speculate that the pendulum length was to be considered divinely inspired and that the linear units were therefore considered holy."[7]

Fascinatingly there is more evidence for this unit provided by the Great Pyramid of Egypt. Several researchers have noted that the Great Pyramid appears to be a geodesic model of the Earth.[8] (See color Fig. 28.) Different dimensions of the Great Pyramid, such as its height and perimeter, are a very accurate 1/43200 model of the dimensions of the earth. This scale model seems to beg the question why? Why a scale model of 1/43,200? Dr. Schoch writes that Livio Stecchini was the first to associate it with a 24–hour day which has 86,400 seconds. Therefore it represents half a day or 12 hours which is equal to 43,200 seconds.[9] I believe that though this may be the case, an additional reason and purpose should be included. In a classic "aha" moment the answer was discovered in the very pendulum used for measurement. The interesting point here is that the "seconds pendulum, " a pendulum with a 2 second period, is a 1/43,200 portion of a mean solar day! Please remember the ancient Egyptians are credited with giving us a 24–hour day. Using the Cayce cubit then, not only gives significant results in its units of measurement for the Great Pyramid, but as a model of the earth and keeper of time.

This is even more appropriate when one examines the survey equipment that may have been used not only to build such structures, but also to measure and transit the stars above. In the case of the Egyptians, this was called a *merkhet* which is translated, appropriately, as an instrument of knowing or an instrument of time keeping. It was known to be used for time keeping by measuring stars, finding north, and for building construction.[10]

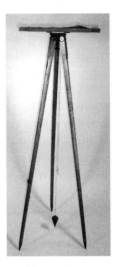

Fig. 13.2–Survey Pendulum/Plumb Bob

As can be seen from its depiction of a surveyor's plane table, an Egyptian *merkhet* also had similar functions and included a plumb line and bob. This would also make a *merkhet* an excellent example of a pendulum.

The Egyptians and the Maya both had "stretching of the cord" ceremonies, used for measurements in the construction of their structures and in some case in measuring the heavens.[11] They shared the purposes of pyramids and quite straightforward serpent symbolism. Both civilizations are also known for their advanced understanding and measurement of time. The builders of Stonehenge are more of an enigma, but if an advanced culture was traveling to the British Isles and sharing such knowledge, it would have been even simpler in distances and waters to navigate.

Below are some of the specifics of this described ancient geodesy and some other significant curious "coincidences" that occur with them.

Geodesy and the Great Pyramid[12]
G.P. perimeter (3023.13 feet) = .5 minute (**30** seconds) of latitude at the equator.
G.P. perimeter at outside sockets (3043.51 feet) = **30** seconds of longitude at the equator

Height of G.P. w/platform = Earth's Polar radius
All this are on a 1/43,200 ratio
360 x 60 x 2

As can be seen here, this exhibit links to other important numbers shown previously to be associated at some of these sites. The 30 seconds of longitude and latitude in the geodesy of the Great Pyramid connects back to the 30 degree longitude and latitude where the Great Pyramid is located and its shared prime numbers in its height and width multiples giving a product of 30. Then at Stonehenge you have the Sarsen stone circle, the second circle, which, in its completed form consists of 30 stone lintels and 30 stone uprights. The Sarsen stone circle is the circle with a Cayce cubit diameter of 44, which equals one arc second of latitude. This circle with its lintel construction was probably used as a horizontal measuring line of sight for celestial viewing and measurements.

The number 44 seems to have significance also at these two sites when looked at from the view of the Cayce readings and speaks of a worldwide international congregation of delegates who met in Egypt. This reading was given in 1925.

> Then we have the gathering together of this group from the farthest places—forty and four (44). As we see. {this number} will run through many numbers, for, as ye find, there is the law pertaining to each and every element significant to man's existence considered and given in one manner or form by the groups as gathered at this meeting.   5748-3

The number 44 not only shows itself in 44 Cayce cubits making one arc second of latitude and the diameter of Stonehenge's Sarsen circle of stones, it is also found in the lowest proportion of the Great Pyramid perimeter over its height; 44/7 and is equal to 2 pi. 2 pi is the constant used to find the circumference of a circle, or a globe such as the earth, by multiplying 2 pi by the radius.

There is a possible 44 connection to the Mayan Kukulcan Pyramid, but it is not as clear as the other sites. The Maya archaeologists who determined the zapal, the length of 2 Cayce cubits, remarked in their research that what helped to confirm this unit of measure was the top of the pyramid being 13 zapals across and the temple being 9 zapals

across was that the Mayas recognized 13 heavens and 9 underworlds. If
one brings these heavens and underworlds together, the sum of 22
zapals equals 44 Cayce cubits. All this seemingly points to messages
that are linked and incorporated at these sites.

So there it is! By being willing to use the information provided by the
psychic readings of Edgar Cayce which included an Egyptian cubit
length ignored by Egyptologists, an advanced ancient civilization that
could travel the world, and that world representatives could even meet
as a council in Egypt, one can find valid confirming evidence for international sharing of information with civilizations. In using the information provided by Edgar Cayce's psychic ability, along with
archaeological and scientific evidence, the theory for a type of international unit of measurement that would be simple to travel with and be
recreated all over the world with a pendulum or just the instructions to
build a pendulum can be submitted. By using the knowledge provided,
exactly what our own scientist suggested doing for an international
unit of measurement, using a pendulum, works the same way for the
Cayce cubit. The clear and compelling evidence of these examined sites
appearing to use the Cayce cubit help validate the theory. It is so elegant, plausible, and simple! As Troy, once considered a fictional city,
became an archaeological reality, so moves in this pendulum, the psychic archaeology of Edgar Cayce. Again there is also another curious
coincidence. This suggested ancient international unit of measurement
based on the spine and representing the kundalini, probably known as
a light unit of measurement spiritually, reflects the modern meter whose
length is now determined as the length of the path travelled by light in
a vacuum in 1/299,792,458 of a second.

Evidence of Correlations Between the Maya Kukulcan Pyramid and the Egyptian Great Pyramid and a Global Unity

The previous section demonstrated the many observable links between the Great Pyramid and Stonehenge. Here will be suggested some
other possible links between the Great Pyramid and the Kukulcan Pyramid. The Kukulcan Pyramid has its famous north staircase and two
serpent heads at its base which create an undulating serpent descending down the pyramid caused by lights and shadows which occur during the year only on the two equinoxes. The Edgar Cayce readings state

that civilizations worldwide visited and were visited by the ancient Egyptian civilization. The readings further state that the Atlanteans had emigrated both to the Yucatan and Egypt. Even aside from such readings, it can be seen that both cultures had a penchant for building pyramids, sharing serpent symbolism, "stretching of the cord" ceremonies, and linear units of measurements as previously mentioned. Also mentioned in an earlier chapter is the not widely known information that the Kukulcan Pyramid has an entrance on the north side to its interior where there is at least one chamber above ground, showing more similarities to the Great Pyramid. Is there further evidence of such sharing traits? The Great Pyramid's original entrance is also on the north side, approximately sixty feet above ground. It seems obvious such an elevated entrance would need a staircase in order to reach the opening—a staircase to reach this entrance and possibly continue up to the top capstone.

Ancient accounts describe the Great Pyramid, in its original state, as being completely covered with white, highly polished gleaming limestone, but no mention of a staircase. Some of the remains of this covering of tura limestone can still be found at its base, but the rest has been cannabilzed and is believed to have been used in the construction of old Cairo. Did the Great Pyramid have on its north side a similar serpernt staircase, only of cobras made of this limestone, now taken away? Possibly a staircase wide at its base and narrowing as it went up, like the hood of a cobra to its narrowing tail? This staircase may have well blended into the face of the pyramid and covered the entrance door. The original entrance shows evidence of having a hinged door to conceal it, which also could have had the limestone staircase as an additional cover.[13] Now with the covering limestone gone is there any possible evidence for such a staircase for the Great Pyramid?

Perhaps the first clues towards this can be seen in an Egyptian heiroglyph.

Fig. 13.3—Bread-Cone Hieroglyph

This is the hieroglyph of conical offertory bread and is translated as
"to give." This fits well in the view of the Great Pyramid as a site of
spiritual initiation—a place to offer oneself, to give oneself, to the Creative Forces. This offertory bread symbol points to such a communion.
Examining the heiroglyph it can be seen as a triangle with a narrow
triangle within it. If this offertory heiroglyph was also emblematic of
the Great Pyramid, then this inner triangle could be an image of a narrowing set of stairs to an offertory entrance.

The most compelling evidence for this possible serpent staircase is
standing in front of the east side of the Great Pyramid between the
paws of the Sphinx. It is the dream stelae! When looking at the carvings
of the stelae, the clues suddenly jump out at you. It is the two human
figures in it and the pyramidal "kilts" they were wearing. Their kilts
were not only triangularly shaped to mirror a pyramid, but they also
had staircases (belts) carved down the middle of them with two cobra
serpent heads at the base! (See color Fig. 30.) Had this stelae captured
the image of the Great Pyramid in its finished form? Could this be a
staircase running down the north side wide at the base and narrowing
to the top? It resonated as a stylizied depiction of it, and it brought back
memories of another pyramid—the Kukulcan Pyramid at Chichen Itza
of the Mayans. (See color Fig. 29.)

Fig. 13.4–Kukulcan Pyramid Serpent Head

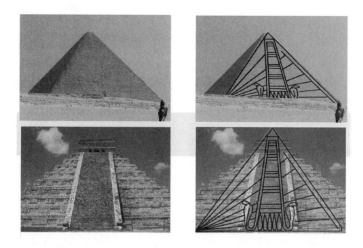

Fig. 13.5–Artist's Depiction of the Great Pyramid Stairway

At this time it cannot be proven that this concept is historically accurate. The limestone finishing blocks and any steps are lost—many to the construction of old Cairo. Yet it makes sense to have had a staircase up to the original entrance and even up to the capstone. There is also an elegant feeling that the north side of the pyramid would also symbolize the same meaning as the offertory hieroglyph. Even the Pharaoh's name given to the Great Pyramid provides us with a clue. It was Khnum-Khufu, meaning "the god khnum protects me." Khnum, the ram god, was their god of Creative Forces. Kukulcan was the Mayan Vision Serpent and the messenger between their kings and gods—their symbol of communion and communication with the Divine, along the lines as I have described the purpose of the Great Pyramid.

All I can ask is that you go inside that still, quiet place in yourself and sense whether this resonates for you, as I felt the resonance in the King's Chamber coffer. Ultimately, each of our own initiations will always be within.

Vibrations and Wave Lengths

Fig. 14.1–Egyptian Headrest

There are the interesting correlations between waves and the functioning of parabolic radio telescopes. As pointed out previously, the Great Pyramid certainly seems to have many similarities to a parabolic dish receiver/transmitter. If we look at the pyramid cubit, depending on the source, its length is considered between 18 to almost 28 inches, similar to a frequency length of a radio wave; this puts it in the range of modern radio telescopes which search the universe and in that narrow window of radio waves which can be received or transmitted from Earth to outer space, the heavens—another comparative link between heaven and earth. For that matter, it appears the spinal lengths of all vertebrae species fall into this same window. (See color Fig. 31.)

The lengths of the male spinal vertebrae lead to another possibility and aspect. The number 71 centimeters (27.9") translates, for sound waves, into 483.0986 Hz, the Cayce cubit of 27.5" equals 491 Hz.[1] Could these sound waves be the note for AUM, the creation chord? To what effect are these waves when sounded in the King's and Queen's Chambers of the Great Pyramid? The note B above middle C is 494 Hz. B-flat is 466 Hz. So both of these lengths fall between the B and B-flat note.[2] Why is this significant? Well, oddly enough scientists have recently discovered a black hole that emits a sound wave in the note of B-flat.

Astronomers have detected the deepest note ever generated in the cosmos, a B-flat flying through space like a ripple on an invisible pond. No human will actually hear the note, because it is fifty-seven octaves below the keys in the middle of a piano.[3]

> The gas is apparently dancing excitedly to the eons-long drone of a deep B-flat.
>
> The note strikes an important chord with astronomers, who say it may help them understand how the universe's largest structures, called galaxy clusters, evolve.
>
> Astronomers were not surprised to find the supermassive black hole making a strong sub-bass sound. Though these greatest known matter sinks are by nature dark and invisible, they create bright and chaotic environments in which many forms of radiation—from radio waves to visible light to X-rays—have been recorded. These electromagnetic waves all travel at the speed of light.
>
> Other studies have shown that the riotous activity around black holes—where gas is accelerated to nearly light-speed—produces many notes that are, all together, much like music. Collectively, the cosmos produces, scientists believe, a cacophonic symphony of inaudible tunes.[4]

Scientists have also discovered what they believe is a black hole in the center of our galaxy, and they postulate that all galaxies have black holes at their centers. Say our black hole resonates to the sound of a B-flat note and, as shown, our spinal column is just off the length of a B-flat note. Is it possible that the Great Pyramid and other sites were not only used for initiation rites, but that the initiation also included a precise attunement of oneself to the B-flat tone astronomers have found reverberating through the universe? The earlier noted Hopi tradition in

Chapter 9 alludes to this possibility:

> Through each ran an axis, man's axis being the backbone, the
> vertebral column . . . Along this axis were several vibratory
> centers which echoed the primordial sound of life throughout
> the universe or sounded a warning if anything went wrong.
> The first of these in man lay at the top of the head.[5]

The ability for living organisms to receive as well as to send sound
and electromagnetic signals is not limited to Hopi lore. This ability is
also recognized by author Stephen Harrod Buhner. Buhner writes that
we are receiving such signals all the time and these signals span the
electromagnetic spectrum. He continues saying that the human body
has its own electromagnetic field which aligns with a person's spine.[6]

Not only does it appear our spines may represent our resonance
with the evolution and creation of a primordial universe, but it may
have an attunement to the cosmos itself in sound. Perhaps there are
other symbolic representations.

The Mayan double–headed serpent bar is also seen as the ecliptic
going across the center of our galaxy according to author John Major
Jenkins. Perhaps this has a correlation with recent work by astronomers
and astrophysicists which shows an angled bar going across the center
of our galaxy. (See color Fig. 32.) This is also similar to the Egyptian
"Raising of the Djed" (Osiris's spine).

> The bar is made of relatively old and red stars, the survey
> shows. It is about 27,000 light-years long or roughly 7,000
> light-years longer than previously thought. Churchwell's team
> also found that the bar is oriented at about a 45-degree angle
> relative to the main plane of the galaxy in which the Sun and
> the other spiral-arm stars orbit . . . , and the Sun sits about
> 26,000 light-years from the center.[7]

Has the alignment to our galactic center of the Earth and our sun on
December 21, 2012 helped begin a global attunement for humankind?
Perhaps it has in a more subtle way than we are aware of as of yet. If
one reflects back to the earlier discussion on the symbolism of the Egyptian tekhenu/obelisk, what may have occurred is a cosmic obelisk or
shaft of light like a baptism and rebirth. The comparison is that from

the primordial bulge (mound) of the center of our galaxy the principal cosmic rays (light) will fall upon the earth. At this center of our galaxy will also be found the constellation Cygnus (the swan), also known as the Northern Cross. A galaxy center and constellation both estimated at approximately 26,000 light years from Earth. This 26,000 light year distance coincides with Plato's Great Year—the amount of time for the full cycle from beginning to end of the precession of the equinoxes. Perhaps we are experiencing a cosmic Alpha and Omega!

The location of the Milky Way's central black hole is well known. Called Sagittarius A*, or Sgr A*, it sits about 26,000 light–years away, *at the heart of the galaxy. It is surrounded by intense radio waves, X-rays* and other radiation. Astronomers know the black hole is smaller than the diameter of Earth's orbit; they suspect it is about 10 times smaller but have not been able to measure it with enough precision to know for sure.[8] [Author's emphasis]

So here we have the Egyptian tekhenu (obelisk) symbolism with its benu bird and the symbolism of the cross on the hill of Golgotha (hill of the skull), both with their resurrections coming to fulfillment in this galactic alignment. Judaic folklore tells us that it was called the hill of the skull because that is where Noah buried Adam's skull after the flood.[9] Are both signifying the alpha and omega completion of a cycle such as the Great Year? On this point more similarities abound. John Major Jenkins writes that "one Hunaphu's head is hung in the dark rift."[10] One Hunaphu is their first father or first sun deity (which in this author's opinion could also be considered as the first light rays), and the dark rift is located in the midst of their cosmic tree (cross). In addition, Andrew Collins enlightens us by saying that Cygnus or the Northern Cross bore the crucified Greek god Orpheus, who also was beheaded, before it was used as the constellation of the cross of Calvary (Golgotha).[11]

If we return to cosmic sound waves, we find that they are not limited to black holes alone. As discussed earlier, scientists now believe that from the vibrations of the Big Bang galaxies were created, and they have described the universe as ringing with the sound of countless cosmic bells. Scientists have discovered the entire universe resounds with what could be called "the music of the spheres"— an apt phrase from the Middle Ages derived from the Pythagorean concept of a cosmic harmony created from the vibrations of celestial spheres in the universe.[12]

Today there remains a residual vibration of the Big Bang called cosmic background radiation. The frequency of this pervading universal note is equivalent to a note between a B and a B–flat.

> The Cosmic Background Radiation is a residual vibration from the explosion of the Big Bang, vibrating at a frequency of 4080 Mega Hertz (4,080,000,000 Hertz). All vibrations can be interpreted as sound. Octaves are defined as the lower frequency being half that of its higher frequency. For example, A 3 = 440 Hz and one octave above is A 4 at 880 Hz. Twenty-two octaves below The Big Note (4,080,000,000 Hertz), is calculated to be 972.75 Hz. This is slightly lower than B 4 at 987.77 Hz and somewhat higher than B Flat 4 at 932.33 Hz, in equal-tempered tuning. Therefore, the Universe is resonating at a tone a little flatter than B, as defined by standard tuning.[13]

Amazingly this universal note is almost exactly the same note for the length of the human spine!!! Is this the sound of a creation note expressed by so many cultures echoing through our central nervous system to our eternal selves, linking us all together in this cosmic symphony? Perhaps we have it in the reverse, is it that we are the instruments created by universal vibrations rather than instruments that create the vibrations?

These "wave front spawning grounds for galaxies" and creations from vibrations also sound very similar to the studies done by Dr. Hans Jenny that he titled: Cymatics; "matters pertaining to waves, wave matters."[14]

> Cymatics, the study of wave phenomena, is a science pioneered by Swiss medical doctor and natural scientist, Hans Jenny (1904-1972). For 14 years he conducted experiments animating inert powders, pastes, and liquids into life-like, flowing forms, which mirrored patterns found throughout nature, art and architecture. What's more, all of these patterns were created using simple sine wave vibrations (pure tones) within the audible range. So what you see is a physical representation of vibration, or how sound manifests into form through the medium of various materials.[15]

Giving heed to the earlier brief discussion on holographic processes, those three-dimensional images are created by pure, powerfully aligned, in-phase light focused on a holographic plate that looks like wave and ripples created by tossing a handful of pebbles in a lake. To reiterate a portion of the previous quote:

> The effect is subtle in another way, because the ringing cosmic bells (the rocks in our analogy) were ubiquitous. So instead of one rock tossed into the pond, "It's more like a handful of gravel," Eisenstein said. "You get overlapping ripples."[16]

As can be seen, a similar action was involved in the creation of our visible universe (regular matter). Such matter accounts for only 5% of our universe. Could the rest of the universe, dark matter and dark energy on a higher dimensional plane, be acting like a hologram for our plane?

Such macrocosmic and microcosmic symbolism and creation follow both the ancient axiom "as above, so below" and the modern science of chaos and fractals. This is also concluded by Jenny in his research. "Now it is beyond a doubt that, where organization is concerned, the harmonic figures in physics are in fact essentially similar to the harmonic patterns of organic nature."[17]

These scientific descriptions are eerily familiar to the biblical creation in Genesis. This adds so much more to the phrase "and God *said* let there be light: and there was light." (Genesis 1:3) along with "And God *said* let us make man in our image, after our likeness." (Genesis 1:26) [Author's emphasis]

Author Andrew Collins in *The Cygnus Mystery* discusses different cultures' tales of the birth of the universe through sound. He notes the Hindu god of creation, Brahma, bringing the universe into existence:

> The entire act of creation is said to have proceeded from *Shabda-brahaman*, the sonic absolute, conveyed by the process of *Naada-brahaman*, the "primordial sound or vibration of Brahma."[18]

Mr. Collins continues noting that Brahma was aided by Hamsa, the swan-goose, similar to the Egyptian creation story with the Great

Cackler. It can be seen that in both Eastern and Western thought the power of sound for creation had similar themes.

In another Far Eastern spiritual theme, the parabola's significance can be noted.

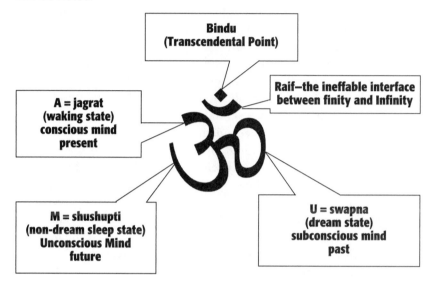

**Bindu
(Transcendental Point)**

**Raif—the ineffable interface
between finity and Infinity**

**A = jagrat
(waking state)
conscious mind
present**

**M = shushupti
(non-dream sleep state)
Unconscious Mind
future**

**U = swapna
(dream state)
subconscious mind
past**

Fig. 14.2—AUM Symbol

This is the Sanskrit glyph for AUM (OM). It is the glyph symbolizing the first vibrations in the universe, the vibration or word of its creation. It is the sacred sound of creation for Hindus and Buddhists.

The Bindu and the Raif. The bindu (Sanskrit, point), symbolized each particle of existence. Each bindu is a catalyst for manifestation. It is also known as the Transcendental Point because each point of existence has intimate contact with the underlying Reality.

The raif is the crescent moon-shaped symbol shown in the glyph (see previous diagram). It symbolized the creative, expressive energy which is generated by or through each bindu, each particle. The raif represents the cosmic hum of the uni-

verse, the means by which Shiva (the Unmanifest, Consciousness or underlying Intelligence) can manifest through Shakti
(Cosmic Energy) to create the world of multifarious objects
which we perceive through the senses. This process takes
place, continuously, moment to moment . . . *The bindu is the
blue-print and the raif is the creative energy.* [Author's empha-
sis] Together, they symbolize the ineffable relationship between the finite and the Infinite, between the part and the
Totality, between the individual and the All, and between time
and the Timeless. Modern quantum physics tells us that each
particle of existence is instantaneously connected to every
other particle. This is independent of time and space—which
suggests that there is an underlying principle (David Bohm,
the well-known quantum physicist, called it the implicate order) which is beyond time and space and which unifies all
things on a deeper level of reality. In Yoga we call this principle Consciousness. In the glyph of it is symbolized by the
formless background on which the symbol is inscribed and by
the ether from which the sound of Aum is created and to
which it returns.[19]

The Bindu and Raif symbols drew my attention. The bindu in the
glyph is shaped like an octahedron (diamond) or turquoise crystal and
the raif with a parabola shape. Not only do the symbols themselves
harken across time, space, and cultures but so do the meanings behind
them. The Bindu "the catalyst for manifestation . . . the blueprint" calls
to the Seal of Solomon, wind, earth, water, and fire, the houses of the
souls. The raif, "the crescent Moon" . . . the creative energy projected
into the Bindu. Such energy that today is focused and projected through
parabolic dishes creating sound and picture, realities, all over the world.
Together they signify the "ineffable relationship between the finite and
the infinite." Also this can be seen in quantum physics, where the wave
(raif) collapses to a particle (bindu). This is the communion with the
saints, the macrocosm and microcosm, and what science has found in
fractals. A perfect match of meaning for the raif and the bindu can be
found in the Cayce reading 2533-7, "The power, then, is in the Christ.
The pattern is in Jesus."

If you are shaking your head and thinking the meaning of these
symbols is overreaching and farfetched, please review the pictures of

the original entrance to the Great Pyramid with its stone carved relief of a parabola shape and the symbols etched into the face of it. After reviewing these pictures, then look at the message communicated in "modern symbols" and sent into space by the Arecibo radio telescope in the same available frequency range that I suggested the pyramid cubit identifies.

The similarities that span thousands of years hopefully allows one to have a more open mind and to take pause. The message consists of 1679 bits, arranged into 73 lines of 23 characters per line (these are both prime numbers and may help the aliens decode the message).[20]

The "ones" and "zeroes" were transmitted by frequency shifting at the rate of 10 bits per second. The total broadcast was less than three minutes. A graphic showing the message is reproduced here. It consists, among other things, of the Arecibo telescope, our solar system, DNA, a stick figure of a human, and some of the bio-chemicals of earthly life.

Fig. 14.3–Arecibo Radio Message

Let us review briefly the case presented for a holographic-like universe where sound and parabolic waves, through their transmission of energy, give birth to a portion of the universe in physicality. This concept for the creation of the universe, as has been shown, is not only a conclusion by today's scientists and cosmologists, but it also echoes back to the noted work of Dr. Hans Jenny and even further back to the Pythagoreans. The makeup of everything physical today is considered a progressive creation of elements through primeval stars. As astronomer, author, and Fellow of the Royal Astronomical Society of London James Mullaney has written: "We've seen that we came from the stars–that our bodies are literally made of stardust."[21]

The concept of our creation from the stars can be seen in the different cultures and the different perspectives that have been discussed here. In Egypt the obelisk stone shaft represented a frozen ray of light from the sun bringing creation to Earth. The Egyptian pyramid texts described the king becoming a star, going back to the heavens, with his head being raised by two (triangular–shaped) Enneads. There are the tables of the Ten Commandments, as triangular shaped, forming a star, and representing the house of the soul. This six–pointed star has been shown to be symbolic of these concepts in Eastern and Western traditions and also representative of the alchemical ancient elements themselves. These aspects are also reflected in the Hermetic philosophy of the heavens mirroring the earth and the earth mirroring the heavens and are encapsulated in the phrase, "as above, so below."

With this recap, now submitted here is a further depiction of the sound waves made by a super nova of star and a PET scan of a human brain. (See color Figs. 33 and 34.) I find that the images are so alike as to be staggering. I think this is a beautiful, modern day depiction of what different ancient cultures were representing symbolically in their philosophies. Now think back upon the discussion of the Mayan cosmic head hung in the heavens or Orpheus beheaded in Greek tradition hung in the heavens or a cosmic head of the alpha and omega skulls at Golgotha. Is what we seem to be in the physical universe a projected manifestation of vibration from the "missing" majority of the universe, a microcosm model of a macrocosm reality? Is our true consciousness and ultimate home found in cosmic vibration rather than the density of particles? Are we actually the vibrations of stars rather than their dust? The evidence is compelling, but you will have to make your own conclusions.

A Coming Age

Even if one feels he must exclude the psychic readings of Edgar Cayce, could the Great Pyramid be a final temple of initiation for spiritual masters and could the Kukulcan Pyramid and Stonehenge function in similar ways? Are these sites for apotheosis, creating a divine human and uniting heaven with earth? Is there an intuition of a coming time for a reuniting of human kind with a spiritual heritage? Is there other evidence for this? These are questions that seem to have been debated, in one form or another, over the millennia.

Author Ralph Ellis puts forth an interesting interpretation concerning Egyptology and the Bible. His premise is that when one sees the terms bull and cattle or sheep and rams used in the Bible or in Egyptology, he should interpret them as references to the constellations of Taurus and Aries. He states that the in ancient times the changes from the Age of Taurus to the Age of Aries created a civil war in Egypt and created an exodus of the Hyksos–Israelite (Shepherd Kings) from the then ruling Egyptian calf worshipers. The Judaic kingdom that sprang from them brought forth the "Rabbi" Jesus who began as the Divine Shepherd and Shepherd of men, but as the constellations proceeded into the Piscean age, became a Fisher of men, as the Roman Catholic Pope is known today.[1]

The fascinating aspect of this, if we continue this interpretation, is that the next age we are on the verge of, or have already begun depending on different sources, is the Age of Aquarius. Aquarius is the water bearer or *cup*bearer. [Author's emphasis] Not only did Jesus in the Bible make the transition from Aries to Pisces, but he also prepared for the Aquarian Age. The cup at the garden of Gethsemane and the cup at the Last Supper come to mind. Then, look at the actual story of Aquarius.

This story is where a perfect man (Ganymede) is seen by God (Zeus) and taken to Mount Olympus by an eagle (the constellation Aquila) to be his cupbearer. In the *Catholic Online Encyclopedia* it states that the eagle is a symbol of Jesus Christ. Oddly enough the Mayan have an astronomical legend of their hawk constellations, identified as our Aquila constellation, lifting the Southern Cross (a.k.a. Thieves' Cross) out of the ocean in April and placing it back in October which corresponds to their planting and reaping seasons.[2] There is a similarity here in Luke's gospel where Jesus (Aquila) tells the good thief (Southern Cross) he will be in paradise with him that day. Biblically the crucifixion of Jesus the Christ and his words to the good thief on the cross occurred during the same season.

Now following the line of thought that author Ralph Ellis inspired and I pursued onward into the Synoptic Gospels of the Bible, specifically, Jesus' prediction and directions to his disciples to seek a water bearer and follow him to the place for the Last Supper in preparation for the transition.

Gospels; King James Version

Matthew 26:17-18 (KJV)

[17]Now the first *day* of the *feast of* unleavened bread the disciples came to Jesus, saying unto him, Where wilt thou that we prepare for thee to eat the passover? [18]And he said, Go *into the city to such a man*, and say unto him, The Master saith, My time is at hand; I will keep the passover at thy house with my disciples.

Mark 14: 13-17 (KJV)

[13]And he sendeth forth two of his disciples, and saith unto them, Go ye into the city, and *there shall meet you a man bearing a pitcher of water: follow him.* [14]And wheresoever he shall go in, say ye to the goodman of the house, The Master saith, Where is the guestchamber, where I shall eat the passover with my disciples? [15]And he will shew you a large upper room furnished *and* prepared: there make ready for us. [16]And his disciples went forth, and came into the city, and found as he had said unto them: and they made ready the passover. [17]And in the evening he cometh with the twelve.

Luke 22: 8-13 (KJV)
Go and prepare us the passover, that we may eat. [9]And they said unto him, Where wilt thou that we prepare? [10]And he said unto them, Behold, when ye are entered into the city, *there shall a man meet you, bearing a pitcher of water; follow him into the house where he entereth in.* [11]And ye shall say unto the goodman of the house, The Master saith unto thee, Where is the guestchamber, where I shall eat the passover with my disciples? [12]And he shall shew you a large upper room furnished: there make ready. [13]And they went, and found as he had said unto them: and they made ready the passover.[3] [Author's emphasis]

Whereas Matthew is more enigmatic, Luke and Mark specifically instruct the disciples to seek a man bearing a pitcher of water. If I may, the gospel cupbearer, the water bearer, is Aquarius! The perfect human in attunement with God, the birthright Jesus told mankind we have. It should be noted that Author Gordon Strachan has also come to the same conclusion.[4]

Signs in the sky and astrological constellations along with other constellations and alignments seem to be playing a significant role. This type of role can be seen from the earlier discussion of the polar triangle of stars that occurred around 10,500 BCE. The Gospel of Luke in the New Testament wrote of signs in the sky. Much attention has been brought upon the rare galactic alignment that has occurred during a period that includes 21 December 2012. This is when the center of our galaxy, then our sun, then the Earth will be in such a position.

Mayan expert and author John Major Jenkins states in his book *Maya Cosmogenesis 2012* that the Mayan saw this alignment as a 26,000 year biological unfolding.[5] Further, that the center of the galaxy was the source of creation.[6] This mysterious galactic center is also seen as a source of our biological unfolding by author Andrew Collins in *The Cygnus Mystery* due to cosmic rays.

It is therefore extremely likely that an exposure to low doses of cosmic radiation, such as that which might be experienced deep underground from point sources such as Cygnus X-3, will have had a long term beneficial effects which would probably not have been available from massive exposures to cosmic radiation on the surface.[7]

Mr. Collins continues about the impact of cosmic rays on human evolution:

> In the end there are two theories that come out of this groundbreaking research concerning the possible accelerated evolution of the human race owing to cosmic rays. Firstly, it may have increased the speed of evolution of the entire human race (i.e. Neanderthals to Homo sapiens sapiens—the Meinels' contention), or more likely, it resulted in enhanced evolution among only some humans, qualifying them for the role of shaman/priests, communicators deep underground with the perceived cosmic source of life and death.[8]

He further strengthens his argument citing Carl Sagan:

> Yet we leave you finally with the words of astronomer and scientific writer Carl Sagan who, I lately find, proposed as early as 1973 that cosmic rays have been essential to the evolution of the human species.[9]

A similar sentiment is put forth by John Major Jenkins for the Mayan 21 December 2012 date with the Maya Sun deity known as First Father or One Hanuhpu. This Maya solar deity is described as a god of a new world age and also represents for first day of the new year and thus for the Maya is seen as the new sun coming forth on the winter solstice on the 21st of December. This is a day of union of First Father with the Milky Way, which the Maya saw as the cosmic mother. We "are also told that as the day of union approaches, the seeding of the womb of all by the penetrating rays of first father will prepare the human alive during the end–times to self–initiate and revive lost knowledge."[10] This Maya alignment of the Sun and the cosmic womb of the Milky Way with its penetrating rays increasing knowledge (evolvement) parallels Mr. Collins' research of cosmic rays and their possible effect.

Mr. Jenkins further reveals to his readers that our galactic center is shown by the Mayans symbolically as a cross and a cup, reminiscent of other similar symbolism such as the Buddhist gem in the lotus and Chartres' stone in the grail.

"The crossroads and the birth portal; the cross and the cup. These two powerful metaphors work together and provide a compellingly clear map to the true astronomical place of Maya Creation."[11]

What needs to be clarified is the specificity of the date 12/21/12. Author Jenkins has presented that though this is a specific date from the Mayans, the astronomical window of this event spans thirty-six years. This is because of the suns width while it would be passing through this alignment window. This window spans the years between 1980 and 2016, with its center date of 1998.[12] The year 1998 is the year that our Sun was actually closer to the center of our galaxy; this is also noted by astronomer James Mullaney FRAS.[13]

To express it in more detail I include this excerpt:

> There has to be a moment when everything's in perfect alignment, but the timescales are so long that astronomers couldn't calculate it. Of course, this alignment with the center of the galaxy doesn't have an effect on the Earth or the Solar System, it's just like crossing an imaginary line in space, like traveling from Canada to the United States in your car.
>
> There's another type of galactic alignment. This is where the Earth, Sun and the center of the galaxy are in perfect alignment from our perspective. This actually happens every year during the winter solstice, on December 21st. Because of a wobble in the Earth's orbit, the positions of the constellations slowly shift from year to year. The most perfect galactic alignment between the Earth, Sun and the center of the Milky Way happened back in 1998, but now we're slowly shifting away from that alignment. In the coming decades, the perfect alignment will shift to another day.
>
> Again, the alignment of these objects is purely a coincidence.[14]

As previously mentioned the time frame for this alignment is described as a window spanning thirty-six years. Astronomers have also pointed out that its most ideal position in this time frame was 1998 and such an alignment is "pure coincidence."

If that is the case, let me add another "coincidence" relating to 1998 from the Cayce readings. The following excerpts are from three Cayce readings referencing what might be considered a spiritual turning point linked to 1998.

Is it not fitting, then, that these must return? as this priest
may develop himself to be in that position, to be in the capac-
ity of a *liberator* of the world in its relationships to individuals
in those periods to come; for he must enter again at that period, or in 1998.   294-151

(Q) Three hundred years ago Jacob Boehme decreed Atlantis
would rise again at this crisis time when we cross from this
Piscean Era into the Aquarian. Is Atlantis rising now? Will it
cause a sudden convolution and about what Year?
(A) In 1998 we may find a great deal of the activities as have
been wrought by the gradual changes that are coming about.
These are at the periods when the cycle of the solar activity, or
the years as related to the sun's passage through the various
spheres of activity become paramount or Catamount [?] [Tan-
tamount?] to the change between the Piscean and the
Aquarian age. This is a gradual, not a cataclysmic activity in
the experience of the earth in this period.
    Hence the awareness of the soul as to its separateness, or
its being separated, only comes through the manifestations of
the principles of that cosmic consciousness in materiality.
    Hence it is as evolution in a part of the development of the
whole of the universe; not this consciousness of our own solar
system, but of that about all solar force, or which our own
system is only a mere part of the whole consciousness. But in
the earth and man's awareness into the three-dimensional
consciousness, only those that have entered same may relieve
or leave same through the awareness of there being those influences through their various spheres of activity, including
not only the earthly sojourns or material sojourns as we know
in a physical consciousness, but the sojourns throughout the
spheres of activity when they are absent from a physical or
material consciousness.   1602-3

In this same pyramid did the Great Initiate, the Master, take
those last of the Brotherhood degrees with John, the forerun-
ner of Him, at that place. As is indicated in that period where
entrance is shown to be in that land that was set apart, as that
promised to that peculiar peoples, as were rejected—as is
shown in that portion when there is the turning back from the

raising up of Xerxes as the deliverer from an unknown tongue
or land, and again is there seen that this occurs in the entrance of the Messiah in this period—1998.   5748-5

These Cayce readings apparently point in the same direction of the
evidence of important changes predicted for the "window of the 2012
era," only more accurately with the use of the year 1998 when the more
perfect alignment occurred. They speak of the Aquarian Age, an age
portending a more spiritually, mentally, physically perfect human. They
bring across that this is a period with an evolution of humans into a
cosmic consciousness and Oneness, that this is a period of the return of
a cosmic Christ-consciousness. Though there is a great deal of activity, it
is occurring through gradual changes with the Sun's passage through
various spheres. I suggest here a passage of the thirty-six years of the
sun noted earlier. The readings certainly seemed to have predicted this
2012 era and its significance.

Is there other evidence for the cause or the trigger of this spiritual
evolution? Is, perhaps, there physical evidence to identify that side of
the spiritual, the below to the as above? Perhaps subtly so, but what I
have not seen discussed by anyone pertaining to this extraordinary
galactic alignment with the Earth and sun is the possibility of the creation of a gravity lens. Albert Einstein predicted that the sun's gravity
should bend the light of background stars, so they would appear to
move outward during a solar eclipse.

As a result, we now believe gravity is not some "magical" force that
pulls on a mass—as Newton theorized—but simply the bending of
spacetime, and this, in turn, led to the acceptance of relativity upon
which our contemporary cosmological ideas are built.

Einstein also theorized that stars and other masses such as galaxies
should also bend light to form points, arcs, and even halos around the
intervening masses. Dozens of such "gravitational lenses," mostly images of quasars deflected by the gravitational fields of whole galaxies
have been discovered to date.[15]

Gravitational lensing not only bends visible light but acts equally on
all electro-magnetic radiation spectrums bending them and *focusing them
from the source point to the focal point.* In this case with our alignment the
focal point could be Earth. (See color Fig. 35.) Such lenses have been
shown to create arcs, rings, and Einstein crosses in the cosmos. These
would certainly be impressive signs in the sky.

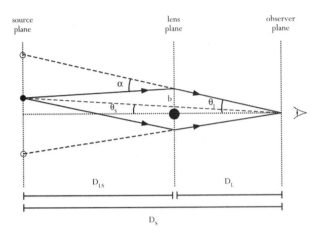

Fig. 15.1–Gravity Lens Geometry

The geometry of gravitational lenses

Fig. 15.2–Gravity Lens Effect I

Actual gravitational lensing effects as observed by the Hubble
Space Telescope in Abell 1689.[16]

Fig. 15.3–Gravity Lens Effect II

An Einstein Cross caused by a gravitational lens. Could it be a
Rosy Cross or Signs in the Sky?

Besides the visible signs such a gravitational lens could create, it
would have the ability to focus anything in the electromagnetic spectrum on the focal point, from light waves, radio waves, through cosmic
rays. This brings us back to the prediction of the Mayans of the coming
penetrating rays of First Father and the evolutionary changing cosmic
rays written about by Andrew Collins. The Pythagoreans have an interesting cosmology that links to both what the authors Jenkins and Collins
have put forth. The Pythagoreans wrote of a central fire or hearth of the
universe, a divine fire that our sun and planets moved around.[17] This is
a hearth concept similar to the Mayan celestial hearth noted on page 44.
They wrote further describing our sun like a disc of glass which reflected this divine fire, very similar to the gravity lens I have described.
Mr. Collins points to the cosmic rays of Cygnus X-3, but there are other
sources. One such source identified at the center of our galaxy is named
Sagittarius A*.

> The complex radio source Sagittarius A appears to be located
> almost exactly at the Galactic Center, and contains an intense
> compact radio source, Sagittarius A*, which many astrono-

mers believe may coincide with a supermassive black hole at
the center of our Galaxy. Accretion of gas onto the black hole,
probably involving a disk around it, would release energy to
power the radio source, itself much larger than the black hole.
The latter is too small to see with present instruments.[18]

Perhaps this alignment with the presented research and the research
of others is showing the end of an age and a birth of another. Are the
Creative Forces of the universe coming into alignment to bring humankind into alignment, an attunement, with such Creative Forces into a
cosmic unity? Rather than isolated initiations through the ages, a global
initiation is on the cusp of occurring. This may well be humankind's
baptism into our birthright of Oneness with God. Consider how science
is plumbing the depths of the cosmos today with radio telescopes.
Through such telescopes they have reached not only deeply into the
universe but back through time as well. Even so they looked through
their lenses darkly. To enhance their viewing resolution they have now
joined radio telescopes into VLBA's, very large base array.

Fig. 15.4–Radio Dish Receiver Arrays

The Very Long Baseline Array[VLBA], part of the National
Radio Astronomy Observatory, is a continent-wide radio-tele-
scope system, with 10, 240-ton dish antennas ranging from
Hawaii to the Caribbean. It provides the greatest resolving
power, or ability to see fine detail, of any telescope in astronomy, on Earth or in space.[19]

Now extend this concept of a VLBA to the spinal columns (central nervous systems) of humankind. Envision millions, if not billions, of central nervous systems aligned and attuned together as this galactic alignment occurs while a gravitational lens is focusing the energy waves emanating from the center of our galaxy on to earth. Acting as living connected VLBA, enhancing the resolution to an unheard of degree, could this be the trigger for the next evolutionary step? Is this a step to a higher consciousness of unity and Oneness, a knowing? Is it recognition of the falsehood of separateness? There is promise of this in the description of such an array's resolving power, also known as its resolution; in music, resolution is the progression of a dissonant tone or chord to a consonant tone or chord. This is a chord that is in harmony. Perhaps the conscious focus of this 2012 alignment that is occurring all over the world both as an end time and as a new age is bringing a larger group consciousness together in focus for a consciousness shift. Much has been written and documented about NDEs (near death experiences) and how such experiences have been a life- and consciousness-changing occurrence for an individual. Is such an event now in the works on a global level?

There is evidence that this spiritual evolution is actually occurring. It is on such a large scale that we do not even realize it is going on. A recent major university study has come to the conclusion that the human race is actually in the most peaceful time it has ever experienced in recorded history.[20] It seems we are so inundated locally and continually by the general media about surrounding war and violence we cannot see compared to our thousands of years of civilization that we are actually becoming more peaceful. We are not seeing the forest for the trees.

A thousand years ago a Christian monk named Niketas Stethatos put this grand concept to paper in the fashion of the ascetic desert fathers of the time:

> Souls that are purified and illuminated by the rays of primordial light in a radiance of mystical knowledge are not only filled with every goodness and luminosity but carried up to the intellective heavens through the contemplation of natural essences. The action of the divine energy does stop here, however, but continues until through wisdom and mystical knowledge of ineffable things, making them abandon their former multiplicity and become one in themselves.[21]

My goal has been to show that the age–old religious and spiritual quest to become aligned, attuned, to be at one with God or the Creative Forces is not limited to metaphysics but can be meshed and corroborated by today's knowledge of sciences; it can be one and the same. Science seems to be catching up, or perhaps better stated, science and spiritual philosophies are starting to share a similar language of Oneness. In addition, I wanted to offer evidence that different civilizations, through the millennia, had more unity and had a much greater grasp of such physics and science in general than has been generally considered possible.

This entire journey among science, symbolism, and spirituality has stretched across time/space and cultures, and it has done so much with the examination of just two symbols—the two symbols of the triangle and the parabolic spiral and their manifestation in different dimensional aspects. These symbols appear to be cosmic archetypes, both for religions and sciences. Ideally this has led to a deepening of the understanding of these symbols. To quote P.D. Ouspensky:

> At the same time the right understanding of symbols cannot lead to dispute. It deepens knowledge, and it cannot remain theoretical because it intensifies the striving towards real results, towards the union of knowledge and being, that is, to *Great Doing*. Pure knowledge cannot be transmitted, but by being expressed in symbols it is covered by them as by a veil, although at the same time for those who desire and who know how to look this veil becomes transparent.[22]

The triangle and parabola are meshed and wedded in many ways. Their creation and connection could well have been known by ancient civilizations just in the fact alone of how a parabola can be created from a triangle.

If you invert and overlap this method of drawing a parabola from a triangle, it is evident that both the vesica pisces and six–pointed star are both created. On page 184 is another example; this time vesica pisces' parabolas are being used to create a triangle.

By stretching a cord between two pegs stuck in the ground, a long straight line was marked out. Then to each peg an equal length of string was tied, more than half as long as the line drawn. By keeping the strings stretched tight and moving the ends around, the Egyptians could

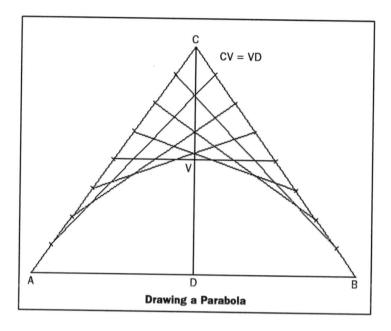

Drawing a Parabola

Fig. 15.5–Drawing a Parabola

To draw a parabola, a good method is shown at above. The
span AB and the height VD are given. Extend VD to C, making VC = VD, and draw CA and CB, which will be the tangents to the parabola at points A and B. Now divide CA and
CB into any number of equal segments (8 in the diagram) by
any of the methods familiar to draftsmen. Connecting points
as shown will draw additional tangents to the parabola, which
makes the curve easy to draw freehand or with a French
curve. In fact, the parabola is quite evident to the eye in the
diagram.[23]

draw parts of two perfect circles. These arcs cross each other at two
points. By drawing a straight line between these two points the original
line is bisected at a right angle and the line is cut into two equal parts.[24]
    (Note this creates the vesica pisces also.)
    There is wholeness, a unity, a completion in these symbols.
    The culmination of the unity of the entire universe and life was de-

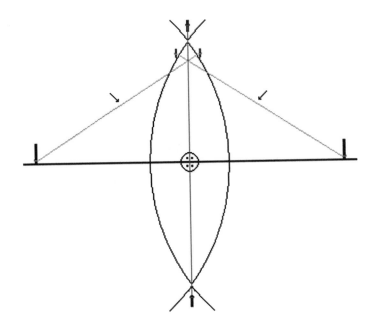

Fig. 15.6—Fixing Right Angles

picted through many ages and many cultures using the aspects of the triangle and the parabola; the accuracy of their knowledge can be now seen in that building block of all life—the DNA molecule. We are almost all familiar with the double helix model by Watson and Crick from the side. But are we familiar with looking at a model of it looking down at it from the vertical? A computer graphic generated picture of such a view is found in color Fig. 36.

When I have shown this computer graphic of the DNA double helix to others, their responses have been very similar to my own reaction. One's entire being seems to pause in acknowledgment, innately recognizing the sacred geometry within our building blocks and wordlessly letting us know that we are One.

Within the basis of all life can be seen the parabolic spiral and the Seal of Solomon, the Creator's Star. This configuration incorporates the cube in the hexagram within a parabolic spiral which, in kind, enfolds and unfolds into all the symbols discussed and then some. The very rungs themselves of DNA which produce this Creator's Star are made up of four separate bases, eerily analogous to the four ancient elements that produced the same star for the alchemists and can be seen formed in the double helix.

This DNA house of the soul geometry is one avenue to see the divine archetype within. Author Greg Braden in his recent book *The God Code* came to similar conclusions approaching DNA from a different perspective. He felt that the letters of God's ancient name "are encoded as the genetic formation in every cell, of every life."[25] Essentially his premise is that the basic elements of DNA—hydrogen, nitrogen, oxygen and carbon—will translate to key letters in the Hebrew or Arabic alphabet. As Mr. Braden notes, alphabets are one symbolic way of communicating deeper meanings, and as I have noted, picture/geometric symbols are also an ancient way of communicating such meanings beyond languages. It appears that our DNA communicates to us in multiple formats.

Fig. 15.7–Geodesic Dome

On the macrocosmic scale scientists are pursuing a theory of a triangular universe with promising results. This theory, technically known as causal dynamic triangulation (CDT), "constructs space-time geometries from simple triangular structures the same way that Buckminster Fuller used triangular surfaces to create geodesic domes."[26] The basic building blocks are described as four-dimensional tetrahedrons. The computer simulations of large scale universes with CDT have matched ones predicted by the standard theory of cosmology.[27]

Causal Dynamical Triangulations

> This approach, the subject of this article, is a modern version of the Euclidean approach. It approximates spacetime as a mosaic of triangles, which have a built-in distinction between space and time. *On small scales, spacetime takes on a fractal shape.*[28] [Author's emphasis]

The point that CDT was compared to geodesic domes which are aspects of triangles and parabolas struck me as a serendipitous synchronicity underling the significance of these core symbols researched here. I will not even attempt to explain the theory or the quantum physics and geometries involved. At best I have only superficial basics of such science gleaned from books and articles written for the general laymen, but I think anyone can appreciate the geometries that are created and their significance in the symbols and hypotheses discussed herein. The beauty of such symbolism is its ability to be grasped by all.

Fig. 15.8—Reconstructing the Universe (see the following examples.)

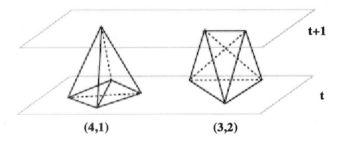

(4,1)   (3,2)

Figure 1: The two fundamental building blocks of causal dynamically triangulated gravity.[29]

Figure 2: Monte Carlo snapshot of a typical universe in phase.[30]

The shape of a cup/chalice. [Author's viewpoint]

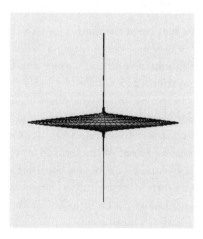

Figure 3: Monte Carlo snapshot of a typical universe in phase B (_0=1.6), . . . The entire universe has collapsed into a slice of minimal time extension.[31]

The shape of a paten/dish [Author's viewpoint]

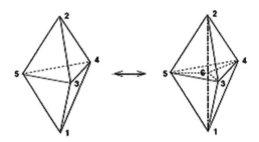

Figure 3: The (2,6)–move in three dimensions.

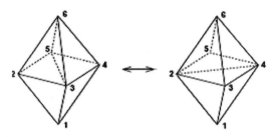

Figure 4: The (4,4)–move in three dimensions.

Fig. 15.9 - Doubled Tetrahedrons and Pentahedrons
(See the turquoise crystal)

(4,4): This move can be performed on a sub-complex of two
(1,3)- and two (3,1)-*tetrahedra forming a "diamond"* (see Fig.
4), with one neighbouring pair each above and below a spatial
slice. The move is then 1235 + 2356 + 1345 + 3456 → 1234 +
2346 + 1245 + 2456. (57) From the point of view of the *spatial "square" (double triangle)* 2345, the move (57) corresponds to a flip of its diagonal. It is accompanied by a
corresponding reassignment of the *tetrahedra constituting the
diamond*. The (2,6)- and (6,2)-moves, together with the (4,4)-
move (which is its own inverse) induce moves within the spatial slices that are known to be ergodic for two-dimensional
triangulations. [Author's emphasis]

The following graphic depiction of the CDT concept of the universe
shows better than I could write the archetypal symbolism in the very
essence of the universal macrocosm. In it you can see the triangles, the
six–pointed star, the axis mundi, and the cube in the hexagram.

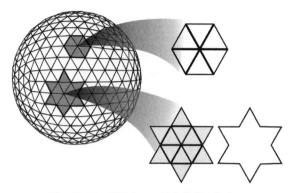

Fig. 15.10–CDT Space Fabric Depiction

A Mosaic of Triangles

To determine how space sculpts itself, physicists first need a way to describe its shape. They do so using triangles and their higher-dimensional analogues, a mosaic of which can readily approximate a curved shape. The curvature at a point is reflected in the total angle subtended by the triangles that surround it. For a flat surface, the angle is exactly 360 degrees, but for curved surfaces it can be less or more.[32] [Author's comment—Think of the axis mundi; cube in the hexagram]

With these views of the Divine archetype mirrored in the microcosm of DNA and the macrocosm of a universe based on CDT and points in between, is it no wonder that these would translate into our consciousness as sacred symbols expressed in our religions and spirituality through all the millennia? The genesis of the latest science of CDT can be read in writings that are 2500 years old! Plato in the *Timaeus* discusses the creation of the universe and matter. He cites the four rudimentary elements as fire, water, air, and earth. He goes on to describe the intrinsic construction of the elements of the universe being made of triangles! What Plato discerned intuitively has returned to cutting edge physics of the universe two–and–a–half millennia later.[33]

And if I may add to these Korzybski's General Semantics core premises: "The map is not the territory; the word is not the thing defined."[34] These are signpost and symbols along the way, not the way itself, or our ultimate destination. Nor is 2012 our final destination, but a way point, a milestone, en route to our home within the Creative Forces.

The hope is that this synthesis was as thought provoking for the reader as the research and writing were for me. The most important aspect of this exercise is to remember that the *Temple is within*. Even with all the external evidence, it is an internal path that one follows to complete the quest, which is the territory. Whether it is within or without, going in or coming out, we are the residents of the One.

Human kind always seems to need to go through an external quest whether it is the Western tradition of the knights of the Holy Grail or the Eastern tradition of Siddhartha searching for higher consciousness or enlightenment. Then after exhausting ourselves with external challenges and experiences, casting about everywhere outside ourselves, we rest. Whether we rest in completion or fatigue, we fall back within ourselves and then the true discovery and knowing begins. We no longer struggle against the current; we begin to flow.

It appears that it is a necessary journey in the macrocosm to know oneself as One in the microcosm. This seems to be a similar journey in physics from Newtonian to Quantum.

> There is that access, then, that way, to the Throne of grace, of mercy, of peace, of understanding, within thine own self. For He has promised to meet thee in thine own temple, in thine own body, through thine own mind . . . And then enter into the holy of holies, within thine own consciousness; turn within; see what has prompted thee. And He has promised to meet thee there. And there shall it be told thee from within the steps thou shouldst take day by day, step by step. Not that some great exploit, some great manner of change should come within thine body, thine mind, but line upon line, precept upon precept, here a little, there a little. For it is, as He has given, not the knowledge alone but the practical application— in thine daily experience with thy fellow man—that counts.
>
> 922-1

If we represent the tabernacle, the "ark," then within us can be seen the laws "imbedded" in our nature, through the Creators' Star. I have described some of this journey: being the jewel in the lotus, the stone in the cup, or the particle in the wave. The biblical New Testament also illustrates this in 1 Peter 2:5 (New International Version) "you also, like living stones, are being built into a spiritual house to be a holy priesthood, offering spiritual sacrifices acceptable to God through Jesus Christ."

The kingdom is within, the fractal infinite within the finite. "I AM" is a fractal and we are "I ams" in this fractal Oneness.

> "Do stay close to the Ark of the Covenant which is within thee . . . "   5177-1

It is important to remember such words and symbolic shapes are guideposts to bring us closer on our journey, like legends on a map, not the destination. As the Cayce reading 707-2 warned about such guideposts:

> These do not give the messages. They only attune self so that the Christ Consciousness may give the message. Listen to no message of a stone, of a number, even of a star; for they are but servants of the Lord and Master of All—even as thou.

And further in reading 587-6

> . . . the understanding that the law was written in the hearts of men, rather than upon tables of stone; that the temple, that the holy of holies was to be within.

So, with this knowledge, these guideposts, hopefully it has shortened one's external quest, which is still important and necessary, and let us go within with confidence, knowing that throughout the universe and ourselves there has been left the evidence of an all–encompassing Oneness. As the ancients recognized this, so can we. Let these symbols strengthen our affirmations of love and unity to meet Him in our tabernacle.

Through contemplative prayer, meditation, *lectio divina*, or whatever terminology is most familiar, remember . . . "the best book is self . . . " (452-3)

Some may want to attribute all of this to my mythological flights of

fancy and the different cultures; to these people I would like to quote
Father Thomas Keating, a Cistercian monk who is credited with helping
bring contemplative prayer (meditation) back into more general practice in the twentieth century:

 "Mythology is not untruth; it is simply the attempt to
speak the truth in a symbolic way that points to a
reality beyond words or concepts."[35]

Appendix

Chapter 20 EXODUS

[1]And God spake all these words, saying, [2]I *am* the LORD thy God, which have brought thee out of the land of Egypt, out of the house of bondage.

[3]Thou shalt have no other gods before me.

[4]Thou shalt not make unto thee any graven image, or any likeness *of any thing* that *is* in heaven above, or that *is* in the earth beneath, or that *is* in the water under the earth: [5]Thou shalt not bow down thyself to them, nor serve them: for I the LORD thy God *am* a jealous God, visiting the iniquity of the fathers upon the children unto the third and fourth *generation* of them that hate me; [6]And shewing mercy unto thousands of them that love me, and keep my commandments.

[7]Thou shalt not take the name of the LORD thy God in vain; for the LORD will not hold him guiltless that

The Egyptian Book of the Dead
1240 BC
The Papyrus of Ani
The Negative Confession

Hail, Fenti, who comest forth from Khemenu, I have not stolen.

Hail, Qerrti, who comest forth from Amentet, I have not committed adultery; I have not lain with men.

Hail, Utu-nesert, who comest forth from Het-ka-Ptah, I have not uttered curses.

Hail, Neba, who comest and goest, I have not uttered lies.

Hail, Tenemiu, who comest forth from Bast, I have not slandered [no man].

Chapter 20 EXODUS

taketh his name in vain.

[8]Remember the sabbath day, to keep it holy. [9]Six days shalt thou labour, and do all thy work: [10]But the seventh day *is* the sabbath of the LORD thy God: *in it* thou shalt not do any work, thou, nor thy son, nor thy daughter, thy manservant, nor thy maidservant, nor thy cattle, nor thy stranger that *is* within thy gates: [11]For *in* six days the LORD made heaven and earth, the sea, and all that in them *is*, and rested the seventh day: wherefore the LORD blessed the sabbath day, and hallowed it.

[12]Honour thy father and thy mother: that thy days may be long upon the land which the LORD thy God giveth thee.

[13]Thou shalt not kill.

[14]Thou shalt not commit adultery.

[15]Thou shalt not steal.

[16]Thou shalt not bear false witness against thy neighbour.

[17]Thou shalt not covet thy neighbour's house, thou shalt not covet thy neighbour's wife, nor his manservant, nor his maidservant, nor his ox, nor his ass, nor any thing that *is* thy neighbour's.

The Egyptian Book of the Dead
1240 BC
The Papyrus of Ani
The Negative Confession

Hail, Kenemti, who comest forth from Kenmet, I have not blasphemed.

Hail, Tutu, who comest forth from Ati (the Busirite Nome), I have not debauched the wife of any man.

Hail, Uatch-rekhit, who comest forth from Sau, I have not cursed God.

Hail, Khemiu, who comest forth from Kaui, I have not transgressed [the law].

About the Author

Donald B. Carroll spent his career working in Fire and Rescue as a district chief, academy instructor, and paramedic. During those thirty years, he raised a family and pursued the meaning of life through extended study into the Cayce readings and other spiritual, scientific, and philosophical materials. Today, Carroll is a regular speaker and writer of metaphysical topics from Cayce to the Kundalini. He spent ten years researching and writing his latest work *Sacred Geometry and Spiritual Symbolism*. Carroll is also an international tour leader for the nonprofit Association for Research and Enlightenment, visiting sites of a spiritual nature across the globe.

Endnotes

Signposts of the Journey, pp. xi-xiii

1. Hugh Lynn Cayce, *Oneness of All Force* (Virginia Beach, VA: A.R.E. Press, 1935), 5.
2. *New Revised Standard Version Bible* (Division of Christian Education of the National Council of the Churches of Christ in the United States of America, 1989), http://www.biblestudytools.com/nrs/.
3. *The Jerusalem Bible, Reader's Edition*, Alexander Jones, ed. (New York: Doubleday & Company, Inc., 1968).

Preface, pp. xv-xvii

1. Shahram Shiva, *Hush Don't Say Anything to God: Passionate Poems of Rumi* (Freemont, CA: Jain Publishing Company, 2000), 17.

Introduction, pp. xix-xxiii

1. *Hamlet*, Act 1, scene 5, 159–167—http://www.enotes.com/ shakespeare-quotes/there-more-things-heaven-earth-horatio.
2. Henry Wadsworth Longfellow, "Excelsior," *Ballads and Other Poems by Henry Wadsworth Longfellow*, 10th edition (Boston: William A. Ticknor and Co., 1848), 129-132.
3. I Corinthians 14 (13–18), *The Jerusalem Bible, Reader's Edition*, Alexander Jones, ed. (New York: Doubleday & Company, Inc., 1968).

Chapter 1, pp. 1-6

1. "Table, Tablet," *Funk and Wagnall's A New Standard Bible Dictionary*, 3rd Revised edition, Melancthon W. Jacobus, Albert C. Lane, and Andrew C. Zenos, eds. (New York and London: Garden City Books, 1936).
2. P.D. Ouspensky, *In Search of the Miraculous* (New York: Harcourt, Inc., 1949), 278.
3. Ibid., 279–281.
4. Mark A. Thurston, *Experiments in SFG: The Edgar Cayce Path of Application* (Virginia Beach, VA: A.R.E. Press, 1976), 34.
5. Aldous Huxley, *The Perennial Philosophy: An Interpretation of the Great Mystics, East and West*, First Perennial Classics edition (New York: Perennial, an imprint of HarperCollins Publishers, 2004), page VIII.

Chapter 2, pp. 7-14

1. Angelo S. Rappoport, *Myth and Legend of Ancient Israel*, Vol. II. (Jersey City, NJ: KTAV Publishing House, Inc., 1966), facing page 316.
2. Manly P. Hall, *The Secret Teachings of All Ages*, Golden Anniversary Ed. (Los Angeles: Philosophical Research Society, Inc., 1977), 65.
3. Ibid., 68.
4. P.D. Ouspensky, *A New Model of the Universe*, 2nd Ed. (New York: Vintage Books, 1971), 190–91.
5. Marie Parsons, "Heliopolis, Egypt's Iunu," http://www.touregypt.net/featurestories/heliopolis.htm.
6. John Anthony West, *Serpent in the Sky: The High Wisdom of Ancient Egypt*, Revised Ed. (Wheaton: Quest Books, 1993), 55.
7. Ray Ellison, "The Pyramid Texts," http://www.touregypt.net/featurestories/pyramidtext.htm.
8. Janice Kamrin, *Ancient Egyptian Hieroglyphs: A Practical Guide* (New York: Harry N. Abrams Inc., 2004), 118–19.
9. Hall, *The Secret Teachings of All Ages*, 173.

Chapter 3, pp. 15-31

1. Professor Schoch has written several books entitled: *Pyramid Quest*, *Voyage of the Pyramid Builders*, and *Voices of the Rocks: A Scientist Looks at Catastrophes and Ancient Civilizations*.
2. Professor Robert Schoch, "The Great Pyramid of Egypt" (Lecture at the A.R.E. Ancient Mysteries Conference, Virginia Beach, VA, October 9, 2004).
3. Lina Eckenstein, *A History of Sinai* (New York: The MacMillan Co. 1921), 67. Can be viewed at http://books.google.com/books/about/A_history_of_Sinai.html?id=yvxPAAAAYAAJ.
4. W.M. Flinders Petrie, *Researches in the Sinai* (E.P. New York: Dutton and Company, 1906), 247.
5. Laurence Gardner, *Lost Secrets of the Sacred Ark* (New York: Barnes and Noble, 2005), 4.
6. Ellis' books are *Tempest and the Exodus* and *Solomon, Falcon of Sheba*.
7. Ralph Ellis, *Tempest and the Exodus* (Kempton, IL: Adventures Unlimited, 2001), 2–3.
8. Ralph Ellis, *Solomon: Falcon of Sheba* (Kempton, IL: Adventures Unlimited, 2002), 11.
9. Ibid., 12.
10. *The Jerusalem Bible, Reader's Edition*, Alexander Jones, ed. (New York:

Doubleday & Company, Inc., 1968).

11. John Van Auken, *Ancient Egyptian Mysticism and its Relevance Today* (Virginia Beach, VA: A.R.E. Press, 1999), 67.

12. Hermes Mercurius Trismegistus, "The Emerald Tablet," *Hermes Mercurius Trismegistus: His Divine Pymander*, Edited by Paschal Beverly Randolph (Des Plaines, IL: Yogi Publication Society, 1972).

13. Brown, Driver, Briggs and Gesenius, "Hebrew Lexicon entry for Ciynay," *The KJV Old Testament Hebrew Lexicon*, <http://www.biblestudytools.net/Lexicons/Hebrew/heb.cgi?number=5514&version=kjv.

14. Brown, Driver, Briggs and Gesenius, "Hebrew Lexicon entry for Choreb," *The KJV Old Testament Hebrew Lexicon*, <http://www.biblestudytools.net/Lexicons/Hebrew/heb.cgi?number=2722&version=kjv.

15. E.A. Wallis Budge, *An Egyptian Hieroglyphic Dictionary*, Vol. 1. (New York: Dover Publications, Inc., 1978), 126.

16. Copper—http://www.csa.com/discoveryguides/copper/overview.php.

17. Adrian Gilbert, *2012—Mayan Year of Destiny* (Virginia Beach, VA: A.R.E. Press, 2006), 219-20.

18. Sine of Great Pyramid—http://www.ies.co.jp/math/java/samples/sinBox.html.

19. John Van Auken, "Ancient Egyptian Mysticism" (A.R.E. staff video lecture given at the headquarters building of the Association for Research and Enlightenment in Virginia Beach, VA. Information confirmed by personal conversation with author 10/06/2007.)

20. Location of Great Pyramid—http://www.gardinersworld.com/content/view/202/39/.

21. Andrew Collins, *The Cygnus Mystery* (London: Watkins Publishing, 2006), 160-61.

22. Ibid., 155.

23. Cybersky 5—http://www.cybersky.com/. These are star alignments and positions for place and date using Cybersky 5 stellarium program Cybersky 5 program software. Cybersky is a planetarium program that allows you to see what was occurring in the heavens anywhere in the world from 15,000 BCE to 15,000 CE either in a still picture or in timed motion. You can see the astronomical aspects of the time and place from stars in the Milky Way to meteor showers from over the Great Pyramids to the Yucatan peninsula.

24. Robert Schoch and Robert Aquinas McNally, *Pyramid Quest* (London: Tarcher/Penguin, 2005), 118.
25. Ibid., p. 137
26. Ibid.
27. Jimmy Dunn, "The Mountains and Horizon of Ancient Egypt" — http://www.touregypt.net/featurestories/horizon.htm.
28. John Major Jenkins, *Maya Cosmogenesis 2012* (Rochester, VT: Bear and Company, 1998), 116–117.

Chapter 4, pp. 33-39

1. Z'ev ben Shimon Halevi, *Kabbalah and Exodus* (York Beach, ME: Red Wheel/Weiser, 1988), 207.
2. Sapphire—Derivation: Middle English saphir, from Old French safir, from Latin sapphîrus, from Greek sappheiros, of Semitic origin; akin to Hebrew *sappîr*, a precious stone. *The American Heritage® Dictionary of the English Language, Fourth Edition* (Boston: Houghton Mifflin Company, 2004). *Answers.com* 19 Aug. 2008. http://www.answers.com/topic/sapphire.
3. Dark blue stone—http://minerals.usgs.gov/minerals/pubs/commodity/gemstones/sp14-95/turquoise.html.
4. Cyril Aldred, *The Jewels of the Pharaoh* (New York: Ballantine Books, 1978), 17.
5. Shelley Kaehr, *Edgar Cayce Guide to Gemstones, Minerals, Metals, and More* (Virginia Beach, VA: A.R.E Press, 2005), 173.
6. Note: Of interest is this reference: S. Kirkpatrick, "Edgar Cayce: The Mysterious Missing." *Venture Inward*, April/May /June 2012, 13. This article shows a reading for azurite which identifies it as Lapis Ligurius. In further Cayce readings, 440-2, 440-9, 440-11 and 440-12 on Lapis vs. Lapis Lingua or Linguis, they show an ambiguity about what the stone really is. It could be azurite or possibly turquoise. The formation of turquoise may hold the answer as it is a secondary mineral that can be created from deposits that include azurite and malachite. This being the case, with the formation of turquoise and the uncertainty of what stone Lapis Linguis was being identified as, turquoise is as valid a candidate.
7. Shelley Kaehr, *Edgar Cayce Guide to Gemstones, Minerals, Metals, and More*, 119.
8. James M. Robinson, gen. ed. *The Nag Hammadi Library in English*. Revised Version (New York: Harper's Collins Publishers, 1990), 326-27.

9. Lora H. Little, Gregory L. Little, and John Van Auken. *Secrets of the Ancient World*. 2nd printing (Virginia Beach, VA: A.R.E. Press, 2005), 157.

10. Lucy Mack Smith, *History of Joseph Smith.*—http://oneclimbs.com/ 2011/02/06/the-all-seeing-eye-symbol-and-the-urim-and-thummim-connection/.

11. Amethyst Galleries—http://mineral.galleries.com/minerals/symmetry/riclinic.htm.

12. Isaac Asimov, *Asimov's Guide to the Bible* (Avenel, NJ: Wings Books, 1981), 204.

13. B. Ernest Frejer, *The Edgar Cayce Companion*. 7th printing (Virginia Beach, VA: A.R.E. Press, 2001), 373.

14. John Van Auken and Lora Little, *The Lost Hall of Records* (Memphis, TN: Eagle Wing Books Inc., 2000), 105 –13.

Chapter 5, pp. 41-48

1. P.D. Ouspensky, *A New Model of the Universe*, 2nd Ed. (New York: Vintage Books, 1971), 390–91.

2. Robert W. Krajenke, *Edgar Cayce's Story of the Old Testament from the Birth of Souls to the Death of Moses* (Virginia Beach, VA: A.R.E. Press, 2004), 17.

3. John Major Jenkins, *Maya Cosmogenesis 2012*, 116.

4. John Major Jenkins, *Maya Cosmogenesis 2012*, 205.

5. Richard Henry Drummond, *A Life of Jesus the Christ* (New York: St. Martin's Paperbacks, 1996), 30–31.

6. *Webster's Third New International Dictionary*, unabridged (Springfield, MA: Merriam-Webster Publishing, 1993).

7. Fractal definition—http://en.wikipedia.org/w/ index.php?title=Fractal&oldid=10025267. *and* Koch snowflake definition—http://en.wikipedia.org/w/ index.php?title=Fractal&oldid=10025267.

8. Self-similar object—http://en.wikipedia.org/wiki/Self-similarity.

9. James Gleick, *Chaos: Making a New Science* (New York: Penguin Books, 1988), 109.

10. Ibid., 110.

Chapter 6, pp. 49-67

1. Sri Yantra—http://alumni.cse.ucsc.edu/~mikel/sriyantra/ joseph.html.

2. Vesica Piscis—http://en.wikipedia.org/wiki/Vesica_piscis.

3. Things represented by the vesica pisces—http://www.ka-gold-jewelry.com/p-articles/vesica-pisces.php.

4. Kevin J. Todeschi, *Edgar Cayce on Vibration: Spirit in Motion* (Virginia Beach, VA: A.R.E. Press, 2007), x.

5. Particle Duality—http://en.wikipedia.org/wiki/Wave%E2%80%93particle_duality.

6. Vibrations Waves—http://science.sbcc.edu/physics/folsom/vibrations_waves/vibrations_waves.pdf.

7. Lawrence Blair, *Rhythms of Vision* (Rochester, VT: Destiny Books, 1991), 75.

8. The Circle—http://symboldictionary.net/?p=1914.

9. Galileo Galilei and Stillman Drake, *Discoveries and Opinions of Galileo*. Selections translated by Stillman Drake (New York: Doubleday & Co., 1957), 237-38.

10. Sound waves—http://www.space.com/661-sound-waves-left-imprint-universe.html.

11. Bill Bryson, *A Short History of Nearly Everything* (New York: Broadway Books, 2003), 172.

Chapter 7, pp. 69-77

1. The Benu (Bennu) by Jefferson Monet—http://www.touregypt.net/featurestories/benu.htm.

2. Ralph Ellis, *Solomon: Falcon of Sheba*, 132.

3. Obelisk—http://core.kmi.open.ac.uk/display/2926263.

4. Ralph Ellis, *Jesus Last of the Pharaohs*, 3rd ed. (Kempton, IL: Adventures Unlimited, 2004), 171.

5. Tekenu—enu or henu—http://www.world-destiny.org/a4an.htm.

6. Daniel Matt, *The Essential Kabbalah* (Secaucus, NJ: Castle Books, 1997), 8.

7. Greg Reeder, "Human Sacrifices," *The Enigmatic Tekenu*—http://www.touregypt.net/featurestories/humansac.htm.

8. Greg Reeder, "Sem Priest," *The Enigmatic Tekenu*—http://www.touregypt.net/featurestories/humansac.htm.

9. Host—*The Columbia Electronic Encyclopedia*, Sixth Edition, Columbia University Press, 2003.

10. King, God-King Hieroglyphs—http://www.omniglot.com/writing/egyptian_det.htm.

11. *The Jerusalem Bible, Reader's Edition*, Alexander Jones, ed. (New York:

Doubleday & Company, Inc., 1968), 110.

12. Greg Reeder, "Effects of the resting *tekenu*," *The Enigmatic Tekenu*—http://www.touregypt.net/featurestories/humansac.htm.

13. *The Egyptian Book of the Dead*, trans. Raymond Faulkner (San Francisco, CA: Chronicle Books 1998), Plate 27.

14. Seven Church Pilgrimage—http://www.catholicpilgrimoffice.com/08d_rome_assisi_7_churches.php.

Chapter 8, pp. 79-91

1. Herbert Silberer, *Hidden Symbolism of Alchemy and the Occult Arts* (New York: Dover Publications, Inc., 1971), 256.

2. Paraboloids—http://en.wikipedia.org/w/index.php?title=Paraboloid&oldid=8439062.

3. Parabolic Dish/Cup—http://www.answers.com/topic/paraboloid.

4. Parabolic Dish Microphone—http://www.howeverythingworks.org/page1.php?QNum=1473.

5. Michael Talbot, *The Holographic Universe* (New York: Harper Perennial, 1992), 1.

6. Joseph E. Kasper and Steven A. Feller, *The Complete Book of Holograms* (New York: Dover Publications, 2001), 1.

7. Close-up photograph of a hologram's surface—http://en.wikipedia.org/wiki/Holography.

8. Michael Talbot, *The Holographic Universe*, 1.

9. Ibid., 11.

10. Ibid., 48.

11. Ibid., 50.

12. Ibid., 51.

13. *Zpower: Zero Point Energy* (Phoenix, Az: Zpower Corporation, May 2003), 5-6—http://www.free-energy-info.co.uk/ZPE.pdf.

14. Lynne McTaggart, *The Field* (New York: HarperCollins Publishers, 2002), XVII.

15. Ibid., 174.

16. Akashic Records—http://medeadbugger.net/2012/12/11/edgar-cayce-glossary/.

17. Waves—http://en.wikipedia.org/wiki/Wave.

18. Lynne McTaggart, *The Field*, 226.

19. Menorah—http://www.jewfaq.org/signs.htm.

20. Louis Charpentier, *The Mysteries of Chartres Cathedral* (New York: Avon Books, 1975), 121.

21. Manly P. Hall, *The Secret Teachings of All Ages*, plate across from p. 177.
22. Wearing a Kippah—http://www.templesan jose.org/JudaismInfo/ faq/kippah.htm.

Chapter 9, pp. 93-98

1. Well, one of the more mystical things Duns accepted was the wearing of conical hats to increase learning. He noted that wizards supposedly wore such things; an apex was considered a symbol of knowledge and the hats were thought to "funnel" knowledge to the wearer. Once humanism gained the upper hand, Duns Scotus' teachings were despised and the "dunce cap" became identified with ignorance rather than learning. Humanists believed learning came from internal motivation rather than special hats and used the public shame of having to wear a dunce cap to motivate slow learners to try harder. Origins of the Dunce Cap—http:// www.straightdope.com/columns/read/1793/whats-the-origin-of- the-dunce-cap.
2. Creating a Dunce Hat—http://en.wikipedia.org/wiki/ Dunce_hat_%28topology%29.
3. Mitre origin—http://www.newadvent.org/cathen/10404a.htm.
4. John Van Auken, *Ancient Egyptian Mysticism and its Relevance Today*, 14.
5. Ibid., plates 7, 12, and 25.
6. Hermes Mercurius Trismegistus, *The Divine Pymander*, 111.
7. Frank Waters, *Book of the Hopi* (New York: Penguin Books, 1977), 10.
8. Andrew Collins, *Gods of Eden* (Rochester, VT: Bear and Company, 2002), 263–64.

Chapter 10, pp. 99-105

1. Henry Gray, *Gray's Anatomy*, 1276.
2. Henry Gray, *Gray's Anatomy*, 1277.
3. Ray Ellison, "The Pyramid Texts"—http://www.touregypt.net/ featurestories/pyramidtext.htm.
4. Functions of a parabolic dish—http:// www.howeverythingworks.org/page1.php?QNum=1473.
5. Coherent Light—http://library.thinkquest.org/27356/ d_coherentlight.htm?tqskip1=1.
6. Michael Talbot, *The Holographic Universe*, 1.
7. Michael Talbot, *The Holographic Universe*, 46–7.

Chapter 11, pp. 107-139

1. Jeffrey Furst, *Edgar Cayce's Story of Egypt* (New York: Berkley Medallion Books, 1976), 80–81.
2. Hermes Mercurius Trismegistus, *His Divine Pymander*, 110–11.
3. Djew—http://www.touregypt.net/featurestories/horizon.htm.
4. Akhet—http://www.eclipse-chasers.com/akhet.html.
5. Use of the number 7 in the Christian world—http://www.newadvent.org/cathen/05590a.htm.
6. Spinal column —http://education.yahoo.com/reference/gray/subjects/subject/25.
7. Henry Gray, *Gray's Anatomy*, 19.
8. Genesis 3—http://www.biblegateway.com/passage/?search=genesis%203&version=KJV.
9. Stecchini—Carrying yoke—http://www.metrum.org/measures/structure.htm.
10. Stecchini—Dimensions of the Great Pyramid —http://www.metrum.org/measures/dimensions.htm.
11. John Van Auken, "Ancient Egyptian Mysticism"(recurring A.R.E. staff video lecture at the Association for Research and Enlightenment, Virginia Beach, VA).
12. E.A. Wallis Budge, *An Egyptian Hieroglyphic Dictionary, Volume 1*, 308.
13. Ibid., 314.
14. Tony Bushby, *The Secret in the Bible* (Queensland, AU: Joshua Books, 2003), 9.
15. C. Staniland Wake, *The Origin and Significance of the Great Pyramid* (London: Reeves and Turner, 1882), IV.
16. Andrew Collins, *Beneath the Pyramids* (Virginia Beach, VA: 4th Dimension Press, 2010), 214.
17. Robert Schoch and Robert Aquinas McNally, *Pyramid Quest* (London: Tarcher/Penguin, 2005), 267 and 296.
18. Houdin—http://www.3ds.com/fileadmin/kheops/renaissance/pdf/PRESSKIT_2011_KHUFU_REBORN.pdf.
19. Aakhu meh cubit—E.A. Wallis Budge, *An Egyptian Hieroglyphic Dictionary, Volume 1*, 24.
20. Craig B. Smith and Kelly E. Parmenter, "Khufu and Kukulcan," *Civil Engineering: The Magazine of the American Society of Civil Engineers*, April 2004, 48.
21. John Major Jenkins, *Maya Cosmogenesis 2012*, 177.
22. Chichen Itza—http://en.wikipedia.org/wiki/Chichen Itza.

23. John Michell, *The Dimensions of Paradise*, Second US ed. (Rochester, VT: Inner Traditions, 2008), 28-33.
24. Hezekiah—http://en.wikipedia.org/wiki/Hezekiah.
25. Nehustan—http://en.wikipedia.org/wiki/Nehustan.
26. Andrew Collins, *The Cygnus Mystery*, 85.
27. Stonehenge acoustics—http://soundsofstonehenge.wordpress.com/conclusions/.
28. Squaring the Circle—http://mathworld.wolfram.com/CircleSquaring.html.

Chapter 12, pp. 141-148

1. Placing The Pineal—http://www.edgarcayce.org/ Cayce Health Database.
2. Shirley Andrews, *Atlantis: Insights from a Lost Civilization*, 1st Ed., (Woodbury, MN: Llewellyn Publications, 2005), 111.
3. Robert Bauval and Adrian Gilbert, *The Orion Mystery: Unlocking the Secrets of the Pyramids*, 1st American Paperback ed. (New York: Three Rivers Press, 1995), 122.
4. Raising the Djed—http://www.touregypt.net/featurestories/djedpillar.htm.
5. John Van Auken, *Ancient Egyptian Mysticism and its Relevance Today*, color plate 7.
6. Crooks and Flails—http://www.touregypt.net/featurestories/crooksandflails.htm.
7. Lawrence Blair, *Rhythms of Vision*, 89.
8. John Major Jenkins, *Maya Cosmogenesis 2012*, xxxix.
9. Tree Goddess—http://www.touregypt.net/featurestories/treegoddess.htm.
10. Tree of Eden—http://www.criticalpages.com/2011/what-fruit-grew-on-the-tree-of-knowledge/.
11. Asherim—http://en.wikipedia.org/wiki/Asherah_pole.
12. Studying under the fig tree—http://www.studylight.org/ls/at/index.cgi?a=257.

Chapter 13, pp. 149-159

1. Clovis people—http://archive.archaeology.org/9907/newsbriefs/clovis.html.
2. Globelki Tepe—http://www.smithsonianmag.com/history-archaeology/gobekli-tepe.html?c=y&story=fullstory.

3. Stone tools—http://www.ldeo.columbia.edu/news-events/humans-shaped-stone-axes-18-million-years-ago-study-says.
4. Stone Age Hunters—http://www.independent.co.uk/news/world/americas/new-evidence-suggests-stone-age-hunters-from-europe-discovered-america-7447152.html.
5. History of the meter—http://en.wikipedia.org/wiki/History_of_the_metre.
6. Georgia State University online pendulum calculator—http://hyperphysics.phy-astr.gsu.edu/hbase/pendl.html#c1.
7. Christopher Knight and Alan Butler, *Before the Pyramids* (London: Watkins Publishing, 2011), 226.
8. Wm. R. Fix, *Pyramid Odyssey* (Urbanna, VA: Mercury Media, Inc., 1984), 26–33.
9. Robert Schoch and Robert Aquinas McNally, *Pyramid Quest* (London: Tarcher/Penguin, 2005), 139.
10. Surveying tools—http://www.surveyhistory.org/egyptian_surveying_tools1.htm.
11. Egyptian ritual—http://www.ancientegyptonline.co.uk/foundationritual.html#stretch;
Maya ritual—http://www.authenticmaya.com/maya_culture.htm.
12. See *Pyramid Odyssey* by WM. R. Fix.
13. G. Maspero, *History of Egypt ,Chaldea, Syria, Babylonia, and Assyria*. Vol. 2, Part B (London: The Grolier Society Publishers, 1903), 181.

Chapter 14, pp. 161-170
1. Wavelength measurement site—http://www.sengpielaudio.com/calculator-wavelength.htm.
2. Frequency to musical note converter site—http://www.phys.unsw.edu.au/music/note/.
3. B–Flat from Space—http://chandra.harvard.edu/press/03_releases/press_090903.html.
4. Black Hole Music—http://www.freerepublic.com/focus/f-news/2316057/posts.
5. Frank Waters, *Book of the Hopi*, 9.
6. Stephen Harrod Buhner, *The Secret Teaching of Plants* (Rochester, VT: Bear and Company, 2004), 50-51 and 87.
7. Milky Way—http://www.space.com/scienceastronomy/050816_milky_way.html.
8. Black Hole—http://www.webpagesbybob.com/blackhole.htm.

9. Hill of the Skull—http://newadvent.org/cathen/03191a.htm.

10. John Major Jenkins, *Maya Cosmogenesis 2012*, 59.

11. Andrew Collins, *The Cygnus Mystery*, 34–35.

12. Music of the Spheres—http://www.merriam-webster.com/dictionary/music%20of%20the%20spheres.

13. Cosmic Background Radiation—http://www.oursounduniverse.com/articles/pulsars.htm.

14. Hans Jenny, *Cymatics: A Study of Wave Phenomena and Vibration*, 2nd printing (Newmarket, NH: MACROmedia Publishing, 2004), 20.

15. Cymatics—http://www.cymaticsource.com/newto.html.

16. Sound waves—http://www.space.com/661-sound-waves-left-imprint-universe.html.

17. Hans Jenny, *Cymatics: A Study of Wave Phenomena and Vibration*. 273.

18. Andrew Collins, *The Cygnus Mystery*, 183.

19. AUM Symbol—http://www.mandalayoga.net/pretty_print.php?rub=what&p=mantra_om&lang=en.

20. Make-up of Arecibo message—http://kbarnett8.tripod.com/temp2.htm.

21. James Mullaney, *Edgar Cayce and the Cosmos* (Virginia Beach, VA: A.R.E. Press, 2007), 110.

Chapter 15, pp. 171-192

1. Ralph Ellis, *Jesus Last of the Pharaohs*, Chapter 6.

2. John Major Jenkins, *Maya Cosmogenesis 2012*, 176 and 168.

3. *The Bible, King James Version*, (Cambridge: Cambridge), 1769.

4. Gordon Strachan, *The Bible's Hidden Cosmology* (Edinburgh: Floris Books, 2005), 119.

5. John Major Jenkins, *Maya Cosmogenesis 2012*, 8.

6. Ibid., 30.

7. Andrew Collins, *The Cygnus Mystery*, 262–63.

8. Ibid., 271.

9. Ibid., 279.

10. John Major Jenkins, *Maya Cosmogenesis 2012*, 307.

11. Ibid., 120.

12. The precise alignment of the solstice *point* (the precise center-point of the body of the sun as viewed from earth) with the galactic equator was calculated to occur in 1998 (Jean Meeus, *Mathematical Astronomy Morsels*, 1997). Thus, the Galactic Alignment "zone" is 1998 +/−18 years = 1980–2016. This is "era-2012." This Galactic

Alignment occurs only once every 26,000 years, and was what the ancient Maya were pointing to with the 2012 end–date of their Long Count calendar. Galactic Alignment #1—http://alignment2012.com/whatisga.htm.

13. James Mullaney, "The Transit of Venus," *Venture Inward*, Apr–June 2012, 24.

14. Galactic Alignment #2—http://www.universetoday.com/30762/galactic-alignment/.

15. Gravitational Lenses—http://archive.seti.org/epo/news/features/detecting-other-worlds-the-flash.php.

16. Gravitational Lensing—http://en.wikipedia.org/wiki/Gravitational_lensing.

17. Pythagoreans' central fire—http://physics.ucr.edu/~wudka/Physics7/Notes_www/node32.html.

18. Galactic Center—http://en.wikipedia.org/wiki/Galactic_center.

19. VLBA—http://www.nrao.edu/pr/2004/sagastar/.

20. Peaceful period—http://lorenzlammens.com/the-most-peaceful-period-in-history/.

21. John Anthony McGuckin, trans., *The Book of Mystical Chapters* (Boston: Shambhala Publications, Inc.), 2003, 170 and 171.

22. P.D. Ouspensky, *In Search of the Miraculous*, 284.

23. Drawing a Parabola—http://mysite.du.edu/~jcalvert/math/parabola.htm.

24. Fixing Right Angles—http://www.cheops-pyramide.ch/khufu-pyramid/pyramid-alignment.html#top.

25. Braden, Gregg, *The God Code* (Carlsbad, CA: Hay House, 2005), xiv.

26. Mark Albert, "The Triangular Universe," *Scientific American*, February 2007, 24.

27. Ibid.

28. Theories of Quantum Gravity—http://www.scientificamerican.com/article.cfm?id=theories-of-quantum-gravity.

29. Reconstructing the Universe—J. Ambjørn a,c, J. Jurkiewicz b and R. Loll c a The Niels Bohr Institute, Copenhagen University Blegdamsvej 17, DK–2100 Copenhagen Ø, Denmark. email: ambjorn@nbi.dk b Mark Kac Complex Systems Research Centre, Marian Smoluchowski Institute of Physics, Jagellonian University, Reymonta 4, PL 30–059 Krakow, Poland. email: jurkiewicz@th.if.uj.edu.pl c Institute for Theoretical Physics, Utrecht University, Leuvenlaan 4, NL–3584 CE Utrecht, The Nether-

lands. email: j.ambjorn@phys.uu.nl, r.loll@phys.uu.nl 06 June 2005.
30. Ibid.
31. Ibid.
32. A Mosaic of Triangles—http://www.sciam.com/
article.cfm?id=describing-the-shape-of-space.
33. Plato, *Plato: Complete Works*, Edited by John M. Cooper (Indianapolis/
Cambridge: Hackett Publishing Company, 1997), 1255–57.
34. Korzybski's General Semantics —http://www.gestalt.org/
semantic.htm.
35. Thomas Keating, *The Human Condition: Contemplation and Transformation* (New York: Paulist Press, 1999), 28.

Bibliography

Bibles

New International Version. Grand Rapids, MI: Zondervan Publishing House, 1988.

New Revised Standard Version. Division of Christian Education of the National Council of the Churches of Christ in the United States of America: http://www.biblestudytools.com/nrs/, 1989.

The Jerusalem Bible, Reader's Edition. Alexander Jones, ed. New York: Doubleday & Company, Inc., 1968.

The King James Version. Cambridge, 1769.

Books

Aldred, Cyril. *The Jewels of the Pharoah.* New York: Ballantine books, 1978.

Andrews, Shirley. *Atlantis: Insights from a Lost Civilization.* 1st Ed. Woodbury, MN: Llewellyn Publications, 2005.

Anonymous. *Secret Symbols of the Rosicrucians of the 16th and 17th Centuries.* Originally published at Altona about 1785–90. Whitefish, MT: Kessinger Publishing, 2010.

Asimov, Isaac. *Asimov's Guide to the Bible.* Avenel, NJ: Wings Books, 1981.

Bauval, Robert, and Adrian Gilbert. *The Orion Mystery: Unlocking the Secrets of the Pyramids.* 1st American Paperback ed. New York: Three Rivers Press, 1995.

Blair, Lawrence. *Rhythms of Vision.* Rochester, VT: Destiny Books, 1991.

Braden, Gregg. *The God Code.* Carlsbad, CA: Hay House, 2005.

Bryson, Bill. *A Short History of Nearly Everything.* New York: Broadway Books, 2003.

Budge, E.A. Wallis. *An Egyptian Hieroglyphic Dictionary,* Vol. 1. New York: Dover Publications, Inc., 1978. Buhner, Stephen Harrod. *The Secret Teaching of Plants.* Rochester, VT: Bear and Company, 2004.

Buhner, Stephen Harrod. *The Secret Teaching of Plants.* Rochester, VT: Bear and Company, 2004.

Bushby, Tony. *The Secret in the Bible.* Queensland, AU: Joshua Books, 2003.

Cayce, Hugh Lynn. *Oneness of All Force.* Virginia Beach, VA: A.R.E. Press, 1935.

Charpentier, Louis. *The Mysteries of Chartres Cathedral*. New York: Avon Books, 1975.

Collins, Andrew. *Beneath the Pyramids*. Virginia Beach, VA: 4th Dimension Press, 2010.

—. *Gods of Eden*. Rochester, VT: Bear and Company, 2002.

—. *The Cygnus Mystery*. London: Watkins Publishing, 2006.

Drummond, Richard Henry. *A Life of Jesus the Christ*. New York: St. Martin's Paperbacks, 1996.

Eckenstein, Lina. *A History of Sinai*. New York: The MacMillan Co. 1921. Can be viewed at http://books.google.com/books/about/A_history_of_Sinai.html?id=yvxPAAAAYAAJ.

Ellis, Ralph. *Jesus: Last of the Pharaohs*. 3rd ed. Kempton, IL: Adventures Unlimited, 2004.

—. *Solomon: Falcon of Sheba*. Kempton, IL: Adventures Unlimited, 2002.

—. *Tempest and the Exodus*. Kempton, IL: Adventures Unlimited, 2001.

Fix, Wm. R. *Pyramid Odyssey*. Urbanna, VA: Mercury Media, Inc., 1984.

Frejer, B. Ernest. *The Edgar Cayce Companion*. 7th printing. Virginia Beach, VA: A.R.E. Press, 2001.

Furst, Jeffrey. *Edgar Cayce's Story of Egypt*. New York: Berkley Medallion Books, 1976.

Galilei, Galileo, and Stillman Drake. *Discoveries and Opinions of Galileo*. Selections translated by Stillman Drake. New York: Doubleday & Co., 1957.

Gardner, Laurence. *Lost Secrets of the Sacred Ark*. New York: Barnes and Noble, 2005.

Gilbert, Adrian. *2012—Mayan Year of Destiny*. Virginia Beach, VA: A.R.E. Press, 2006.

Gleick, James. *Chaos: Making a New Science*. New York: Penguin Books, 1988.

Gray, Henry. *Anatomy of the Human Body*. Philadelphia: Lea & Febiger, 1918.

—. *Gray's Anatomy*. 1901 Edition. New York: Barnes and Noble, 1995.

Halevi, Z'ev ben Shimon. *Kabbalah and Exodus*. York Beach, ME: Red Wheel/Weiser, 1988.

Hall, Manly P. *The Secret Teachings of All Ages*. Golden Anniversary Ed. Los

Angeles: Philosophical Research Society, Inc., 1977.

Host—*The Columbia Electronic Encyclopedia*, Sixth Edition. New York: Columbia University Press, 2003.

Huxley, Aldous. *The Perennial Philosophy: An Interpretation of the Great Mystics, East and West*. First Perennial Classics edition. New York: Perennial, an imprint of Harper Collins Publishers, 2004.

Jacobus, Melancthon W., Albert C. Lane, and Andrew C. Zenos, eds. *Funk and Wagnall's A New Standard Bible Dictionary*. 3rd revised ed. New York and London: Garden City Books, 1936.

Jenkins, John Major. *Maya Cosmogenesis 2012*. Rochester, VT: Bear and Company, 1998.

Jenny, Hans. *Cymatics: A Study of Wave Phenomena and Vibration*. 2nd printing. Newmarket, NH: MACROmedia Publishing, 2004.

Josephus, Flavius. *The Antiquities of the Jews*. Translated by William Whiston. Blacksburg, VA: Unabridged Books, 2011.

Kaehr, Shelley. *Edgar Cayce Guide to Gemstones, Minerals, Metals, and More*. Virginia Beach, VA: A.R.E Press, 2005.

Kamrin, Janice. *Ancient Egyptian Hieroglyphs: A Practical Guide*. New York: Harry N. Abrams Inc., 2004.

Kasper, Joseph E., and Steven A. Feller. *The Complete Book of Holograms*. New York: Dover Publications, 2001.

Keating, Thomas. *The Human Condition: Contemplation and Transformation*. New York: Paulist Press, 1999.

Knight, Christopher, and Alan Butler. *Before the Pyramids* London: Watkins Publishing, 2011.

Krajenke, Robert W. *Edgar Cayce's Story of the Old Testament from the Birth of Souls to the Death of Moses*. Virginia Beach, VA: A.R.E. Press, 2004.

Little, Gregory L., Lora Little, and John Van Auken. *Mound Builders: Edgar Cayce's Forgotten Record of Ancient America*. Memphis, TN: Eagle Wing Books, Inc., 2001.

Little, Lora H., Gregory L. Little, and John Van Auken. *Secrets of the Ancient World*. 2nd printing. Virginia Beach, VA: A.R.E. Press, 2005.

Longfellow, Henry Wadsworth. "Excelsior." *Ballads and Other Poems by Henry Wadsworth Longfellow*. 10th edition. Boston: William A. Ticknor and Co., 1848.

Maspero, G. *History of Egypt ,Chaldea, Syria, Babylonia, and Assyria.* Vol. 2, Part B. London: The Grolier Society Publishers, 1903.

Matt, Daniel. *The Essential Kabbalah.* Secaucus, NJ: Castle Books, 1997.

McGuckin, John Anthony, trans. *The Book of Mystical Chapters.* Boston: Shambhala Publications, Inc., 2003.

McTaggart, Lynne. *The Field.* New York: HarperCollins Publishers, 2002.

Michell, John. *The Dimensions of Paradise.* Second US ed. Rochester, VT: Inner Traditions, 2008.

Mirdad, Michael. *The Seven Initiations of the Spiritual Path.* Virginia Beach, VA: A.R.E. Press, 2005.

Mullaney, James. *Edgar Cayce and the Cosmos.* Virginia Beach, VA: A.R.E. Press, 2007.

Ouspensky, P.D. *A New Model of the Universe.* 2nd Ed. New York: Vintage Books, 1971.

—. *In Search of the Miraculous.* New York: Harcourt, Inc., 1949.

Petrie, W.M. Flinders. *Researches in the Sinai.* E.P. New York: Dutton and Company, 1906.

—. *The Pyramids and Temples of Gizeh.* Chestnut Hill, MA: Elibron Classics, Adamant Media Corporation, 2007.

Plato. *Plato: Complete Works.* Edited by John M. Cooper. Indianapolis/Cambridge: Hackett Publishing Company, 1997.

Rappoport, Angelo S. *Myth and Legend of Ancient Israel.* Vol. II. Jersey City, NJ: KTAV Publishing House, Inc., 1966.

Robinson, James M., gen. ed. *The Nag Hammadi Library in English.* Revised Version. New York: Harper's Collins Publishers, 1990.

Schoch, Robert, and Robert Aquinas McNally. *Pyramid Quest.* London: Tarcher/Penguin, 2005.

—. *Voices of the Rocks: A Scientist Looks at Catastrophes and Ancient Civilizations.* New York: Harmony Books, 1999.

—. *Voyage of the Pyramid Builders.* New York: Tarcher/Penguin Books, 2003.

Shiva, Shahram. *Hush Don't Say Anything to God: Passionate Poems of Rumi.* Freemont, CA: Jain Publishing Company, 2000.

Silberer, Herbert. *Hidden Symbolism of Alchemy and the Occult Arts.* New

York: Dover Publications, Inc., 1971.

Strachan, Gordon. *The Bible's Hidden Cosmology.* Edinburgh: Floris Books, 2005.

Talbot, Michael. *The Holographic Universe.* New York: Harper Perennial, 1992.

The Egyptian Book of the Dead. Translated by Raymond Faulkner. San Francisco, CA: Chronicle Books 1998.

Thurston, Mark A. *Experiments in SFG: The Edgar Cayce Path of Application.* Virginia Beach, VA: A.R.E. Press, 1976.

Todeschi, Kevin. *Edgar Cayce on Vibration: Spirit in Motion.* Virginia Beach, VA: A.R.E. Press, 2007.

Trismegistus, Hermes Mercurius. "The Emerald Tablet." *Hermes Mercurius Trismegistus: His Divine Pymander.* Edited by Paschal Beverly Randolph. Des Plaines, IL: Yogi Publication Society, 1972.

Van Auken, John. *Ancient Egyptian Mysticism and its Relevance Today.* Virginia Beach, VA: A.R.E. Press, 1999.

Van Auken, John, and Lora Little. *The Lost Hall of Records.* Memphis, TN: Eagle Wing Books Inc., 2000.

Wake, C. Staniland. *The Origin and Significance of the Great Pyramid.* London: Reeves and Turner, 1882.

Waters, Frank. *Book of the Hopi.* New York: Penguin Books, 1977.

Webster's Third New International Dictionary. Unabridged. Springfield, MA: Merriam–Webster Publishing, 1993.

West, John Anthony. *Serpent in the Sky: The High Wisdom of Ancient Egypt.* Revised Ed. Wheaton: Quest Books, 1993.

Lectures

Schoch, Robert. "The Great Pyramid of Egypt." Lecture presented at the A.R.E. Ancient Mysteries Conference, Virginia Beach, VA, October 9, 2004.

Van Auken, John. "Ancient Egyptian Mysticism." ARE staff video lecture given in the headquarters building of the ARE in Virginia Beach, VA. Information confirmed by personal conversation with author 10/06/2007.

Zpower: Zero Point Energy. Phoenix, Az: Zpower Corporation, May 2003.— http://www.free-energy-info.co.uk/ZPE.pdf.

Magazines

Albert, Mark. "The Triangular Universe." *Scientific American*, February 2007, 24.

Kirkpatrick, S. "Edgar Cayce: The Mysterious Missing." *Venture Inward*, April/May /June 2012, 13.

Mullaney, James. "The Transit of Venus." *Venture Inward*, Apr–June 2012, 24.

O'Brien, Patricia J., and Hanne Christiansen. "An Ancient Maya Measurement System." *America Antiquity*, January 1986, 48.

Smith, Craig B., and Kelly E. Parmenter. "Khufu and Kukulcan." *Civil Engineering: The Magazine of the American Society of Civil Engineers*, April 2004, 48.

Web Addresses

Akashic Records—http://medeadbugger.net/2012/12/11/edgar-cayce-glossary/.

Akhet—http://www.eclipse-chasers.com/akhet.html. A Mosaic of Triangles—http://www.sciam.com/article.cfm?id=describing-the-shape-of-space.

Amethyst Galleries—http://mineral.galleries.com/minerals/symmetry/riclinic.htm.

Arecibo Radio Message—Author Pengo Original Monochrome version of Image: Arecibo message.svg by Arne Nordmann (norro), edited by User:Pengo depicting the w:Arecibo message. Original file's licensing remains: {{self2|GFDL|cc-b http://en.wikipedia.org/wiki/File:Arecibo_message_bw.svg.

Arecibo telescope—http://kbarnett8.tripod.com/temp2.htm.

Asherim—http://en.wikipedia.org/wiki/Asherah_pole.

AUM Symbol—http://www.mandalayoga.net/pretty_print.php?rub=what&p=mantra_om&lang=en.

B-Flat from Space —http://chandra.harvard.edu/press/03_releases/press_090903.html.

Black Hole—http://www.webpagesbybob.com/blackhole.htm.

Black Hole Music—http://www.freerepublic.com/focus/f-news/2316057/posts.

Bread–Cone Hieroglyph—http://en.wikipedia.org/wiki/Bread-cone_(hieroglyph).

Brown, Driver, Briggs Gesenius. "Hebrew Lexicon entry for Choreb." *The KJV Old Testament Hebrew Lexicon.* http://www.biblestudytools.net/Lexicons/Hebrew/heb.cgi?number=2722&version=kjv.

—. "Hebrew Lexicon entry for Ciynay." *The KJV Old Testament Hebrew Lexicon.* http://www.biblestudytools.net/Lexicons/Hebrew/heb.cgi?number=5514&version=kjv.

Chichen Itza—http://en.wikipedia.org/wiki/Chichen Itza.

Close–up photograph of a hologram's surface–http://en.wikipedia.org/wiki/Holography.

Clovis people—http://archive.archaeology.org/9907/newsbriefs/clovis.html.

Coherent Light—http://library.thinkquest.org/27356/d_coherentlight.htm?tqskip1=1.

Copper—http://www.csa.com/discoveryguides/copper/overview.php.

Cosmic Background Radiation–http://www.oursounduniverse.com/articles/pulsars.htm.

Creating a Dunce Hat—http://en.wikipedia.org/wiki/Dunce_hat_%28topology%29.

Crooks and Flails—http://www.touregypt.net/featurestories/crooksandflails.htm.

Cybersky 5—http://www.cybersky.com/.

Cymatics—http://www.cymaticsource.com/newto.html.

Dark blue stone—http://minerals.usgs.gov/minerals/pubs/commodity/gemstones/sp14-95/turquoise.html.

Djew—http://www.touregypt.net/featurestories/horizon.htm.

Doubled Tetrahedrons and Pentahedrons—AEI-2001-049 24 May 2001 Dynamically Triangulating Lorentzian Quantum Gravity J. Ambjørn a, J. Jurkiewicz b and R. Loll c1 a The Niels Bohr Institute, Blegdamsvej 17, DK–2100 Copenhagen Ø, Denmark email: ambjorn@nbi.dk b Institute of Physics, Jagellonian University, Reymonta 4, PL 30–059 Krakow, Poland email: jurkiewi@thrisc.if.uj.edu.pl c Albert-Einstein-Institut, Max-Planck-Institut f'ur Gravitationsphysik, Am M'uhlenberg 1, D-14476 Golm,

Germany email: loll@aei-potsdam.mpg.de.

Drawing a Parabola—http://mysite.du.edu/~jcalvert/math/parabola.htm.

Dunn, Jimmy. "The Mountains and Horizon of Ancient Egypt"—http://www.touregypt.net/featurestories/horizon.htm.

Earth Globes—http://upload.wikimedia.org/wikipedia/commons/6/62/Latitude_and_Longitude_of_the_Earth.svg.

EgyptianHeadrest—http://commons.wikimedia.org/wiki/File:Egyptian_-_Headrest_-_Walters_61301.jpg.

Egyptianritual—http://www.ancientegyptonline.co.uk/foundationritual.html#stretch.

Ellison, Ray. "The Pyramid Texts"—http://www.touregypt.net/featurestories/pyramidtext.htm.

Fixing Right Angles—http://www.cheops-pyramide.ch/khufu-pyramid/pyramid-alignment.html#top.

Fractal definition—http://en.wikipedia.org/w/index.php?title=Fractal&oldid=10025267.

Frequency to musical note converter site—http://www.phys.unsw.edu.au/music/note/.

Functions of a parabolic dish—http://www.howeverythingworks.org/page1.php?QNum=1473.

Galactic Alignment#1—http://alignment2012.com/whatisga.htm.

Galactic Alignment#2—http://www.universetoday.com/30762/galactic-alignment/.

Galactic Center—http://en.wikipedia.org/wiki/Galactic_center.

Genesis 3—http://www.biblegateway.com/passage/?search=genesis%203&version=KJV.

Georgia State University online pendulum calculator—http://hyperphysics.phy-astr.gsu.edu/hbase/pendl.html#c1.

Globelki Tepe—http://www.smithsonianmag.com/history-archaeology/gobekli-tepe.html?c=y&story=fullstory.

Gravitational Lenses—http://archive.seti.org/epo/news/features/detecting-other-worlds-the-flash.php.

Gravitational Lensing—http://en.wikipedia.org/wiki/Gravitational_lensing.

Gravity Lens Effect I—http://en.wikipedia.org/wiki/
File:Abell.lensing.arp.750pix.jpg.

Gravity Lens Effect II—http://en.wikipedia.org/wiki/
File:Einstein_ring.jpg.

Gravity Lens Geometry—http://en.wikipedia.org/wiki/
File:Gravity_lens_geometry.png.

Hamlet, Act 1, scene 5, 159–167—http://www.enotes.com/shakespeare-
quotes/there-more-things-heaven-earth-horatio.

Hezekiah—http://en.wikipedia.org/wiki/Hezekiah.

Hill of the Skull—http://newadvent.org/cathen/03191a.htm.

History of the meter—http://en.wikipedia.org/wiki/
History_of_the_metre.

Houdin—http://www.3ds.com/fileadmin/kheops/renaissance/pdf/
PRESSKIT_2011_KHUFU_REBORN.pdf.

Human Brain PET Scan—http://en.wikipedia.org/wiki/
File:PET_Normal_brain.jpg.

King, God-King Hieroglyphs—http://www.omniglot.com/writing/
egyptian_det.htm.

Koch snowflake definition—http://en.wikipedia.org/w/
index.php?title=Fractal&oldid=10025267.

Korzybski's General Semantics -http://www.gestalt.org/semantic.htm.

Kukulcan Pyramid Serpent Head—http://en.wikipedia.org/wiki/
File:Head_of_serpent_column.jpg#file.

Location of Great Pyramid-http://www.gardinersworld.com/content/
view/202/39/.

Make-up of Arecibo message—http://kbarnett8.tripod.com/temp2.htm.

Maya ritual—http://www.authenticmaya.com/maya_culture.htm.

Menorah—http://www.jewfaq.org/signs.htm.

Milky Way—http://www.space.com/scienceastronomy/
050816_milky_way.html.

Mitre origin—http://www.newadvent.org/cathen/10404a.htm.

Music of the Spheres—http://www.merriam-webster.com/dictionary/
music%20of%20the%20spheres.

Myth and Legend of Ancient Israel. WWW.KURLRadio.Com.

Nehustan—http://en.wikipedia.org/wiki/Nehustan.

North Side of Chichen Itza—http://en.wikipedia.org/wiki/
File:Chichen_Norte.JPG.

Obelisk—http://core.kmi.open.ac.uk/display/2926263.

Online pendulum calculator http://hyperphysics.phy-astr.gsu.edu/
hbase/pendl.html#c1.

Origins of the Dunce Cap—http://www.straightdope.com/columns/
read/1793/whats-the-origin-of-the-dunce-cap.

Parabolic Dish/Cup—http://www.answers.com/topic/paraboloid.

Parabolic Dish Microphone—http://www.howeverythingworks.org/
page1.php?QNum=1473.

Paraboloids—http://en.wikipedia.org/w/
index.php?title=Paraboloid&oldid=8439062.

Parsons, Marie. "Heliopolis, Egypt's Iunu." http://www.touregypt.net/
featurestories/heliopolis.htm.

Particle Duality—http://en.wikipedia.org/wiki/
Wave%E2%80%93particle_duality.

Peaceful period—http://lorenzlammens.com/the-most-peaceful-pe-
riod-in-history/.

Pendulum—http://commons.wikimedia.org/wiki/
File:Simple_gravity_pendulum.svg#file.

Pendulum—http://en.wikipedia.org/wiki/
File:Simple_gravity_pendulum.svg.

Placing The Pineal—http://www.edgarcayce.org/ Cayce Health Database.

Pythagoreans' central fire -http://physics.ucr.edu/~wudka/Physics7/
Notes_www/node32.html.

Radio frequency—http://www.answers.com/topic/radio-frequency.

Raising the Djed—http://www.touregypt.net/featurestories/
djedpillar.htm.

Reconstructing the Universe—J. Ambjørn a,c, J. Jurkiewicz b and R.
Loll c a The Niels Bohr Institute, Copenhagen University
Blegdamsvej 17, DK-2100 Copenhagen Ø, Denmark. email:
ambjorn@nbi.dk b Mark Kac Complex Systems Research Centre,
Marian Smoluchowski Institute of Physics, Jagellonian University,

Reymonta 4, PL 30-059 Krakow, Poland. email: jurkiewicz@th.if.uj.edu.pl c Institute for Theoretical Physics, Utrecht University, Leuvenlaan 4, NL-3584 CE Utrecht, The Netherlands. email: j.ambjorn@phys.uu.nl, r.loll@phys.uu.nl 06 June 2005.

Reeder, Greg. "Effects of the resting *tekenu*." *The Enigmatic Tekenu*. http://www.touregypt.net/featurestories/humansac.htm.

—. "Human Sacrifices." *The Enigmatic Tekenu*. http://www.touregypt.net/featurestories/humansac.htm.

—. "Sem Priest." *The Enigmatic Tekenu*. http://www.touregypt.net/featurestories/humansac.htm.

Sapphire—*The American Heritage® Dictionary of the English Language, Fourth Edition*. Boston: Houghton Mifflin Company, 2004. *Answers.com* 19 Aug. 2008. http://www.answers.com/topic/sapphire.

Self-similar object—http://en.wikipedia.org/wiki/Self-similarity.

Seven Church Pilgrimage—http://www.catholicpilgrimoffice.com/08d_rome_assisi_7_churches.php.

Sine of Great Pyramid—http://www.ies.co.jp/math/java/samples/sinBox.html.

Smith, Lucy Mack—*History of Joseph Smith*. http://oneclimbs.com/2011/02/06/the-all-seeing-eye-symbol-and-the-urim-and-thummim-connection/.

Sound waves—http://www.space.com/661-sound-waves-left-imprint-universe.html.

Spinal column -http://education.yahoo.com/reference/gray/subjects/subject/25.

Squaring the Circle—http://mathworld.wolfram.com/CircleSquaring.html.

Sri Yantra—http://alumni.cse.ucsc.edu/~mikel/sriyantra/joseph.html.

Stecchini—Carrying yoke–http://www.metrum.org/measures/structure.htm.

—. Dimensions of the Great Pyramid—http://www.metrum.org/measures/dimensions.htm.

Stone Age Hunters—http://www.independent.co.uk/news/world/americas/new-evidence-suggests-stone-age-hunters-from-europe-discovered-america-7447152.html.

Stone tools—http://www.ldeo.columbia.edu/news-events/humans-shaped-stone-axes-18-million-years-ago-study-says.

Stonehenge acoustics—http://soundsofstonehenge.wordpress.com/
conclusions/.

Studying under the fig tree—http://www.studylight.org/ls/at/
index.cgi?a=257.

Survey Pendulum/Plumb Bob –http://gallery.usgs.gov/photos/
07_22_2009_j51Qi76Hgb_07_22_2009_12.

Surveying Tools—http://www.surveyhistory.org/
egyptian_surveying_tools1.htm.

Tekenu—enu or henu—http://www.world-destiny.org/a4an.htm.

The Benu (Bennu) by Jefferson Monet–http://www.touregypt.net/
featurestories/benu.htm.

The Circle—http://symboldictionary.net/?p=1914.

Theories of Quantum Gravity—http://www.scientificamerican.com/
article.cfm?id=theories-of-quantum-gravity.

Things represented by the vesica pisces—http://www.ka-gold-
jewelry.com/p-articles/vesica-pisces.php.

Tre Goddess—http://www.touregypt.net/featurestories/
treegoddess.htm.

Tree of Eden—http://www.criticalpages.com/2011/what-fruit-grew-
on-the-tree-of-knowledge/.

Use of the number 7 in the Christian world—http://
www.newadvent.org/cathen/05590a.htm.

Vesica Piscis—http://en.wikipedia.org/wiki/Vesica_piscis.

Vibrations Waves—http://science.sbcc.edu/physics/folsom/
vibrations_waves/vibrations_waves.pdf.

VLBA—http://www.nrao.edu/pr/2004/sagastar/.

Wavelength measurement site—http://www.sengpielaudio.com/calcu-
lator-wavelength.htm.

Waves—http://en.wikipedia.org/wiki/Wave.

Wearing a Kippah—http://www.templesan jose.org/JudaismInfo/faq/
kippah.htm.

Color Illustration Credits

1. **Mount Ta Dehent**—Photo by author.
2. **Copper Ore**—Rob Lavinsky, iRocks.com – CC–BY–SA–3.0 http://upload.wikimedia.org/wikipedia/commons/c/cf/Copper-Cuprite-226396.jpg.
3. **Original Entrance of the Great Pyramid**—Courtesy of Robert Schoch.
4. **The Summer Triangle**—http://commons.wikimedia.org/wiki/File:Summer_triangle_map.png#file.
5. **Egyptian Skies 10,400 BCE**—Planetarium program Cybersky5 courtesy of Stephen Michael Schimpf –http://www.cybersky.com/.
6. **Six-Pointed Star**—http://openclipart.org/detail/138559/6-color-diamond-hexagram-by-10binary.
7. **Turquoise Crystal System**–http://www.metafysica.nl/turing/promorphology_2a.html.
8. **Tekhenu Hieroglyph Depiction**–http://commons.wikimedia.org/wiki/File:Souls_of_Pe_and_Nekhen.svg#file.
9. **Baptism of Jesus**—Neoclassical altar with altar painting by Anton Hitzenthaler Sr. showing the Baptism of Christ (1793) at Ss. Giles and Leonard Parish Church in Peilstein, Austria. http://commons.wikimedia.org/wiki/File:Peilstein_Kirche_-_Taufaltar_2a_Altarbild.jpg.
10. **The obelisk that emits a tone! Karnak, Egypt (obelisk on side)**—Photo by author.
11. **Tekhenu /Obelisk at Karnak, Egypt (obelisk upright)**—Photo by author.
12. **Broken Hologram**– Photograph of holographic reconstructions of two different sections of a broken hologram. http://en.wikipedia.org/wiki/File:Broken_hologram.jpg.
13. **Menorah**—http://en.wikipedia.org/wiki/File:Menorah_0307.jpg.
14. **Great Pyramid Entrance Inscription**—Courtesy of Robert Schoch.
15. **Great Pyramid and Sphinx**—Photo by author.
16. **Predicted Pyramid Shafts**—http://www.3ds.com/fileadmin/kheops/renaissance/pdf/PRESSKIT_2011_KHUFU_REBORN.pdf.
17. **Djed Hieroglyph**—The Djed pillar, an ancient Egyptian symbol meaning "stability," is the symbolic backbone of the god Osiris.

http://commons.wikimedia.org/wiki/File:Djed.svg.

18. **Mayan Kukulcan Pyramid**—Photo by author.
19. **Kukulcan Pyramid "Serpent of Light"**—http://commons.wikimedia.org/wiki/File:ChichenItzaEquinox.jpg#file.
20. **Maya Serpent Bar**—Cast of Stela A, Maya site of Copan, made by Alfred Maudslay, Department of the Americas, British Museum. Current location is the British Museum. http://commons.wikimedia.org/wiki/File:Stela_A_Copan.jpg#file.
21. **Raising the Djed**—Photo by author.
22. **Stonehenge**- Photo by author.
23. **Djed on a Pillar at the Philae Temple, Egypt**- Photo by author.
24. **Djed with Serpent**—Photo by author.
25. **Egyptian Crook and Flail**—This symbolize signifies leadership and a powerful ruler. http://commons.wikimedia.org/wiki/File:Crook_and_flail.svg#mw-head.
26. **Sycamore Figs**—http://commons.wikimedia.org/wiki/File:Ficus_sycomorus_0003.jpg#file.
27. **Pituitary Gland**—http://jpkc.gdmc.edu.cn/blx/10jxwz/tupu/bltp/15nfb19.htm.
28. **Earth Globes**—http://commons.wikimedia.org/wiki/File:Latitude_and_Longitude_of_the_Earth.svg#file.
29. **Kukulcan Pyramid Staircase**—http://commons.wikimedia.org/wiki/File:Chichen_Norte.JPG.
30. **Dream Stelae—Sphinx**—Photo by author.
31. **Electro-Magnetic Spectrum**—http://en.wikipedia.org/wiki/File:Atmospheric_electromagnetic_transmittance_or_opacity.jpg.
32. **Milky Way**—http://commons.wikimedia.org/wiki/File:The_Galaxy.jpg#file.
33. **Super Nova Sound Waves**—Courtesy of Professor Adam Burrows, Princeton University.
34. **Human Brain PET Scan**—http://en.wikipedia.org/wiki/File:PET_Normal_brain.jpg.
35. **Gravity Lens Depiction**—http://en.wikipedia.org/wiki/File:Gravitational_lens-full.jpg.
36. **DNA-Star**—open source tutorial.

Black-and-White Illustration Credits

Figures

1.1. **Moses with the Tablets**—http://www.sacred-texts.com/eso/sta/index.htm.

2.1 **Tetractys**—http://www.sacred-texts.com/eso/sta/index.htm.

2.2 **Tetragrammaton**—http://www.sacred-texts.com/eso/sta/index.htm.

2.3 **Ennead**—Courtesy of Carol Hicks.

2.4 **"A Priest Carrying a Scroll" Hieroglyph**- Temple at Edfu, Egypt—Photo by the author.

3.1 **Exodus Route**—Courtesy of Carol Hicks.

3.2 **Statue of Hathor in the Cairo Museum**—Personal picture of Gérard Ducher- http://en.wikipedia.org/wiki/File:GD-EG-Caire-Mus%C3%A9e091.JPG.

3.3 **Serabit al-Khadim**—"Serabit Al-Kadim" image courtesy of Mysterious World—http://www.mysteriousworld.com/Journal /2008/Spring /Artifacts /ExodusRevelationPart2-TheExodus.asp.

3.4 **A Benben Stone**—photo by Kurohito— http://upload.wikimedia.org/wikipedia/commons/c/c1/Dahchour0019.jpg.

4.1 **Six-Pointed Star in Sun Disc**—The U.S. Bureau of Ethnography 2nd Annual report of 1881 by J.W. Powell, Vol. II p. 57, illustration no. 5: stone, sun symbol, uxmal published by the Washington Government printing office 1883.

5.1 **Om Mani Padme Hum lotus**—https://commons.wikimedia.org/wiki/File:OM_MANI_PADME_HUM-bw.svg.

5.2 **Cube and Star in Hexagram**—http: //en.wikipedia.org/wiki/Hexagon.

5.3 **The Mercaba**—This image was generated by Vladimir Bulatov's Polyhedra Stellations Applet—http://bulatov.org/polyhedra/stellation_applet.

5.4 **Koch Snowflake Fractal**—SVG version of

Image:KochFlake.png. Chas zzz brown– http://en.wikipedia.org/wiki/File:KochFlake.svg.

5.5   **Symbolic Unity of Spirit and Matter**—Courtesy of Carol Hicks.

6.1   **Sri Yantra**—http://upload.wikimedia.org/wikipedia/commons/a/a2/Sri_Yantra_256bw.gif.

6.2   **Axis Mundi**—http://upload.wikimedia.org/wikipedia/commons/8/8a/Star_polygon_6-3.svg.

6.3   **Hexagon/cube and the axis mundi/hexagram/cube/triangle**—http://www.sacred-texts.com/eso/sta/index.htm.

6.4   **Chi Rho I**—http://en.wikipedia.org/wiki/File:Simple_Labarum2.svg.

6.5   **Chi Rho II**—http://en.wikipedia.org/wiki/File:Labarum.png.

6.6   **Chi Rho III**—http://commons.wikimedia.org/wiki/File:Chi-rho_mensa_Louvre_Ma_3023.jpg#file.

6.7   **Turquoise crystal system**—http://www.metafysica.nl/turing/promorphology_2a.html.

6.8   **Orthogonal Projections**—http://en.wikipedia.org/wiki/Octahedron.

6.9   **Flower of Life**—http://en.wikipedia.org/wiki/File:Flower-of-Life-small.svg.

6.10   **Seed of Life**—http://en.wikipedia.org/w/index.php?title=File:Seed-of-Life.svg&page=1.

6.11   **Vesica Pisces/Ichthys**—http://en.wikipedia.org/wiki/File:Vesica-P-Constr-Diagram.png.

6.12   **Vesica Pisces Form Generator**—Courtesy of Carol Hicks.

6.13   **Circumpunct/Ra symbol**—http://en.wikipedia.org/wiki/Image:Circumpunct.png (en:User:Abdulmajid).

6.14   **Vesica Pisces**—http://upload.wikimedia.org/wikipedia/commons/b/bd/Vesica_Piscis.svg.

6.15   **Vesica Pisces in Ripples**—http://commons.wikimedia.org/wiki/File:Ripple_-_in_rail.jpg#file.

6.16   **Vesica Pisces**—http://upload.wikimedia.org/wikipedia/commons/b/bd/Vesica_Piscis.svg.

6.17   **Flower of Life**—http://en.wikipedia.org/wiki/File:Flower-of-Life-small.svg.

6.18   **Flower of Life in Wave Ripples**—http://commons.wikimedia.org/wiki/File:Constructive_interference.jpg#file.

6.19 **Weed Lines from Wave Actions**—http://
commons.wikimedia.org/wiki/
FileSea,_sand,_weed,_horizontal_concrete_castellations_and_sunlight,_Broadsands_-
geograph.org.uk-_1046999.jpg#file.

6.20 **Hexagrams in Vesica Pisces**—http://commons.wikimedia.org/
wiki/File:Decad.svg#file.

6.21 **Six-Pointed Star from the Seed of Life and Symbolic
Unity of Spirit and Matter**
Six-Pointed Star—http://openclipart.org/detail/138559/6-color-
diamond-hexagram-by-10binary.
Seed of Life—http://en.wikipedia.org/w/
index.php?title=File:Seed-of-Life.svg&page=1.
Symbolic Unity of Spirit and Matter—Courtesy of Carol Hicks.

7.1 **Benben Stone from Pyramid of Amenemhet III—Cairo
Museum**—http://upload.wikimedia.org/wikipedia/commons/
c/c1/Dahchour0019.jpg.

7.2 **The Tekenu**—courtesy of Greg Reeder—http://
www.egyptology.com/reeder/.

8.1 **Parabolic dish**/cup—http://en.wikipedia.org/wiki/
File:Paraboloid_of_Revolution.png.

8.2 **Holographic swirls**—http://en.wikipedia.org/wiki/
File:Holographic_recording.jpg.

8.3 **Fermat parabolic spiral**—http://en.wikipedia.org/wiki/
File:Fermat%27s_spiral.svg#file.

8.4 **Chartres labyrinth**—http://commons.wikimedia.org/wiki/
File:Labychartres.jpg#file.

8.5 **Yin-yang symbol**—http://commons.wikimedia.org/wiki/
File:Esoteric_Taijitu.svg.

9.1 **Wizard's Hat**—Thinkstock #71394068.

9.2 **Witch's Hat** —Thinkstock # 95049203.

9.3 **Dunce's Cap** —Thinkstock #78455046.

9.4 **Gold Cone Hat 900 BCE**—http://commons.wikimedia.org/
wikiFile:C%C3%B4ne_d%27Avanton,_mus%C3%A9e_des_Antiquit%
C3%A9s_Nationales.jpg.

9.5 **Triangle to Cone**—Courtesy of Carol Hicks.

9.6 **Mitre Evolution**—http://en.wikipedia.org/wiki/

File:Mitre_evolution.gif#file.

9.7 **Egyptian Hieroglyph Amenta**—the underworld/west horizon
9.8 **Chinook Flathead Skull**— http://commons.wikimedia.org/ wiki/File:Flathead_(Chinook)_skull.png.

10.1 **Parabolic Radio Receiver Dish**—http://putra-design.blogspot.com/2009_02_01_archive.html.
10.2 **Great Pyramid Outline**—http://commons.wikimedia.org/ wiki/File:Great_Pyramid_Diagram.jpg#file.
10.3 **Great Pyramid, Cairo, Egypt**—Courtesy of Robert Schoch.
10.4 **Radio Receiver Dish Array**—http://commons.wikimedia.org/ wiki/File:LOFAR,_ITS_Test_Station.png#file.
10.5 **Bindu and Raif symbol**—Courtesy of the author.
10.6 **Radio Receiver Dish**—Thinkstock #135940052.
10.7 **Great Pyramid Entrance** —Courtesy of Robert Schoch.

11.1 **Satellite Dish**—Thinkstock #78457366.
11.2 **Eucharist Communion**—Thinkstock #90272475.
11.3 **Da Vinci's Vitruvian Man**—http://en.wikipedia.org/wiki/ File:Vitruvian_Man_Measurements.png#file.
11.4 **Moses and Aaron with Pharaoh**—http:// commons.wikimedia.org/wiki/File:Foster_Bible_Pictures_0060-2_Aaron%27s_Rod_Changed_into_a_Serpent.jpg#file.
11.5 **Moses Raising the Serpent**—http://commons.wikimedia.org/ wiki/ File:Figures_Moses_fixes_the_brazen_Serpent_on_a_pole.jpg#file.
11.6 **Spine**—http://www.niams.nih.gov/health_info/scoliosis/.
11.7 **Snake**—Courtesy of the author.
11.8 **Vertebrae**—
A—http://commons.wikimedia.org/wiki/File:Gray84.png#mw-head.
B—http://commons.wikimedia.org/wiki/File:Gray82.png#mw-head.
C—http://commons.wikimedia.org/wiki/File:Gray94.png#file.
11.9 **Pelvic Girdle**—http://commons.wikimedia.org/wiki/ File:Illu_pelvic_girdle.jpg#file.
11.10 **Spine**—http://www.niams.nih.gov/health_info/scoliosis/.
11.11 **Right Triangle**—http://commons.wikimedia.org/wiki/ File:Sohcahtoa.svg.

11.12 **Smyth map**—http://archive.org/details/ ourinheritancei00unkngoog.

11.13 **Hebrew Lamed**—http://commons.wikimedia.org/wiki/ File:Hebrew_letter_lamed.svg#file.

11.14 **Stonehenge Diagram**—http://en.wikipedia.org/wiki/File:Y-Z.jpg#filehistory.

11.15 **Star in the Stonehenge Depiction**—http://en.wikipedia.org/ wiki/File:New_Jerusalem_(Michell)_Sacred_Geometry.svg#file.

11.16 **Avebury Serpent**—Courtesy of author Andrew Collins.

12.1 **Cervical Vertebra**—http://en.wikipedia.org/wiki/ File:Gray86.png.

12.2 **Osiris with Crown**—http://commons.wikimedia.org/wiki/ File:Bronze_figurine_of_Egyptian_god_Osiris.jpg#file.

12.3 **Cervical Vertebra II**—http://en.wikipedia.org/wiki/ File:Gray88.png.

12.4 **Egyptian Peschent Crown**—http://commons.wikimedia.org/ wiki/File:Pschent.svg#file.

12.5 **Cauda Equina**—http://en.wikipedia.org/wiki/Cauda_equina.

12.6 **Spinal Cord and Cauda Equina**—http:// upload.wikimedia.org/wikipedia/commons/b/b4/NHM_-_Central_nervous_system_2.jpg.

12.7 **Tree System**—http://upload.wikimedia.org/wikipedia/commons/c/c9/Arbor-scientiae.png.

13.1 **Pendulum**—http://commons.wikimedia.org/wiki/ File:Simple_gravity_pendulum.svg#file.

13.2 **Survey Pendulum/ Plumb Bob**—http://gallery.usgs.gov/ photos/07_22_2009_j51Qi76Hgb_07_22_2009_12.

13.3 **Bread-Cone Hieroglyph**—http://en.wikipedia.org/wiki/ Bread-cone_(hieroglyph).

13.4 **Kukulcan Pyramid Serpent Head**—http://en.wikipedia.org/ wiki/File:Head_of_serpent_column.jpg#file.

13.5 **Artist's Depiction of the Great Pyramid Stairway**—Courtesy of Carol Hicks.

14.1 **Egyptian Headrest**—http://commons.wikimedia.org/wiki/ File:Egyptian_-_Headrest_-_Walters_61301.jpg#file.

14.2 **AUM Symbol**—http://www.mandalayoga.net/

pretty_print.php?rub=what&p=mantra_om&lang=en.

14.3 **Arecibo Radio Message**—http://en.wikipedia.org/wiki/
File:Arecibo_message_bw.svg.

15.1 **Gravity Lens Geometry**—http://en.wikipedia.org/wiki/
File:Gravity_lens_geometry.png.

15.2 **Gravity Lens Effect I**—http://en.wikipedia.org/wiki/
File:Abell.lensing.arp.750pix.jpg.

15.3 **Gravity Lens Effect II**—http://en.wikipedia.org/wiki/
File:Einstein_cross.jpg.

15.4 **Radio Dish Receiver Arrays**—http://images.nrao.edu/im-
ages/vlba_montage_lo.jpg.

15.5 **Drawing a Parabola**—http://mysite.du.edu/~jcalvert/math/
parabola.htm.

15.6 **Fixing Right Angles**—http://www.cheops-pyramide.ch/khufu-
pyramid/pyramid-alignment.html#top.

15.7 **Geodesic Dome**—Photo by the author.

15.8 **Reconstructing the Universe**—J. Ambjørn a,c, J. Jurkiewicz b
and R. Loll c a The Niels Bohr Institute, Copenhagen University
Blegdamsvej 17, DK–2100 Copenhagen Ø, Denmark. email:
ambjorn@nbi.dk b Mark Kac Complex Systems Research Centre,
Marian Smoluchowski Institute of Physics, Jagellonian Univer-
sity, Reymonta 4, PL 30–059 Krakow, Poland. email:
jurkiewicz@th.if.uj.edu.pl c Institute for Theoretical Physics,
Utrecht University, Leuvenlaan 4, NL–3584 CE Utrecht, The
Netherlands. email: j.ambjorn@phys.uu.nl, r.loll@phys.uu.nl 06
June 2005.

15.9 **Doubled Tetrahedrons and Pentahedrons**—AEI–2001–049
24 May 2001. Dynamically Triangulating Lorentzian Quantum
Gravity J. Ambjørn a, J. Jurkiewicz b and R. Loll c1 a The Niels
Bohr Institute, Blegdamsvej 17, DK–2100 Copenhagen Ø, Denmark email: ambjorn@nbi.dk b Institute of Physics, Jagellonian
University, Reymonta 4, PL 30–059 Krakow, Poland email:
jurkiewi@thrisc.if.uj.edu.pl c Albert–Einstein–Institut, Max–
Planck-Institut f¨ur Gravitationsphysik, Am M¨uhlenberg 1, D–
14476 Golm, Germany email: loll@aei-potsdam.mpg.de.

15.10 **CDT Space Fabric Depiction**—Courtesy of Carol Hicks.

4TH DIMENSION PRESS

An Imprint of A.R.E. Press

4th Dimension Press is an imprint of A.R.E. Press, the publishing division of Edgar Cayce's Association for Research and Enlightenment (A.R.E.).

We publish books, DVDs, and CDs in the fields of intuition, psychic abilities, ancient mysteries, philosophy, comparative religious studies, personal and spiritual development, and holistic health.

For more information, or to receive a catalog, contact us by mail, phone, or online at:

4th Dimension Press
215 67th Street
Virginia Beach, VA 23451-2061
800-333-4499

4THDIMENSIONPRESS.COM

EDGAR CAYCE'S A.R.E.

Who Was Edgar Cayce?
Twentieth Century Psychic and Medical Clairvoyant

Edgar Cayce (pronounced Kay-Cee, 1877-1945) has been called the "sleeping prophet," the "father of holistic medicine," and the most-documented psychic of the 20th century. For more than 40 years of his adult life, Cayce gave psychic "readings" to thousands of seekers while in an unconscious state, diagnosing illnesses and revealing lives lived in the past and prophecies yet to come. But who, exactly, was Edgar Cayce?

Cayce was born on a farm in Hopkinsville, Kentucky, in 1877, and his psychic abilities began to appear as early as his childhood. He was able to see and talk to his late grandfather's spirit, and often played with "imaginary friends" whom he said were spirits on the other side. He also displayed an uncanny ability to memorize the pages of a book simply by sleeping on it. These gifts labeled the young Cayce as strange, but all Cayce really wanted was to help others, especially children.

Later in life, Cayce would find that he had the ability to put himself into a sleep-like state by lying down on a couch, closing his eyes, and folding his hands over his stomach. In this state of relaxation and meditation, he was able to place his mind in contact with all time and space—the universal consciousness, also known as the super-conscious mind. From there, he could respond to questions as broad as, "What are the secrets of the universe?" and "What is my purpose in life?" to as specific as, "What can I do to help my arthritis?" and "How were the pyramids of Egypt built?" His responses to these questions came to be called "readings," and their insights offer practical help and advice to individuals even today.

The majority of Edgar Cayce's readings deal with holistic health and the treatment of illness. Yet, although best known for this material, the sleeping Cayce did not seem to be limited to concerns about the physical body. In fact, in their entirety, the readings discuss an astonishing 10,000 different topics. This vast array of subject matter can be narrowed down into a smaller group of topics that, when compiled together, deal with the following five categories: (1) Health-Related Information; (2) Philosophy and Reincarnation; (3) Dreams and Dream Interpretation; (4) ESP and Psychic Phenomena; and (5) Spiritual Growth, Meditation, and Prayer.

Learn more at EdgarCayce.org.

What Is A.R.E.?

Edgar Cayce founded the non-profit Association for Research and Enlightenment (A.R.E.) in 1931, to explore spirituality, holistic health, intuition, dream interpretation, psychic development, reincarnation, and ancient mysteries—all subjects that frequently came up in the more than 14,000 documented psychic readings given by Cayce.

The Mission of the A.R.E. is to help people transform their lives for the better, through research, education, and application of core concepts found in the Edgar Cayce readings and kindred materials that seek to manifest the love of God and all people and promote the purposefulness of life, the oneness of God, the spiritual nature of humankind, and the connection of body, mind, and spirit.

With an international headquarters in Virginia Beach, Va., a regional headquarters in Houston, regional representatives throughout the U.S., Edgar Cayce Centers in more than thirty countries, and individual members in more than seventy countries, the A.R.E. community is a global network of individuals.

A.R.E. conferences, international tours, camps for children and adults, regional activities, and study groups allow like-minded people to gather for educational and fellowship opportunities worldwide.

A.R.E. offers membership benefits and services that include a quarterly body-mind-spirit member magazine, *Venture Inward*, a member newsletter covering the major topics of the readings, and access to the entire set of readings in an exclusive online database.

Learn more at EdgarCayce.org.

EDGARCAYCE.ORG